D 5·1 ,P 3

Sir William Gell in Italy

I Sir William Gell, 1830, by T. Uwins

Sir William Gell
in Italy

Letters to the Society of Dilettanti,
1831–1835

EDITED BY
EDITH CLAY
in collaboration with Martin Frederiksen

HAMISH HAMILTON · LONDON

First published in Great Britain 1976
by Hamish Hamilton Ltd
90 Great Russell Street London WC1B 3PT

Copyright © 1976 by Edith Clay

SBN 241 89467 0

Printed in Great Britain by Thomson Litho Ltd., East Kilbride, Scotland

CONTENTS

Illustrations

Acknowledgments

We wish to record our deep gratitude to the Trustees of The Marc Fitch Fund who have made a grant of £1,000 towards the expenses of the publication of this book and to the Society of Dilettanti for giving us permission to publish these Letters by Sir William Gell, also to the Council of the British School at Rome for allowing us to study the Gell notebooks in their possession, and to reproduce from them.

Our warm thanks go to Mrs. Philip Gell, who together with her husband, the late Colonel Philip Gell, generously made all their archives relating to their ancestor available to us, and to whom Edith Clay is indebted for their hospitality on several pleasurable occasions.

In addition to the persons mentioned in the text, we offer our thanks to the following: Sir Harold Acton; Mr John Boardman; Prof. J. M. Cook; Mr. Roger Fulford; Dr. Kenneth Garlick; Mr. Robin Jasper, lately H. B. M. Consul General at Naples; Mr. Scott Medd; Mr. Michael Rea; Dr. Francis Steer; Prof. J. M. C. Toynbee; Mr. Raleigh Trevelyan; Mr. John Ward-Perkins, lately Director of the British School at Rome; Mr A. W. H. Pearsall, Custodian of MS, National Maritime Museum at Greenwich; Commander Sattherwaite, Secretary of the Garrick Club; Mr. J. R. Seaton and Mr. I. F. Maciver of the National Library of Scotland at Edinburgh; the Biblioteca Nazionale, Naples; Prof. A. De Franciscis, Soprintendente alle Antichità della Campania, Naples; and Dr. Horst Blanck of the German Archaeological Institute at Rome.

Mr. Andrew Wilton discovered the pencil drawing of Sir William Gell in a dealer's folio and generously gave it to Edith Clay. He dated the drawing about 1810, but Gell was knighted in 1814: the signature on the drawing does not appear to be that of Gell.

In preparation of this edition, Martin Frederiksen has been mainly responsible for the parts concerning the archaeological discoveries and Gell as archaeologist, and Edith Clay for editing the Letters for publication and the parts concerning Gell's life and friendships.

Abbreviations used in *Introduction* and *Notes*:

Bullettino = *Bullettino dell'Instituto di Corrispondenza archeologica di Roma* (from 1829 onwards)
Annali = *Annali dell'Instituto di Corrispondenza archeologica* (from 1829)
Memorie = *Memorie dell'Instituto di Corrispondenza Archeologica* (from 1832)
PAH = G. Fiorelli, *Pompeianarum antiquitatum historia*, vols. i–iii (Naples, 1860–1864)

Introduction

These *Letters*, which are interspersed with sketches, are the property of the Society of Dilettanti,[1] and were written by Sir William Gell to the Society's Secretary between 8 April 1831 and 25 March 1835; but there seem to be gaps in the correspondence and the replies to Gell are lost. Gell had been appointed in 1830 as the Society's resident minister plenipotentiary at Naples and thereafter he wrote monthly letters to its Secretary recording archaeological discoveries and the activities of the 'fashionables' at Naples.

' The Society's Secretary at this time was Mr. William Richard Hamilton (1777–1859), the son of the Rev. Anthony Hamilton, Archdeacon of Colchester and Anne, daughter of Richard Terrick, Bishop of London. At the age of twenty-two, Hamilton was appointed by the Earl of Elgin as his chief private secretary. His sponsor wrote of him, 'He has much good sense, and a great activity of mind; he is industrious and in the highest degree anxious to render himself useful. His manners are pleasing and his principles perfectly good so you may use him at once as your companion, your confidant, and your fag.'[2] He accompanied Lord Elgin on his mission to Constantinople and took part in the proceedings which led to the acquisition of the Elgin Marbles by the Nation. From 1809 to 1822, Hamilton was Permanent Under-Secretary for Foreign Affairs and from 1822 to 1825 was Minister and Envoy Plenipotentiary at the Court of Naples. He helped to compel Louis XVIII to return to Italy art treasures which had been despoiled by Napoleon. He was twice rejected as a member of the Society,

1. 'In the year 1734 some gentlemen who had travelled in Italy, desirous of encouraging at home a taste for those objects which had contributed so much to their entertainment abroad, formed themselves into a society under the name of Dilettanti, and agreed upon such resolutions as they thought necessary to keep up the spirit of the scheme.' *History of the Society of Dilettanti* by Lionel Cust and Sidney Colvin. London, Macmillan, 1898, p. 4.
2. Col. Anstruther to Elgin. 19 March 1799. Elgin Papers.

but in 1830 was appointed its Secretary as successor to Sir Thomas Lawrence and remained in office until his death. Hamilton was Member of Parliament and a Fellow of the Royal Society. His letters to Gell have not survived in the Society's archives.

A considerable part of this correspondence is concerned with the struggle in which Gell was engaged to secure publication of *The Topography of Rome and its vicinity with accompanying Map*. As a result of his persistent efforts the Society of Dilettanti 'agreed to assist him in the publication of a valuable work on the topography of Rome, a kind of gazateer accompanied by a map'. The Map, which had been engraved at Rome, was re-engraved by the Society in London and Gell was voted £200 towards his expenses. Arrangements were finally made with Messrs. Saunders and Otley, who published the work in 1834, Gell receiving £300 for the sale of the copyright of the book and map.[1]

In order to preserve Gell's often quaint and very personal manner of expressing himself, the spelling and use of capitals in these *Letters* has been altered as little as possible, although he does at one point modestly invite Mr. Hamilton to make any necessary corrections. The punctuation, however, has been slightly augmented for the sake of clarity. Where place-names occur, their more usual modern form is given enclosed in square brackets. As far as it has been possible to do so, identification of persons mentioned in the correspondence appears in the Notes; it has been thought best generally to record titles as in their country of origin.

Although this book is only concerned with Sir William Gell's last years in Italy, a brief account of his earlier life should be given. He was born at Hopton Hall near Wirksworth in Derbyshire in 1777 being a member of an old County family, and was the son of Philip Gell and his wife, Dorothy Milnes, who later married Thomas Blore, the topographer of Derbyshire. He was educated at Jesus College, Cambridge; later became a Fellow of Emmanuel College, and studied at the Royal Academy of Arts. He was elected a Fellow of the Society of Antiquaries of London in 1800 and in the following year started on his travels by visiting the Troad. In 1803 he was sent on a diplomatic mission to the Ionian Islands, and from 1804 to 1806 travelled in Greece and the neighbouring islands. He was elected a Member of the Society of Dilettanti and a Fellow of the Royal Society in 1807. Four years later the Society of Dilettanti commissioned him to undertake an

1. Cust and Colvin, *op. cit.*, pp. 174–76.

exploration of Greece and Asia Minor in pursuance of the Society's policy of continuing the study of the classical antiquities of those regions. Gell was accompanied, as draughtsmen, by Mr. John Peter Gandy (who later assumed the name of Deering) and by Mr. Francis Bedford, both of them being well-known architects. As a result of these travels, Gell wrote and published several books, which are listed in the *Bibliography*, and achieved fame in scholarly circles as a classical topographer. Byron in *English Bards* referred to Gell in the well-known couplet:

> Of Dardan tours, let dilettanti tell,
> I leave topography to classic Gell.

Byron and Gell were acquainted, and the former, who had written 'coxcomb' in his MS, altered the word to 'classic' before publication. However, in the fifth edition of this work, Byron altered 'classic' to 'rapid' with the note, 'RAPID, INDEED!'.

Gell (Pl. II) was Knighted on 11 May 1814. Cust, the *D.N.B.* and the *Gentleman's Magazine* (June 1836) state that he received the Knighthood 'on his return from a mission to the Ionian Islands' and give the year 1803 for the bestowal of this honour. It appears that all three sources confused the Ionian Islands with the Ionian coast of Asia Minor.

For the next few years Gell seems to have resided chiefly in London where he and his life-long friend, Mr. Keppel Craven, became members of the intimate circle which surrounded Princess Caroline of Wales. Lady Charlotte Campbell, a lady-in-waiting to the Princess, makes many references, and records numerous amusing anecdotes relating to Sir William Gell in her Diary[1] which she published as Lady Charlotte Bury after her second marriage. Writing in October 1811, Lady Charlotte, describing the Princess of Wales's dinners, says,

> Very frequently, the dinners at Kensington were exceedingly agreeable, the company well chosen, and sufficient liberty was given to admit of their conversing with unrestrained freedom. This expression does not imply licentious mode of conversation; although sometimes, in favour of wit, discretion and modesty were trenched upon. Still that was by no means the general turn of discourse, Mr. Gell and Mr. Craven, in particular,

---

1. There were two editions of this book, but the second one was revised and is of more interest to the modern reader: *The Diary of a Lady-in-Waiting* by Lady Charlotte Bury, edited by A. Francis Steuart. London, John Lane, The Bodley Head, 1908, 2 vols.

though often very droll, were never indecorous. I think I never knew a man of a more kind and gentle turn of mind, nor one so humanised by literature and the particular pursuits to which he devoted himself, as Mr. Gell. He was affectionate in the highest degree, and willing to impart all he knew (no common stock of information) in the least pedantic and most agreeable manner; if ever he indulged in a joke that was questionable, it was in a manner so devoid of real vice, that the most punctilious or delicate female could scarce take offence at it.

Later on, Lady Charlotte remarks that 'of all these people, Mr. Gell is, I believe, my favourite: I think he is really good, and I cannot like any one long, that has not a stable foundation whereon to rest.'

In 1814 when Princess Caroline decided to leave England to travel on the Continent and in the Middle East, Sir William Gell accompanied her as one of her Chamberlains; in fact, when she embarked in August from Worthing she gave a ball on board *Jason* which she opened on the arm of Sir William. The Princess was joined a little later in Germany by Keppel Craven, but both he and Gell left her suite after the Party's arrival in Italy, the former pleading increasing infirmity due to recurring attacks of gout from which he seems to have suffered from an early age. Lady Bessborough writing to her sister, Georgiana, Duchess of Devonshire from Marseilles on 21 December 1814 says:

Keppel Craven writes his Mother word that he has galloped thro' Italy with the Pss. of Wales, who just stops long enough to receive Royal Honours everywhere. At Rome, after a triumphal entry, she went first to dine with Lucien Buonaparte, who gave her a ball. Next day an Audience of the Pope, and a dinner with the old King of Spain and Queen of Etruria—the Queen of Spain very ugly, and still very coquettish. Next day trots to Naples, where K. Joachim persists in taking her coming as an acknowledgment of his title by the English Government. Mr. Craven says nothing ever was so Magnificent as her Court— the men's dresses exactly like his and Dr. Gell's à la Henri Quatre, only cover'd with gold and silver Embroidery. What can make the Pss. dress them up so?[1]

1. *Private Correspondence of Lord Granville Leveson Gower, 1781–1821*, ed. by Castalia, Countess Granville. London, 1916, 2 vols; vol. ii, pp. 517–18.

Although Gell did not settle permanently in Italy until 1820, it would appear that he spent most of his time there in the five years prior to that date, and he was certainly in attendance on the Princess of Wales for short periods when she was at Rome and Naples in 1816 and 1817. Princess Caroline obviously had a high regard for Gell, and there is in existence a series of very entertaining letters from her to Sir William which are at Hopton Hall. These letters are unpublished.

In his earlier days Gell must have been a frequenter of the Devonshire House Circle because Lady Elizabeth Foster (later Duchess of Devonshire) writing to her son, Augustus Foster, from Chiswick on 9 November, 1808 says she 'had just seen interesting letters from Mr. Gell'; and in 1806 in correspondence between Lord Aberdeen and Augustus reference is made to Gell 'having gone off to Zante'.[1] Gell kept in touch with Elizabeth, Duchess of Devonshire after her widowhood when she was living at Rome during the last years of her life.

Gell returned to England in order to give evidence for the Defence at Queen Caroline's Trial in October 1820,[2] but from that time onwards he lived either at Rome or in his 'beautifully situated and elegantly arranged villa' at Naples. Here he was busily occupied in preparing further editions of his *Pompeiana* and *The Topography of Rome* as well as entertaining, and acting as *cicerone* to, the many English visitors who were travelling in Italy at that time in spite of the fact that he was seldom free from pain, and was so crippled by gout and rheumatism that he had to be carried about in a chair. He died at Naples on 4 February 1836. Writing to Lady Blessington from Naples on 17 April, Keppel Craven says of the last days of Gell.

> He was not aware of his increasing debility; and as the functions of his stomach continued unimpaired until within two days before the sad event, when a general and rapid decay of all the vital functions occurred, I don't think that his reflection dwelt upon the dissolution as being very near. Nevertheless, his last will, about which he was very anxious, was executed little

1. *The Two Duchesses*, ed. by Vere Foster. London, 1892, 2 vols; vol. i, pp. 187, 189; vol. ii, p. 313.
2. Lady Granville referring to this on 7 October 1820 says: 'Sir William and Keppel Craven, God help their souls, giving the most entire and cordial testimony in her favour, confuting much of the previous evidence against her.' *Letters of Harriet Countess Granville, 1810–1845*. London, 1892, 2 vols; vol. i, p. 153.

more than a week before his decease, and occasionally he would allude to the event itself in an indirect manner; for on receiving some books about a month before it happened, and my asking to lend some to me, he said, 'You had better read them when they are your own—and you are not likely to wait long'. ... He never ceased, I don't think for an hour, but an *instant*, to have a book open before him; and though he sometimes could not fix his eyes for two minutes at a time on its contents, he nevertheless understood it, and could afterwards talk of the work in a manner which proved that, while his mental powers were awake, they were as strong as ever—more especially his memory; but the state he was in caused much confusion in his ideas of time and distance, of which he was aware, and complained of.

Sir William Gell was buried in the Protestant Cemetery at Naples (Pl. Va) on the day after his death in the tomb of the Margravine of Anspach, the mother of his greatest friend. This tomb is in the form of a small doric temple. Keppel Craven, who was his sole executor, followed him there sixteen years later.

It is interesting to read of the affection in which Gell was held by Craven's mother, who wrote in her Memoirs,[1]

> The refined taste of Sir William Gell, the bosom friend of my aimable Keppel, and whom I almost considered as another son, has led him to pass his life in exploring the antiquities of Greece and Rome, and to display an unremitting assiduity in all his researches. I have been accustomed to his society for years; and his universal knowledge and various acquirements have endeared him to all who really knew how to esteem his qualities. Keppel and Sir William have been inseparable friends. I lament to say, that the gout has made such violent inroads on the constitution of Sir William that his health has lately been totally undermined.

The Honourable Keppel Richard Craven was born in 1779 being the third and youngest son of William, sixth Baron Craven and Elizabeth, daughter of the fourth Earl of Berkeley. When only three years old, his parents separated and Lady Craven took Keppel with her to France and thereafter lived abroad. However, in June 1791 she returned to England to send Keppel to school at Harrow under an assumed name. In September of that year, Lord Craven died, and at the end of the year Lady Craven married Christian Frederick Charles Alexander, Margrave of Brandenburg, Anspach

1. *Memoirs of the Margravine of Anspach formerly Lady Craven written by Herself.* Paris. A. and W. Galignani, 1826, 2 vols; vol. ii, p. 260.

and Bayreuth, Duke of Prussia, Comte de Sayn and nephew of Frederick the Great. Very soon after the marriage, the Margrave renounced his German possessions, and he and his wife took up residence in England at Brandenburg House on the Thames, which later was leased to Queen Caroline and where she died. The Margrave died in 1806, and thereafter the Margravine and Keppel Craven went to live abroad. In 1819 Ferdinand I of Naples gave a grant of land at Posillipo near Naples to the Margravine where she built the Villa Craven, and where she spent the rest of her life until her death on 13 January 1828. Richard, Duke of Buckingham and Chandos, nephew of the Margravine, who had arrived at Naples on the day of her death describes her Villa as being,

> beautifully situated, hanging over the bay, and looking over it and commanding Nicida (sic) and part of Baiae. The lodge of entrance is a neat Doric pavilion, looking on Naples. Here she caught her death. Her great amusement was in the garden, and she persisted, about three weeks ago, in remaining digging in it in a wet day until she get wet through, and caught a chill and fever.[1]

The Margravine left all her real property to Keppel Craven for his life.

Keppel Craven seems to have made his chief residence with his mother. He travelled a good deal, and in 1814 accepted the post of Chamberlain to Princess Caroline of Wales. Although he did not retain this appointment for long, he kept in constant touch with the Princess and her suite until her death in 1821. In 1834, Craven bought the *Convento* of La Penta near Salerno. He travelled extensively in Italy and was the author of *A Tour through the Southern Provinces of the Kingdom of Naples*. London, 1821 and *Excursions in the Abruzzi and Northern Provinces of Naples*. London, 1837, 2 vols. Lady Blessington[2] said that Craven 'had a highly-cultivated mind, manners at once distinguished and graceful, and exercises an elegant hospitality, that renders his house the most attractive here.' While Madden[3] remarks of Gell and Craven that

1. *Private Diary of Richard, Duke of Buckingham and Chandos, K. G.*, London, Hurst and Blackett, 1862, 3 vols; vol. i., pp. 243-4. See also F. Alvino. *Regno di Napoli e di Licolia (La Collina di Posillipo)*. Napoli, 1945.
2. *The Idler in Italy* by Marguerite, Countess of Blessington, Paris, Baudry's European Library, 1839 — 1 vol. edition, p. 293.
3. *The Literary Life and Correspondence of the Countess of Blessington* by R. R. Madden. New York, Harper and Brothers, 1855, 2 vols; vol. i, p. 416.

'Their tastes, habits, pursuits, and inclinations were identical. There never were friends more united in sentiment and affection. Mr. Craven was a classical scholar, had an excellent taste for drawing, was a great lover of books, and had all the feelings, refined manners, and the gentle, winning, easy address of an accomplished gentleman'.

Sir William Gell left all his personal effects to Keppel Craven who wrote to Lady Blessington on 17 April 1836 after Gell's death,

> The drawings I have placed in two cabinets, in drawers, except those forming a series of his 'Travels in Greece', which I knew he wished finally to bestow upon the British Museum; these are all in one case, with his initials, and at my death shall be removed to that destination, more worthy, perhaps, of their merits than their present position, but not more honoured by their owner.

On Craven's death, his papers and personal documents were bequeathed to his Italian secretary, by name, Andrea Pasquini. We have been quite unable to trace the whereabouts of Sir William Gell's Italian sketch and note books apart from those at the British School at Athens and the British School at Rome.[1] The British Museum received Gell's Bequest in March 1853 where it is now housed in the Department of Greek and Roman Antiquities.

It has not been possible to find out exactly where Sir William Gell lived at Naples when he was writing these letters. In a MS copy of Vol. IV of his *Roman Topography* at the British School at Rome, a letter is inserted from Mr. Laing Meason (p. 46) addressed to him at 'Piazza S. Teresa, Chiaja, Napoli' and dated 2 August 1832. Another letter of 12 May 1833 is addressed 'Lago S. Tereselle a Chiaja', and Gell's letter to the Society of Dilettanti of 12 May 1833 (p. 119, n. 2) records that 'Lord de Tabley has taken the Pavillion of the Villa Salicetti just above me'. The Villa Saliceti, built by Lalò, later transformed by Niccolini and re-named the Villa Floridiana, was bought by Ferdinand IV in 1817 and given to his morganatic wife, Lucia Migliaccio, duchessa di Floridia. The pavilion in the grounds must be the Villa Lucia (*palazzina Pompeiana*) built by Maresca. Ferdinand bought the Villa Saliceti from the Principe di Torella, who had inherited it from his wife's family: they had purchased the property from Lalò in 1807.

1. See *Bibliography*.

The whole area around the Church of S. Teresa a Chiaia is now greatly changed. In Gell's time the Vomero hill was unbuilt upon, and the houses or *palazzi*, which formerly surrounded the Church, have been pulled down and apartment blocks erected in their place. From the piazza Amedeo, close by the Church, it is still possible to look up and see the Villa Lucia perched on top of the Vomero. In Gell's day a path wound down the hillside from it to the Chiaia (Pl. IV), which confirms his remarks about Lord de Tabley's residence and he himself must have been living not far from the Church of S. Teresa.

During one of the editor's first visits to Hopton Hall, a small sketchbook of Gell's was seen containing a drawing of his house bearing the inscription (of which a note was taken), 'Chiaja sotto il palazzo Calabrito, No. 44', but on a later visit this sketch-book was unaccountably missing. There is, however, at Hopton an album which contains, amongst many others of different places, two drawings by Gell bearing the words, 'Our House' (Pls. IIIa, b), but with no indication of date. The palazzo Calabritto stands now on the south side of the piazza dei Martiri. This *piazza* (originally called, we believe, the piazza della Pace) was created in the middle of the last century by the destruction of S. Maria a Cappella Nuova (Pl. IIIc): not to be confused with S. Maria a Cappella Vecchia which still exists next to the palazzo Sessa where Sir William Hamilton lived. Opposite p. 257 of the 4'th volume of the 4th edition (1792) of Carlo Celano *Notizie del Bello...della Città di Napoli* is an engraving of the Chiaia at that time. No individual church is identified, but there is one which is probably S. Maria a Cappella Nuova, which has a dome and what appears to be a square tower as in Gell's drawings.[1] If this identification is correct, it would be possible to see the Certosa di S. Martino in the centre background as depicted by Gell, and 'Our House' could well be 'sotto il palazzo Calabrito, No. 44'; but could, of course, be an earlier apartment where Gell was then living. It is possible that this abode is the one Gell described in a letter he wrote to Lady Charlotte Bury when he says:

Scene—a charming little room with the windows open looking out on the lovely bay, Orange trees, myrtles, and flowers under my window. The sun shining as it can only shine at Naples. Present, an individual dressed in an orange and blue-coloured dressing gown, a red velvet nightcap upon his head, his countenance nearly the same he as his gown, perhaps a little more

1. We are indebted to Professor Sir Ellis Waterhouse for this identification.

resembling a citron colour: his feet rolled up in flannel, and deposited upon a stool. He exclaims occasionally with much anger and vehemence, as a twinge of the gout makes itself severely felt.[1]

And when Madden was at Naples he says that Gell was living:

with his drawing room, library, studio, museum, all combined in a very moderately-sized apartment, with such a store of rarities, old folios in vellum, modern topography and illustrated travels richly bound, caricatures, charts, maps and drawings ... so many models too, of ancient structures, so many things in so small a space that still folks wondered Gell had one small room could hold so much so well.[2]

Both of Gell's drawings are inscribed 'Our House', and we must presume that at that time he was sharing house with Keppel Craven; at one time Gell wrote that Craven was 'tacked to his mama's apron'. On his mother's death in 1828, Craven inherited both the Villa Craven at Posillipo and her apartment at 6bis Via Chiatamone, but in 1834 he bought the *convento di Penta* near Salerno which he seems to have made his main residence. Later on Augustus Craven and his wife Paolina lived in the Chiatamone establishment[3]—Augustus was the natural son of Keppel whom he always acknowledged.

Although Gell had various other lodgings in his earlier days at Rome, from the time when he resided permanently in Italy he lived with Mr. Charles Mills at the Villa Spada or Mills on the Palatine Hill (Pl. Vb) (p. 81, n. 1). Writing on 14 November 1828, the Duke of Buckingham and Chandos says that he

visited the Villa Spada, on the Palatine Hill and forming part of the ruins. August's palace stood on the spot, and part of the vaulted apartments below remain as in the Emperor's time. The house is pleasantly fitted up, and commands a beautiful prospect. The gardens are very beautiful; and the terrace, which overhangs the site of the Curius Maximus, with all Rome to the right hand, and the Apennines, with Albano, Frescati (sic), etc., to the left, is the most enjoyable spot I have seen in Rome. It is the property of Mr. Mills, famous for having come over at the head

1. Lady Charlotte Bury: *op. cit.*, vol. ii, p. 237.
2. *op. cit.*, vol. i, pp. 322–23.
3. See *Paolina Craven e la sua famiglia* by Teresa Raveschieri. Napoli, Cav. Antonio Morano, 1892.

of the Queen's witnesses during her trial and as having perjured himself more than most.[1]

And the Diarist, Charles Greville, records on 24 May 1830 that he 'called on Sir William Gell at his egg-shell of a house and pretty garden which he planted himself ten years ago, and called Boschetto Gellio. He was very agreeable, with stories of Pompeii, old walls, and ruined cities, besides having a great deal to say on living objects and passing events.' The next day Greville went to breakfast with Gell 'under a treillage of vines, and surrounded by fruits and flowers'.[2] When Lady Granville visited this villa on 3 November 1842 she wrote that the garden was 'all full of roses, Cape jessamines and heliotrope; himself (Mr. Mills) and Lady Charlotte Bury driving off from his front door rather damaging the effect.'[3]

There is no doubt that Gell inspired great affection among his many friends, and was the centre of a wide circle at Naples. Although Lady Charlotte Lindsay (another lady-in-waiting to Princess Caroline of Wales) said, 'he has become a coffee-house for the idle and the nothing-to-do arians', he was surrounded by innumerable persons of learning and culture, and was in great demand as *cicerone* by English visitors. In fact, it would seem that few people of note coming to Naples did not seek his acquaintance.

In spite of being plagued by gout and rheumatism from a very early age—he remarked that he was beset by 'a dozen gouts and as many agues besides swelled glands' and had 'breakfast with his feet tied in a red silk handkerchief'—he was always full of fun and jokes. Lady Blessington called him her 'laughing philosopher', and said that he never spoke an unkind word of any one. The whimsical aspect of his character and strong sense of humour must have endeared him to many other people; and the correspondence between Gell and his friends is often very amusing. Princess Caroline used to sign her letters to him, 'Miss Julia Grundy', 'Grundy Thompson', 'Griselda Grundy', 'Alsimadere Pastorelle', 'St. Catherine Martyr'; and when writing to Lady Charlotte Campbell (Bury), Gell's signature appears among other oddities as 'Anacharsis', 'Adonis', 'Edmund Ironside', 'Blue Beard'; also 'Your humble servant and tame dog' and 'Your affectionate grandmother, John Julius Angerstein'. Gell's sense of fun is also well-illustrated by this note to Lady Charlotte Campbell: 'Mr. Trinsberg (Gell)

1. Duke of Buckingham, *op. cit.*, vol. iii, p. 17.
2. Greville, *Memoirs* ed. H. Reeve, vol. i, pp. 380, 383.
3. *Letters, op. cit.*, vol. ii, p. 340.

has requested me to enclose to you a letter to the Princess's cook, Mrs. Grundy Thompson (the Princess herself), maker of stews and sauces—please to deliver the same'.

Indeed, one can appreciate Gell's sense of humour in this series of *Letters*: for instance when he 'sighs for Tom Hope's new book and a new map of the moon value 3 or 4£', or when he refers to the 'present state of my rents from my Chateaux en Espagne' and remarks, 'I am happy to inform you that all the little boys in America will be whipped if they don't know what I say in some subjects for there is a new Lemprière full of me published there so that tho' the Prophet have no honour in his own country he may be revenged in the other or next world'. Even at the sad and solemn moment of the death of his old friend Dodwell, he is able to relate that Dodwell 'has had extreme unction which he told me this morning was his passport and the absolution his clean boots.'

Apart from Gell's abiding interest in classical studies of every kind, the assessment of which is undertaken in the latter part of this *Introduction*, his general knowledge covered a very wide field: he never seems to have been at a loss to discourse on any subject. Volcanoes interested him; that the inhabitants of Avellino had 'yellow and light hair—true Germans—not black as the Neapolitans'; the exhumation of Raphael's skull; politics and, of course, the weather. Even in the last years of his life his fertile mind was full of ideas for further publications—to illustrate new editions of Virgil, Homer and Pausanias; to draw 'maps of value' of Greece and Italy, and there is even his detailed scheme for 'making out what could be discovered of the cities conquered by Joshua' and in constructing a real map of that country. All this when he could not 'put a foot to the ground but must trust to slaves and asses for loco-motion'.

Gell's personal comments are often amusing and apt. 'I very much doubt whether Sir Walter was a very extraordinary man, and secondly if he were so I think the history of his decay would be quite as interesting as the account of his glory, and would give an air of truth to the account which it must want without it,' so he remarks of Sir Walter Scott. Of Bulwer Lytton, he says, 'I don't much admire writing or writers who merely pander to the passions of the mob and who if the Soup is not good lay it to the influence of the Aristocracy, but he seems in person quite different from England and the English so I should tell you in this what new lights he may throw on the science of Publication...By the bye one of the best things in His book[1] is the unmasking of who are the British Public who pronounce what is the opinion of the English nation—He says these are tenth rate scribblers who write from garrets and who can get no other employment than writing such nonsense'.

Another human side of Gell is his love of animals: he was always surrounded by dogs. Writing to Lady Blessington in 1832 from Naples, he says, 'My dog family consists of *Ticati*, who is my companion, his son and heir, *Monsu Qua*, a youth of promising talents—I have also a white terrier, *Monsu Bo*, of Craven breed'. He is also supposed to have taught at least one of his dogs to sing, because he said, 'My dog was in the habit of howling when loud music was performing and Sir Walter laughed till his eyes were full of tears at the idea of the dog singing "My mother bids me bind my hair", by the tune of which the animal seemed most excited'.[2] Gell himself was very musical and Madden says he had a light guitar which 'he had recourse to so often in moments of torture'. In these *Letters* we are told that Sir Charles Monck presented him with an organ; also Gell makes allusion to the operas of Mozart and Rossini.

So many persons have referred to Gell in terms of appreciation, affection and friendship that it is not easy to choose from whom one should quote to bear testimony. There is his obvious friendship with Princess Caroline of Wales and her lady-in-waiting, Lady Charlotte Campbell, the evidence for which is already in print; as is also that of Mr. R. R. Madden who knew him well at Naples and who in his book on Lady Blessington devotes the whole of Chapter XV in Vol. 1 to Gell, and in the following three chapters prints his letters to Lady Blessington; also he prints a Note on Sir William Gell by Mr. James Ramsay which is given here as *Appendix B*. Madden describes Gell as 'accomplished, witty, ever jocund and facetious' as well as drawing attention to his scholarship and learning, he also remarks that his 'indolent easiness of temper had something in it of a philosophical calmness of an Epicurean character'.

As for Lady Blessington herself, she relates many accounts of her meetings and excursions with Gell in her Neapolitan journals which form part of her book *The Idler in Italy*. Lord and Lady Blessington, Count D'Orsay, Lady Blessington's niece, Miss Mary

1. This must refer to his novel *Pelham*.
2. *Reminiscences of Sir Walter Scott's residence in Italy* by Sir William Gell, ed. by James C. Corson. London and Edinburgh, Nelson, 1957, p. 10.

Ann Power, and Charles James Matthews, the young architect whom Lord Blessington had employed on his Irish estate, arrived at Naples in July 1823. They at first rented the Villa Belvedere, then later the Villa Gallo, and continued to reside at Naples until February 1826. During that time a warm friendship developed between Lady Blessington and Sir William Gell, and after the Blessingtons left Naples, the two kept up a lively correspondence which was only ended by Gell's death. Since Lady Blessington so fully recounts the course of this friendship in her book, it is unnecessary to quote here more than the following tribute she paid to him:

> Sir William Gell is so universally esteemed and beloved. . . . He is a great acquisition to Naples. His house is the *rendez-vous* of all the distinguished travellers who visit it, where maps, books, and his invaluable advice, are at the service of all who come recommended to his notice. The extent and versatility of his information are truly surprising, and his memory is so tenacious, that the knowledge of any subject once acquired is never forgotten. Although a prey to disease, gout and rheumatism having deprived him of the power of locomotion, his cheerfulness is unvarying, and his temper unalterable. He opposes an unconquerable stoicism to the assaults of pain; but it is only against pain that the existence of this stern quality is made known, for a kinder heart, or one more ready to sympathise with the cares of others, does not exist. His society is justly appreciated at Naples, and universally sought. It is curious to see him supported into a room by two persons, his body offering the melancholy picture of cureless decrepitude, while his face still preserves a youthful and healthy appearance. He is the most lively and amusing companion imaginable; possessing a perfect knowledge of life, without having lost the least portion of the freshness of mind or goodness of heart which such a knowledge is supposed to impair.[1]

The visit of Sir Walter Scott to Naples between 17 December 1831 and 11 May 1832 resulted in the two knights becoming great friends, Sir William accompanying Sir Walter almost daily and conducting him to all the places of interest at Naples and in the surrounding countryside. Sir William Gell's *Reminiscences* of this

1. Lady Blessington, *op. cit.*, pp. 265–66.

visit, referred to in these *Letters*, have been admirably published by Dr. Corson and need no amplification here.

In order not to give the impression that Sir William Gell was a paragon of all the virtues, reference should be made to the remarks of Henry Fox whom Archbishop David Mathew referred to in *Lord Acton* as 'little delicate bitter'. Writing from the Villa Muti at Frascati where he was then living, Fox[1] on 13 July 1828 said

> Gell came for a night, unwell and out of sorts. After every one went to bed except Ed (Edward Cheney, see p. 84) and myself; he told us amusing stories of Dr. Parr[2] by whom he was educated and whom he justly described as a ridiculous fantastic mountebank, mad with vanity and imposed upon by the grossest and most apparent deceptors . . . Gell betrayed a most wonderful piece of ignorance with the respect to the Queen's Trial. Tho' attached to her for many years as one of her gentlemen-in-waiting, tho' in England at the time as a witness, he steadfastly denied the whole trial being caused by her unwillingness to drop the title of Queen. Gell speaks of no one with gratitude or kindness. Tho' unable to deny a thousand benefits from her, he invariably mentions the Queen with derision and contempt. He denies her liberality, and told a story of her meanness and ingratitude, towards Torlonia (see p. 65), tho' they gave her money in her hour of need without bond and when she had no credit.

1. *Journal of Henry Edward Fox, afterwards last and fourth Lord Holland, 1818–1830*, edited by the Earl of Ilchester, London, Thornton and Butterworth, 1923. p. 308.
2. Dr. Samuel Parr (1747–1825). Eminent Whig man of letters. Parr went to Harrow as assistant-master in 1767, but in 1771, after a quarrel in which he was disappointed at not being made head-master, he set up his own school at Stanmore. In 1776 he became head-master of Colchester Grammar School and in 1783 was made a Prebend of St. Paul's. In 1785 he accepted the perpetual curacy of Hatton, Co. Warwick, where he took private pupils, and 4 years later became rector of Wadenhoe. We are indebted to the Bursar of Harrow School, who most kindly has searched his archives, but can find no record of Gell being at the School. We must therefore suppose that he was one of Dr. Parr's private pupils.

It is of interest to note that Parr's last public act was on the occasion of the Trial of Queen Caroline when he wrote a solemn protest in the parish prayer-book at Hatton against the omission of her name in the liturgy. Lady Bessborough writing to Lord Granville Leveson Gower on 1 October 1811 remarks that 'he would not be a pleasant *companion*, but it is amusing enough to see so great an oddity for a short time'. (*op. cit.*, vol. ii, p. 400).

It is as well to record what Lady Charlotte Bury has to say about Torlonia when she refers to an assembly at his *palazzo* at Rome. She says he had two palaces, the old one for his banking business and his money-bags, the new for his *festas*, and continues:

> It would be unjust not to acknowledge that the duca di Torlonia, though purse-proud and a *parvenu*, is a very useful and hos-pitable person, and his family render themselves equally service-able and agreeable to all strangers who visit Rome, especially to the English... Torlonia whom Napoleon created a duke, bought valuable jewellery from Princess Caroline of Wales; and some pearls of priceless value, which belonged to H.R.H., decorate the ample bosom of the citizen's wife.[1]

However, in spite of the barbs which Fox aimed at Gell, he saw a good deal of him, entertained him, and went on excursions with him. An account of one of these excursions to Veii is given in *Appendix C*. Rather more critical comments come from the poet, Thomas Moore, who said Gell was 'full of jokes—still a coxcomb, but rather amusing', and the American traveller, George Ticknor, referred to him as 'a man of learning and taste, but a consummate fop in person and letters'.

Sir William Gell lived at Naples under three Bourbon Kings. At first, during the closing years of the long and strife-torn reign of Ferdinand I, and then during those of his son Francis I, who reigned from 1825–30. Thus it was that Ferdinand II, known as King 'Bomba', was ruling when these *Letters* were written.

Gell was too crippled to travel far afield in the latter part of his life, but he was a keen observer of the political scene, both in England, in Italy and other parts of the world. In spite of the fact that he attempted many reforms which would be beneficial to his people, Ferdinand II's reign was characterised by an uninterrupted succession of internal struggles, partly in Naples and partly in Sicily, especially after 1848. However, during the early years most of the political troubles in the Kingdom had little effect in Naples itself, where things were relatively calm.

Harold Acton[2] tells us that the dawn of Ferdinand's reign was like 'a clear patch of sunlight surrounded by storms'. On his accession, the King made great efforts to alleviate the hardships of his subjects. For instance, he renounced 100,000 ducats of his

1. Lady Charlotte Bury, *op. cit.*, vol. ii, pp. 4–5.
2. For the most comprehensive and admirably written account of this later period of Bourbon rule see *The Last Bourbons of Naples*, by Harold Acton, London, 1961, and see here pp. 51–52.

allowance; abolished some of his father's hunting preserves which were to be thrown open to the public to promote agriculture, and is recorded as having remarked that 'he would leave the crown and abandon Naples rather than subscribe to a constitution in the backward state of civilisation in his country, since its only result would be to encourage excesses and disorders, plunging the land into a sea of woes'.

In May 1833 Gell writes that 'The King had been on a Tour and having discovered the nakedness of the land is going they say to redress grievances in the Augean stable, and a pretty job it must be, but nevertheless the people are happier under a Brummagen salon'. During the earlier part of his reign Acton says the King made 'lightning tours of the province without pomp or preparation, staying in monasteries, dining with mayors and magistrates, to find out their requirements and see things for himself'. It must have been one such tour to which Gell refers. In June of the following year Gell reports that 'Capua has capitulated to escape the sacking and ravishing that would have evoked from a more obstinate resistance and the two armies during the armistice had a fête champêtre under the trees at Carditella' (p. 152, n. 1). Since his interests were not only confined to Naples, at this same period of time, he tells us that Rome has an 'appearance of prosperity greater than usual' and goes on to describe the improvements in the housing situation. We are also given an interesting account of the restorations at the Villa Borghese, and of Prince Borghese granting the public greater facilities in his park. Earlier in June 1832, Gell refers to trouble outside the Kingdom of Naples commenting that 'there would be the devil to pay because all the prisoners to the number of 300 at Spoleto had broken out and gone to Ancona' (p. 84).

Personal comments on the Neapolitan Royal Family are few in these *Letters* (Pl. VIII). Gell, however, remarked that 'the King's habits of frugality are so praiseworthy in these degenerate times', and goes on to describe an amusing incident when the King put his 'tent and conveniences' at the disposal of General Filangieri 'if he had a mind to ask his friends to dinner'. The unfortunate General then discovered that although Royal pots, pans, dishes and plates were provided, the cost of all the provisions fell on him. An example of King Bomba's impetuosity and disregard for personal convenience is given when Gell writes that during army manoeuvres the King dismounted from his horse and plunged up to his neck in the River Sebeto, his anger and disgust having been aroused on seeing his troops making a diversion to ford the river at a shallower place.

It is strange that we are not told anything about Court cere-
monies, Royal balls and similar entertainments considering how
social Gell and Craven were. They had innumerable friends
amongst the Neapolitan nobility and other Court personages, and
practically all English visitors to Naples of any note called on
them there. They must surely have received many Royal commands, but none of these are mentioned to the Society of
Dilettanti—perhaps by then Gell was too ill to stand the strain of
such functions. Madden, however, quotes the following extract
from an undated letter written by Keppel Craven from Naples,
'I was tête-à-tête with Gell over our tea, which we have like two
washerwomen, and am ashamed to say we prefer it to ices that
are handing about in the Royal Box which we quitted half-an-hour
ago'.[1]

Sir William Gell must have been a lovable and amusing person
with originality and whimsicality of mind which undoubtedly made
him an entertaining companion; his eccentricities probably en-
dearing him all the more to his friends. It is much to be regretted
that apart from these *Letters* and his correspondence with Lady
Blessington, no other such series has yet come to light.

Gell as Archaeologist

In considering Gell's position in the story of archaeology, we
must recognise that there were two sides to him. On the one hand
he was a populariser, especially of Italian classical antiquities; on
the other he made contributions in his own right as a classical
topographer. It is the former side that emerges, perhaps, the more
clearly in these *Letters*; and we catch many glimpses of the amusing
talker who commanded friendships among English and Italian
notables, the gouty but ebullient *cicerone* who guided many English
travellers around Rome and Naples, and the correspondent and
liaison-officer for the Society of Dilettanti. But the more serious
side must also be reckoned with; Gell the tireless traveller, the
recorder of monuments, and the cartographer and, in his way,
scholar, whose friendships could also include the learned men of
four nations. On this topic the *Letters* contain several interesting
allusions, and more is to be gleaned from Gell's other publications.
We must estimate this side of Gell, if only to understand why the
Society of Dilettanti placed such continuous confidence in him.

1. *op. cit.*, vol. i, p. 285.

With the founding of the Society of Dilettanti in 1733, as has been often observed, a new era in archaeology had begun, and in the course of the eighteenth century the Society had assumed a unique position in encouraging the study and collection of classical art.[1] The times favoured such an enterprise. The English aristocracy was among Europe's wealthiest; they felt acutely the obligation to make the journey abroad to Europe, the 'pilgrim martyrs, condemned to make their grand tour', as Laurence Sterne describes them. Many a great collection of statues and vases was created, nearly always with the help and connections that the Society provided. Rome was for long the main centre of their interest; the declining power of the Papacy and the impoverishment of aristocratic families made ideal conditions for the market in antiquities. The English buyer, moreover, could avail himself of expert advice. Two resident artists had dedicated themselves lucratively to the trade in antiquities. One was a Scotsman respected for his honesty, Gavin Hamilton, who had undertaken excavations at Hadrian's Villa and at Ostia. The other, Thomas Jenkins, operated with less scruple and grew more wealthy; he even became a private banker to visiting nobles, the Torlonia of his day. Whole villas— the Villa Mattei, the Villa Negroni, the Villa d'Este—passed through their hands, and quantities of statues, vases, coins and medals left Italy for English houses. In most cases the buyers were Dilettanti; so originated the Townley collection, the Thomas Hope collection (later at Deepdene), and that of Henry Temple at Broadlands (the family home of Viscount Palmerston). Others— who might not be able to accept the very whig complexion of the Society itself—nonetheless used the same agents, as did Shelburne, the later Lord Lansdowne. In Naples there was a member in the British minister himself, Sir William Hamilton, who negotiated some outstanding purchases.[2] Through him the British Museum obtained its first fine collection of vases in 1772; the Hope vases (1801) were also supplied by Hamilton, as was the famous Portland Vase. He had sent bronzes to Townley, and helped Payne Knight

1. To the basic work of Cust and Colvin (for which see above, p. 1, n. 1) we may add the earlier sketch by W. R. Hamilton, *Historical Notices of the Society of Dilettanti* (1856) with the review by Lord Houghton in the *Edinburgh Review* CV (1857); the remarkable appreciation by A. Michaelis, 'Die Gesellschaft der Dilettanti in London', *Jahrbuch für bildende Kunst* XIV (1879); and also his *A Century of Archaeological Discovery* (Eng. ed. London, 1908).
2. On Sir William Hamilton's long term in Naples (1764–1801), see the appreciation of H. Acton in *The Bourbons of Naples* i, 163 f. And now see the study of B. Fothergill, *Sir William Hamilton, Envoy Extraordinary* (1969).

to build up a great coin collection; both men were very influential figures in the Society of Dilettanti.

The golden age of English collectors, though it had begun earlier in the time of Lord Arundel, coincided above all with the eighteenth century. By the end of the century it was already starting to fade. Most of the early giants had died; in 1805 Townley's collection passed to the British Museum, and Payne Knight's was to follow before long (1824). There are signs, too, of the change of taste and a shift of interest that art-historians have often connected with the effects of the French Revolution and the Napoleonic Wars; many of the ancestral collections that were auctioned or seized consisted largely of paintings; English buyers with equal enthusiasm now turned to these, and the Picture Gallery came to be as common as the Sculpture Gallery had been before. Furthermore, and not least through the efforts of the Society of Dilettanti, the remains of Greece and Asia Minor were now being revealed to explorers, opening up new horizons. But a more realistic explanation is to be found in the French occupation of Italy, which shattered the English monopoly. Gavin Hamilton died in 1797, of grief at the French invasion, it is said. Thomas Jenkins was actually hounded from Rome and died almost immediately afterwards (1798). Sir William Hamilton fled with the Court from Naples in 1799, and was recalled to London in 1801. Among the savage clauses of the Treaty of Tolentino (1797) there were demands that the greatest treasures of Rome, sculptures, pictures, and manuscripts, should be sent to Paris to adorn the capital of the new Empire; nor were they all retrieved by the Treaty of Paris (1815). It is true that after the Wars the English buyers re-asserted themselves to a limited extent. To the years following 1815 belong the collections of the Dukes of Bedford at Woburn Abbey and the Duke of Buckingham at Stowe, which were sumptuous indeed. But even though Italy was accessible to English travellers once more they no longer commanded the market, and it is hard to resist the feeling that in these respects as in others an age had passed away.

But it would be wrong to suggest that English travellers in Italy had in any way grown less numerous. The intellectual ideas of the age were contagious, and the many groups of political or literary exiles helped to spread knowledge of foreign parts; and the romantic movement itself discovered new reasons for travel. These travellers were no longer the specialised *collezionisti* of the previous century, or gentlemen in search of culture or erudition; they were a wider circle of writers, artists and others, moved by enthusiasms of more varied kinds, or impelled by simpler curiosities. The Shelleys, who visited Naples in 1818–19, were among the first and most remarkable of the new brigade. For the French, the Napoleonic occupation had meant discovery of a new past; and for Germany, an antiquarian diary *Viaggio in Italia* by Goethe's father, J. Caspari Goethe (1740), was later answered, in the new romantic vein, by the *Italienische Reise* of his more famous son. The tour of Italy in this new atmosphere took on other meanings, and became for many a voyage of psychological discovery. The monuments of classical antiquity were not only objects of rational study, they were appeals to the imagination, like nature itself. One might not understand, but one could at least commune. 'A sweet languor enters the soul, and instead of studying nature we contemplate it; we should like to reflect, but instead we dream dreams' (Chateaubriand). Pompeii and Herculaneum were becoming a necessity for poets as well as scholars and *érudits*.[1]

Gell's letters give us some interesting glimpses of the new-style tourist that characterised the early nineteenth century. Their tone is very informal, and they deal briefly with a wide range of information, social and antiquarian. This was presumably what he was engaged to supply. Gell at several points asked whether the Society was satisfied with the content of his letters, and was answered in the affirmative. The social news was important to the Society's membership, and it was hardly available elsewhere. Serious reports of discoveries could wait for formal publications. It is rather to Gell's books that we should turn; they were written— what books were not in that time?—with an eye upon the cultivated public of gentlemen whom the Society of Dilettanti symbolised. But they give us the serious side of Gell that he has not given us in the *Letters*.

Under the intelligent guidance of Townley and Payne Knight, the Society had chosen William Gell, then a young man, to lead a mission of exploration in Ionia. Gell had already travelled widely in Greece. In 1801, at the age of twenty-four, he had studied the site of Troy and published his account of it with his own sketches (1804); this was what moved Byron to observe, 'Rapid indeed! He topographised and typographised King Priam's dominions in three days'. Other tours followed in the later years (1802, 1805–6, etc.),

---

1. See also E. Cione, *Napoli Romantica* (3rd ed. Naples, 1957); and the interesting study by R. Michéa, 'Les ruines, l'Italie et le préromantisme', *Rev. des études italiennes* 1945. J. C. Goethe's *Viaggio in Italia* was republished in 1932 (Rome).

and publications on Ithaca (1807), the Itinerary of Greece (1810), and at a later stage the two descriptive works on the Morea (published 1817, 1823). His sketches were usually accurate rather than artistic, though he allowed himself now and then the indulgence of an 'imaginative reconstruction' as of the palace on Ithaca; his descriptions were in keeping, clear, sober, circumstantial, neither too erudite nor too rhetorical. In an age where these lands were being revealed for the first time, these were not inconsiderable qualities.[1]

These, and the undeniable fact that Gell worked fast, may have moved the Society of Dilettanti in appointing Gell to head the mission to explore Ionia and Athens. The first expedition to Ionia, that of Chandler, Revett and Pars in 1764, also financed by the Society of Dilettanti, had suffered crucial delays in the publication of its results, and the memory was no doubt keen. The results of Gell's expedition were splendid, but this time the costs were unexpectedly large—£6,500. The reasons are unknown; but they probably lay in the unrest of the time and the unfavourable exchange-rate of English currency, and there is no hint that the mission had been unduly extravagant. The Society at any rate rose to the occasion, and a ten-guinea levy was paid by its members to make good the loss. In 1817 the antiquities of Attica saw the light, and in 1821 the best of the Ionian material (the remainder of it did not appear until 1840, after Gell's death). All in all the Society had much to be pleased with: Gell and his colleagues had acted quickly and worked tirelessly. The prestige of the Society had been lately somewhat tarnished during the debate about the Elgin marbles, wherein Payne Knight had loudly proclaimed them mere Roman copies; the five publications did much to restore its reputation. This may be measured by the fact that in 1816 Gell, along with Hamilton, Payne Knight, W. M. Leake and Dodwell, was elected to honorary membership of the Royal Academy in Berlin.[2]

1. Michaelis called Gell 'dry but indefatigable'; Lord Houghton describes Gell as 'the accurate and lucid traveller who has furnished the material for every subsequent traveller of Hellenic explorers'. His drawings still have value; see those now in the British Museum in the Department of Greek and Roman Antiquities listed by Hasluck in *Annual of the British School at Athens* XVIII (1911–12), 272. His notebooks were published by A. M. Woodward and R. P. Austin, 'Some Note books of William Gell', in *Annual...* XXVII and XXVIII (1925–6 and 1926–7).
2. Ad. Harnack, *Geschichte der königlich-preussischen Akademie der Wissenschaften zu Berlin* (Berlin 1900) I, p. 969. Gell was most appreciative of the honour and

Gell's work in Italy began immediately upon his arrival in the following of Queen Caroline in 1814. His movements in these years are somewhat obscure. But in 1814 he surely began his work with Gandy on Pompeii which was to emerge in 1819 as the first *Pompeiana*, and it may be assumed that he made repeated visits to Naples until he settled there in 1820.[1] We must suppose some time spent in Rome, where he drew a set of sketches of the city walls which appeared in his joint publication of them with Antonio Nibby in 1820; by this year, too, as we learn from the title-page of that work, he had already been elected to the 'Accademia Romana di Archaeologia', and was therefore well-known in Rome.[2]

But for a man of Gell's tastes and temperament, Naples had the advantages. Above all it was near Pompeii, on which Gell soon made himself the English expert. The first series of *Pompeiana* were a great success (1817-19; further edns. 1821, 1824 (Pls. X, XIa, b, XII, XIIIb). The excavations were now over half a century old, and had been actively promoted in the years of French rule; they were not yet available to an English public.[3] Gell remedied this lack with skill and knowledge. The book was openly welcomed by Italians as well, and a French adaptation was soon undertaken

some years later, after having submitted in 1827 his study of Cyclopean Walls, he wrote, 'I have dedicated and given this to the Royal Society of Berlin out of gratitude for their unsought protection and election of myself when I was yet young and unknown.' (Gell to Lady Blessington, 29 December 1829; Madden, vol. ii, p. 60). He was later elected a member of the Leipzig academy; Madden ii, 54 (6 June 1828).

1. The basic work by Gell and Gandy for the first *Pompeiana* was done 1817-19. In its second edition, p. 4, Gell reports a reading of an Oscan inscription he made in 1814. cf. Madden,[2] ii, 8-11.

2. *Le Mura di Roma disegnate da Sir William Gell, illustrate con testo da A. Nibby* (Rome 1820). The work was dedicated to, and no doubt subsidised by, 'Sua Eccellenza, Elisabetta Duchessa di Devonshire che le ricerche antiquarie ama e protegge'. It was she to whom, rather unexpectedly, the historian Gibbon had once proposed marriage. From 1814 to 1824 she had lived in Rome; she fostered excavations and lavish publications, and maintained a variegated salon. Gell was known in this circle, but the Duchess was not a cultivated woman and he joked about 'her admiration for the purity of the Roman government' (see, under August 1820, Moore, *Memoirs* iii, p. 137).

3. There were few books on Pompeii of any kind. C. Celano had included some notices in his *Notizie del bello, dell'antico* etc., vol. IV (Naples 1792); and there was a popular work by D. Romanelli, *Viaggio a Pompei, a Pesto*, etc. (1811; 2nd ed. 1817). The volume of engravings by Piranesi junior (Naples 1804-5) was simply illustrative. The works of H. Wilkins, *Suite de vues pittoresques des ruines de Pompéi* (Rome 1819) and of W. B. Cooke and Lieut.-Col. Cockburn (London 1818-27) were relatively worthless. F. Mazois began his work in 1812, but his first publication appeared only in 1824.

(publ. 1827). Gell was unlikely to be indifferent to the material advantages of his work; these letters show he had financial worries as did most writers of his age.

In addition, however, Naples was the first city of Italy at this time, 'Italy's only capital' according to Stendhal. The rule of the Bourbons after their restoration was hardly a model of enlightenment; but there was not much choice in Metternich's Europe. In Rome the withdrawal of French rule brought about a period of reaction and stagnation, creating the dreary city that appears in Leopardi's *Letters* or the memoirs of Massimo D'Azeglio. Gell was himself not blind to the fact. 'I find this kingdom quite green and everything in a most flourishing condition after that worn out, misgoverned, unfortunate representative of the Mistress of the World' (Gell to Lady Blessington, 2 June 1834; Madden ii, 86 f.). Naples by comparison seemed lively and almost liberal; dissident opinions could at least be expressed, and among aristocrats and administrators there were distinct Anglophile currents of feeling.[1] Gell moved with easy familiarity among the foreign colony and among Italian aristocrats. The English ministers, Sir William Drummond (retired), the Hon. William Noel Hill (1824–33) and William Temple (1833–55), Lord Palmerston's brother, were known to him, and were all keen students of antiquities. He attended major social events such as the *soirées* of the aged Monsignor Capecelatro, Archbishop of Taranto; until his death in 1836 at the age of ninety-two, that amiable eccentric held a brilliant and variegated Court in the Palazzo Sessa, Sir William Hamilton's old residence, surrounded by rich antiquities and a company of cats. Gell knew the antiquarians of the time; F. M. Avellino, the ageing Michele Arditi, composer and archaeologist, the architect Carlo Bonucci, the German artist M. Ternite. Wilhelm Zahn he mentions in *Pompeiana* as an acquaintance (see pp. 92, 111); this remarkable artist devoted his long life to the publication of Pompeian paintings; he exercised a deep influence on the future emperor of Germany, Frederick William IV, and so created an epoch of neo-classical art. Gell's allusions to him lack warmth; he thought him ignorant, and it is clear that the artist by training

1. Gell's opinion on Naples was surprisingly echoed by the historian Macaulay on his visit in 1839; see *Life and Letters of Lord Macaulay* (London 1876) ii, 43. Imports from England in the 1830's accounted for over 35 per cent of the total in the Kingdom of Naples. The political currents of the time were complex and oddly contradictory: see recently R. Romeo, *Mezzogiorno e Sicilia nel Risorgimento* (Naples 1963), 51 ff.; and G. Cingari, *Problemi del risorgimento meridionale* (Messina-Firenze 1965), 7 ff.

and outlook did not mix with the antiquarian.[1] As for his connections with English visitors and with the colony at Naples, the *Letters* themselves give us our best information.

After his arrival in Italy Gell visited Rome frequently, where his connections were more influential. The Roman revival was slower since the period of French rule, whatever its virtues, had virtually killed all antiquarian pursuits. Many English residents had left by 1800 and after 1815 influential figures did not return.[2] The leading scholar in learning and judgment had been the Danish agent Georg Zoega, who denounced the French sack of the city's treasures, and died in 1809; another enthusiast, the Prussian Minister Wilhelm von Humbolt, was recalled to Berlin in 1808. James Millingen alone of English scholars seems to have lasted out the occupation in Rome; he was the author of many works on coins, medals and vases in inaccessible private collections; but he had lived earlier in France and so may have been politically acceptable to the French. A true revival, however, began with the arrival of Niebuhr as Prussian ambassador in 1816. A Dane by origin and earlier career, Niebuhr had moved into the service of Prussia as lawyer and economist, and had already found time to produce his *Roman History* (first edn., 1811–12). In Rome his stay was, perhaps, less productive in scholarship than diplomatically; certainly, it was not until he left Rome in 1823 and became professor at Bonn that his second, and decisive, edition of the *Roman History* appeared (vols 1–2, 1827–8; vol. 3, 1832). His scepticism, and radical rejection of the most famous legends of early Rome, seemed deeply shocking; but his new methods mark an epoch in the study of ancient history, and he encouraged others generously. Gell must have met him, but nothing suggests that he knew him well; indeed it is

1. His main works were *Neu entdeckte Wandgemälde in Pompeii* (Munich 1828); and *Die schönsten Ornamente und merkwürdigsten Gemälde aus Pompeii, Herculaneum und Stabiae* (3 vols, Berlin 1828–1852). In *Pompeiana* (2nd series, 2nd ed.) vol. i, p. 54, Gell mentions Zahn as 'an indefatigable and exact artist who will contribute much to the embellishment of his native country on his return, and who kindly permitted the Author to copy and publish his picture'. Gell also mentions his acquaintance with Th. Panofka (II *Pompeiana*, vol. ii, p. 157); the Canonico Iorio (ibid. p. 197); the Cav. Carelli, secretary of the Royal Academy (ibid. p. 199); and Arditi and Bonucci (ibid. vol. 1, p. viii ff.).

2. For the German and other residents in Rome, apart from the *Allgemeine Deutsche Biographie*, the facts are in A. Michaelis, *Storia dell'Instituto Archeologico Germanico 1828–1879* (Rome 1879) and F. Noack, *Das Deutschtum in Rom seit dem Ausgang des Mittelalters*, vol. ii, esp. pp. 113 ff. English residents, to judge from the memoir literature, were fewer though visitors were more frequent than ever.

apparent that Niebuhr in Rome stood rather apart from the other scholars who had begun to work there.

Twice in these letters Gell mentions dining with Bunsen. This is Baron Christian von Bunsen, who had been posted as secretary to the Prussian embassy in Rome with Niebuhr, and followed him as minister (1823–1838). Bunsen's wife was English, one Frances Waddington of Monmouthshire; and it is remarkable that his later service as ambassador in London (1842–54) was also a heyday of warm feelings between England and the liberal Germany of the day. His term in Rome was no less fruitful, especially after Niebuhr's departure; combining scholarship, a passion for antiquities and great social gifts, he virtually created the first international archaeological body, which was known in its early phase as the Istituto di Corrispondenza Archeologica. Its periodical Gell refers to in these letters, with quaint parochialism, as 'Bunsen's Archaeologia'; and his references to Bunsen himself show that they were on warm terms (see pp. 48, 89). The same was also true of another German resident, August Kestner, in the Hanoverian embassy in Rome from 1817, and full ambassador after 1827. He was a man of less learning, but his interest in art and religion was real and active. As England had no official representation at the Holy See, the duty naturally fell to Kestner who knew the English well. Gell happens not to mention him in the letters, but he dedicates his study, *Gli Avanzi di Veji* (1831), to 'Augusto Kestner, consigliere ed incaricato d'affari di sua maestà Britannica il re di Annovera presso la S. Sede', and was plainly on close terms with him.[1] Gell's *entrée* into the circle of Roman antiquarians was doubly assured.

The 1820's were significant for the emergence of the Instituto di Corrispondenza Archeologica, a major landmark in the history of archaeology. Its origins lay among an informal group of dedicated scholars and amateurs known as the *Iperborei romani*, the 'Romans from north of the Alps'. In fact, its founding members were mainly Germans. Most important were two scholars Eduard Gerhard and Theodor Panofka, who had embarked on a huge project of publication of material in Roman and Italian Museums. But

---

1. *Gli Avanzi di Veji* (1831) first appeared in vol. i of the *Memorie* and was later incorporated in *The Topography of Rome and its Vicinity* as the article on 'Veii'. Kestner's mother had been the original of Charlotte, the central character in Goethe's *Leiden des Jungen Werthers*; and Kestner himself had earlier written a tragedy called *Sulla*, 'in the style of Shakespeare'. His close friendship with Bunsen is movingly related in the *Memoirs* of her husband by Frances Baroness Bunsen (London 1867).

they included also the veteran explorer of Greece Stackelberg, who had excavated years before at Bassae, his old companion there, the Dane Brondstedt, and of course Kestner and Bunsen. Bunsen's untiring efforts bore fruit, despite some opposition from the Pontifical authorities, when he succeeded in convincing the Prussian Crown Prince, the future Kaiser Federick William IV, and the Institute was finally born in 1829. Gell's relations with the *Iperborei romani* were quite close; apart from Bunsen and Kestner, he knew Stackelberg and Brondstedt and may have met them in Greece. Panofka he had known in Naples, Gerhard he knew later, at least, as secretary of the Institute (see p. 88). But these men were Germans and romantics; they knew their Goethe, they had learned mythology from Heyne, and they had fallen under the spell of Fr. Creuzer and thought that myths were symbolic and the relics of a primitive revelation of divine truth of mankind.[1] The stolid Gell would hardly have shared such heady notions. The English scholars in Italy were of another kind, travellers and explorers, and typically solitary. But the *Iperborei romani* could hardly ignore the new monuments they discovered and did much to help publish their first-hand accounts and drawings. Gell generously made available to them his own and his colleagues' drawings.[2]

Another important friend in Rome was Antonio Nibby (1792–1839), young, brilliant, and at the time professor of archaeology at Rome University. Nibby was the author of a great many topographical studies; but they were rather in the Italian tradition of topography, and aimed at giving a full repertory of sources and documents about each site in the fashion later culminating in the work of Tomasetti. Gell and Nibby, despite the difference in their ages, complemented one another. We do not know when they met, but a few years after Gell's arrival in Italy they produced a joint study of the walls of Rome (1820), Gell's sketches accompanying Nibby's text.[3] Soon the further plan was hatched to which these

1. Creuzer's book, *Symbolik and Mythologie der alten Völker* (1810–12), had enormous influence in Germany and France; cp. A. Rumpf, *Archäologie* (Samml. Göschen) i, pp. 69 f., 86.
2. Gell's paper, submitted in 1827 to the Berlin Academy ('Probestücke von Städtemauern des alten Griechenlands, von Sir William Gell, Mitglied der königlichen Gesellschaft zu Berlin', publ. 1831), included not only his own drawings but others by Craven (Alba, Arpino, Bovianum), Dodwell (Empulum), and Lady Mary Deerhurst (Norba). In vol. i of the *Memorie* there were more drawings by several hands, including Fox.
3. Nibby's interest in things English goes back at least to 1810, when at the age of eighteen he published an Italian translation of Oliver Goldsmith's *History*

letters refer (see p. 43 ff.). Gell, as cartographer, was to prepare a map of the Roman Campagna, and Nibby was to supply an extended commentary on the places. The task of producing a map of the Roman Campagna from the beginning, including the basic triangulation, was a formidable one, and even the 'rapid Gell' spent five years over the expeditions and readings that it involved. In advance of Nibby's part of the work, he arranged for the preliminary publication of the map in Rome, having been fortunate in procuring a subsidy towards it from Lord Blessington. It was engraved by the Roman engraver Troiani and appeared in 1827 as the *Tentamen Geographicum*. Troiani's map soon appeared to Gell to be very unsatisfactory technically, as these letters reveal. But Gell's map had required a huge copperplate and a mass of very minute detail, and it is no surprise, in the straitened conditions of Roman life, that the map had imperfections.[1]

Nibby's part of the work, meanwhile, languished; in his perfectionist zeal for full documentation he was led far afield into medieval sources, and was dogged increasingly by ill health. Finally each resolved to publish separately. Gell's struggle with the Society of Dilettanti over the map and its accompanying text is related in the Letters that follow, and it was not until 1834 that his *Topography of Rome and its Vicinity* finally appeared. Nibby, using the earlier and imperfect map, produced his explanatory text in 1837;[2] two years later he was to die in poverty. Gell speaks forcefully of Nibby's delays in these letters (pp. 61), but we must remember that he was hoping for money from the Society and was bound to

---

of England, and he had since produced several topographical works.

It should be recorded here that about a dozen letters of Gell's to Nibby are preserved in the Biblioteca dell'Instituto di Architettura e Storia d'Arte in the Palazzo Venezia, Rome (ref. MS Lanciani 66). Most are undated, but the earliest dated one is of 1821, and seems to presuppose a long acquaintance. The letters and sketches are mostly concerned with the forthcoming map of the Campagna, and were preserved by Nibby for that reason. Nibby also kept the phrenologist's 'report' on him (compare these *Letters*, p. 153) that Gell had sent him; he was diagnosed, wrote Gell, as 'sanguineous, bilious, lymphatic, nervous'. The tone of these letters, half in Italian, half in English, is strikingly warm, and show the real affection that Gell felt towards his 'Caro Nibbsbuhriano', as he jokingly calls him.

1. The *Iperborei romani* found similar difficulties in publishing in Rome, see Michaelis, *Storia*, pp. 14 and 39; as did James Millingen, see his *Some Remarks on the State of Learning and the Fine Arts in Britain* (London 1831). Papal censorship had encouraged much printing to migrate elsewhere.

2. The *Analisi storico-topografico-antiquaria della Carta de' Dintorni di Roma* (1837; 2nd ed., 1848).

give prominence to his own virtues. Certainly no quarrel had occurred, since Nibby in his introduction speaks very generously of Gell and Gell followed Nibby's opinions and identifications with a rare respect.

About Gell's other connections we can only speculate. In a letter of 1832 (p. 79) he mentions under humorous disguise the great Italian excavator Carlo Fea, now bent with his eighty-nine years of age, a remarkable survivor of an earlier generation. Gell's contacts with French scholars seem to have been less close—they, too, went in for the *archeologia simbolica* that afflicted the Germans —but he mentions with pride his election to an honorary membership of the French Institute (p. 95). His closest contacts were with other Englishmen. He did much to encourage Keppel Craven in his travels. The intelligent but shy Dodwell he helped to make known, and generously published his drawings. We get little reference to James Millingen (p. 107), the *doyen* of English expatriates; he had lived long in Rome and Naples, though it is true that in 1832 he moved to Florence and his interests ran towards coins and smaller *objets* that were not to Gell's taste. Gell showed no enthusiasm at all for Thorwaldsen (p. 153). Yet it becomes clear why, when the Instituto di Corrispondenza was founded, second only to Millingen, Gell was appointed an honorary member of the Directorate. For that enterprise, next to the backing of Prussia, the French contingent was probably the most important, but English representatives were well to the fore.[1] Gell continued to enjoy Bunsen's confidence, as these letters reveal; he sent many notices to the Institute, and in the early volumes of the *Bullettino* and *Annali*, as well as in Volume I of the *Memorie*, his name appears repeatedly. Gell thought that 'Bunsen was worth all the rest put together'. The obituary notice of Gell published in the *Bullettino* in 1836 is surely by Bunsen.[2]

Gell's more general, and more durable, contribution was as a populariser. His two sets of *Pompeiana* were each followed by later editions and offered the first account in English of Pompeii. His plates and sketches were appreciated in their own right; and he

1. Millingen became Secretary of the English section; the early meetings were also attended by Lord Lovaine (later 2nd Earl of Beverley), Lord Northampton and Dr. Nott. English membership of the Institute rose from 27 in 1830 to 71 in 1832, see the figures in Michaelis, *Storia*, p. 55; and for a list of members at this time, see *Bullettino* 1836, at the end.
2. Gell to Lady Blessington, 6 June 1828 (Madden ii, p. 55). *Bullettino* 1836, pp. 16 and 22.

supplied maps and house-plans with unusual profusion. As he admitted, they were not meant as a scientific record that could compete with the younger Piranesi's engravings, or with the great survey undertaken by Mazois. But for the time they were very accurate; Gell used a *camera lucida* (he calls it 'the prism of Dr. Wollaston') and avoided imaginative excesses.[1] The text was clear, sane, well-informed; the books attempted to cover the life of the city in all its aspects. Their success with the English public was immediate; and we may say that Gell's most successful pupil was Edward Bulwer, the later author of the *Last Days of Pompeii*. Gell was a plain man giving an account that was interesting and avoided rhapsodies or poetic languors. As many small touches show, Pompeii had stirred a real curiosity in him; he pursued topics deeply, he changed his mind between editions. The books were solid and trustworthy, and admirable value for those who wished to know.

Gell was said to have had the same virtues as *cicerone*, and he was accurate, entertaining and undidactic. To those who sought information Gell gave full value. But in the first flush of the romantic movement not all visitors wanted instruction; many had obscurer reasons for travel. Here is the kind Lady Blessington, in 'poetic' mood:

> Glad as I was to profit by the *savoir* of Sir William Gell..., yet I could have wished to ramble alone through the City of the Dead, which appealed so forcibly to my imagination, conjuring up its departed inhabitants instead of listening to erudite details of their dwellings and the use of each article appertaining to them.[2]

Sir Walter Scott, who visited Naples in 1832, just before his death, displayed similar symptoms in a more striking form:

> There is a point in going toward the Arco Felice whence at a turn of the road a very extensive and comprehensive view is obtained of the Lake of Avernus. The Temple of Apollo, the Lucrine Lake, the Monte Nuovo, Baiae, Misenum and the sea are all seen at once, and here I considered it my duty in quality of *cicerone* to enforce the knowledge of the locality. I observed

1. *Pompeiana*, second series, vol. i, p. xxiv. We may here quote the judgement of the architect in the Pompeian excavations, Carlo Bonucci (*Pompei Descritta*, 3rd ed., 1827, p. 13); 'Le vedute pittoresche del Cavaliere Gell, da lui stesso designate sul luogo, offrono la piu ragguardevole collezione de monumenti di Pompei che finora si conosca: l'effetto di questi quadri è magico.'

2. Lady Blessington, *The Idler in Italy* (Paris 1839, ii, p. 280).

to Sir Walter that several of the places he would hear mentioned in society, and that I was therefore anxious that he should remember something of their respective situations. He submitted to my representations, and attended to the names I repeated to him; and when I asked whether he felt himself sure of remembering the spot, he replied that he had it perfectly in mind. I found however that something in the place had inspired him with other recollections of his own beloved country and the Stuarts, for, on proceeding, he immediately repeated in a grave tone and with great emphasis,

'Up the craggy mountain and down the mossy glen
We canna gang a-milking for Charlie and his men'.

I could not help smiling at this strange commentary on my dissertation upon the Lake of Avernus . . .[1]

Opinions about Gell were clearly bound to vary according to the prejudices of his listeners. Henry Fox, apart from seeing in Gell a degree of rancour that few others found, has left a rather waspish account of a picnic at Veii under Gell's guidance, see *Appendix* C. It is only fair in this context to put the other side of the case. In narrating the incident of the Latin inscription, Fox has badly misspelled the personal names involved, whereas Gell's record of the same inscription renders them correctly. More important, the inscription was never seen again, so that for this interesting text with its curious nomenclature we are solely dependent upon Gell's copy that he took on that day of the picnic.[2] The honours of the incident, as so often, lie rather with Gell.

To a wider estimate of Gell's work these letters add some useful new insights. It is of course clear that much of the information and gossip they contain is of an ephemeral kind; and his accounts of discoveries at Pompeii are often the same as in the official reports, which were sent to the Instituto di Corrispondenza, and so appeared regularly in the *Bullettino*.[3] On Etruscan tombs and the cemeteries of Etruria, which were among the sensational discoveries of these years, Gell's accounts seem to have come largely from

1. Sir William Gell, *Reminiscences of Sir Walter Scott's residence in Italy* (p. 13, n. 2).
2. *Gli Avanzi di Veji*, p. 12; see *Corpus Inscriptionum Latinarum*, vol. XI, no. 3840. For a full appreciation of Gell's work on Veii, see J. B. Ward-Perkins, *Papers of the British School at Rome*, XXIX, 1961, 82–84.
3. The reports were later published by G. Fiorelli, *PAH, passim*. But from the second *Pompeiana*, vol. I, p. xvii, it is to be presumed that Gell had direct access to them in Naples.

Bunsen, Gerhard and other friends, and again his reports largely corroborate those of the *Bullettino*. But Gell's eye would often notice something that we miss in the official texts; and his wider circle of informants often gave him information we cannot find at all elsewhere. The most important new notices are probably those concerning the terracottas of Calvi (p. 4) and the Roman baths at Torre Annunziata (p. 95 ff.).

This latter discovery offers several points of interest. The modern town of Torre Annunziata overlies an ancient settlement by the name of *Oplonti*, which was presumably destroyed, like Pompeii, in the eruption of A.D. 79, and virtually vanished from record. Its presence here has been confirmed by the recent and widely-reported discovery of a Roman villa of outstanding beauty and condition (see, for instance, the *Illustrated London News*, October, 1973). But the site was first located when General Vito Nunziante, using the services of an Englishman, Colonel Robinson, was excavating the foundations of his own thermal establishment, which today still bears the name of Terme Nunziante. The only record of these finds is the rather vague account given by R. Liberatore in the *Annali Civili del Regno di Napoli*, VI, 1834; Gell's notices valuably supplement them. The big square building known to Gell formed part of a larger bath-complex, as we know from Liberatore. Gell reports a well-like recess with a descending stairway ending in a pentagonal chamber, lined with Roman brickwork, that served bathers as a sort of plunge-bath. Gell's first account was based on hearsay and was plainly fanciful (p. 141); he was misled by talk of columns and entablature, and thought that the spring had first been housed in a round columnar building, which was then destroyed in the eruption, but re-used in later antiquity with a brick casing reinforcement; 'I have little doubt that my theory will prove true' (p. 142). But a later visit to the site produced correction—there had been exaggerated talk of columns, 'not one of which exists' (pp. 144–5); the fragment of Doric entablature was an earlier fragment re-used; his hopes had turned out to be false, as he honestly admitted. We are probably dealing with a round thermal chamber of the type that exists at Baiae.

Gell's works on topography have ceased to be read except by a few scholars. He had, perhaps, his faults. His speed was too great; writing often in the field, he was casual in citing texts and authors, and relied too much on memory. His works on Greece show that he knew Homer, Pausanias and Strabo well, but he was too credulous about the legendary past. The defects naturally do not appear in his works on Pompeii, which rested on his own observations, but they mar his work on the *Topography of Rome and its Vicinity*. Gell was in this the creature of his time, the last age of the non-professional scholar. When the *Topography of Rome* was re-published after Gell's death (1846), its editor Bunbury had to protest several times about Gell's wayward methods. And James Ramsay's judgement, contained in his notice of Gell here printed as *Appendix* B, that Gell was neither original nor profound, is anachronistic and severe. A new generation of scholarship had arisen in the interval, forgetful of what the earlier topographers had aimed to do and the conditions in which they had worked.

Yet Gell, as these Letters make plain (p. 58 f.), saw himself neither as historian nor antiquarian. He was a traveller who recorded what was there, a cartographer who aimed at accuracy and honesty. To modern scholars these virtues will seem somewhat unheroic, but at the time, when the lands of classical antiquity were not ex-plored and there were few maps and no photography, they were more justly appreciated. Like many who have treated of Italian topography, Gell was deeply moved by the continual destruction of Italy's classical heritage; hence his wish to record, even if sum-marily and imperfectly. This dominated his attitude to map-making. In the long argument in these *Letters* about the form in which Gell's map was to appear, we can detect two opposed views. Was the map to present a reader with a clear, legible view of general topography? or was it to be a total physical record of the Campagna, even at the expense of legibility? Gell has no doubts. 'Every turn of every mountain or eminence has been inserted from actual drawing and observation on the spot . . . so that a student reading the account of any battle may be certain that here stood such a height & there ran such a brook.' 'I have left the place blank instead of imagining anything to make the map look prettier' (p. 59). 'The map has *trees marked where trees exist*' (p. 63). Gell had himself shown what could be done on a smaller scale with his map of Veii in which we find the close detail that would nowadays be expected only in an air-photograph. But for the whole area of the Campagna the detail was excessive, as the English engravers at first feared and finally accepted. Yet Gell's map of Rome and Vicinity was a remarkable feat. There

1. The fullest account of these labours is that of Nibby in the 'Discorso pre-liminare' to his *Analisi storico-topografico-antiquaria* etc., pp. v–xii. At the time it was made, Gell's map was unique: see the comments of Th. Ashby in *The Roman Campagna in Classical Times*, p. 6.

were no true maps of any kind at the time; Gell personally undertook the surveying of the whole large area; his triangulations for it and antiquarian tours, even with Nibby's help, lasted for five years. It is a testimony to strong convictions.

Much of Gell's interest in topography may be related to his background as an English gentleman of Derbyshire. Most English travellers had been taught to draw and carried a sketchbook; English, again, is Gell's feeling for natural things, and grasp of landscape, rocks and vegetation, as is also his love of travelling by horse or mule in remote places. Travelling was good for his health, as he wrote to Nibby after a strenuous tour around Arpino, Sora and Veroli.[1] But his curiosities surely ran deeper than that. He had the eye of the true topographer, for whom men and events became real when placed in their natural or geographical setting. 'Whether schoolboys or others read Roman history, they will now be enabled to understand & clearly perceive how much of the early conquests of the Romans, of which so confused an idea existed, are really reducible to the test of locality, and are no longer romances... Until another account, equally probable in all its bearings with those of Livy and Dionysius, can be offered, it cannot be denied that a great step is gained by proving that as many Cities & Towns did exist as names can be found for in the most authentic history' (p. 59).

There is no doubt that the thrusts are directed against Niebuhr, whose *History* Gell had read with rising indignation. 'There is a good deal of information in the book,' he wrote to Lady Blessington in 1828, 'and several jokes and vulgarities not proper for history.'[2] Gell criticised individual arguments: Niebuhr had not looked at Etruscan monuments in talking of their sports (p. 67), he had placed Fidenae on the right bank of the Tiber in defiance of geography (p. 138), he did not know that the soil at Veii would have easily permitted Camillus' tunnel.[3] 'Some big wig will say

1. Unpublished letter to Nibby (above, p. 28, n. 1), contents datable to 1826.
2. Gell to Lady Blessington, 6 June 1828 (quoted in Madden, 2nd edn., ii, 54).
3. See the notes below, p. 140. It is worth quoting here from a note in Gell's handwriting that is included in a copy of *Gli Avanzi di Veji* that is now in the Biblioteca Nazionale, Naples (ref. 186.L.16).

'Niebuhr writes that the cuniculus of Camillus was a mere fable. He says timbers must have been employed under the walls of Veii to support them till the said timbers being burned the walls would fall in and cause a break, but the tufa though easily cut would have supported the walls if only a foot or two of the rock were left... The obstinacy of N. proceeds from his total ignorance of the place and his want of curiosity and local knowledge though he resided at Rome for several years.'

Rome never existed till 3 centuries before Christ, that it is all a folly and my map a dream' (p. 117). It is too simple to dismiss Gell as old-fashioned, for there were harder elements in his antipathy. Even Mommsen was to blame Niebuhr for his ignorance of monuments. Gell was more shocked by Niebuhr's sheer speculative presumption in bending facts to suit a pre-ordained Method, and there can be no denying this charge against the historian. A topographer's approach to evidence was bound to be more respectful. A single example must suffice: in his long contribution for the Berlin Academy on Cyclopean Walls, Gell insisted that the masonry by itself cannot be dated and occurs in all periods, and that no safe conclusions could be drawn until much more study of remains had been achieved. Given the heat with which Cyclopean walls were being discussed at the time, such sanity was unfashionable. An Anglo-Saxon distaste for speculation was combined with an archaeologist's sense of fact; at the same time there was the optimism of those for whom there is always new evidence to conquer. The clash of principles or temperaments, historian *versus* archaeologist, is not entirely spent in classical studies today.

Where Gell recorded a monument or inscription since destroyed he still may offer factual information to the modern scholar. The contributions he himself took seriously, his drawings and maps, would nowadays be better done by photography or by other new techniques, though they contain much precise observation; but his *Pompeiana*, though bound to become out-of-date in some respects as excavations progressed, are still worth reading for their accounts of the older areas of excavation. As often happens with scholars of earlier generations, it is easier to see what Gell was not than what he was. The new enthusiasms of his age he viewed with irony and detachment;[1] he had small artistic sense save in music; the new German scholarship, still in its groping infancy, he did not really appreciate. Gell's interests harked back to the earlier century of collectors and explorers; he was the typical gentleman scholar, honest but unexacting. There is some truth in the shrewd, if severe, judgements of Madden and James Ramsay that Gell squandered his talents on talk and social pastimes, and that his books

1. The irony is best seen in his *Reminiscences of Sir Walter Scott*. 'It was surprising,' he wrote, 'how quickly he caught at any romantic circumstance, and I found in a very short time he had converted the Torre di Chiunso [above Nocera] into a feudal residence and already peopled it with a Christian host' (p. 17); the sly tone is maintained. Gell had met Byron and read widely, but remained unmoved.

were too big for any but aristocratic purses. They remembered the amusing and flippant conversationalist; they forgot the rather old-fashioned honesty of the books. But perhaps, too, the comments reflect the change that had come over academic studies after Gell's death. A new generation of scholars, ensconced now in institutes and universities, was firmly on its way; the centres of gravity were shifting. The older amateurs, with their careless methods and rather juvenile enthusiasms, were harshly criticised by the new professionals who no longer needed to cast about for patronage. It was symptomatic that, when the young Theodor Mommsen arrived at the Archaeological Institute in Rome in 1844, he had nothing but derision for the earlier 'segretari fondatori' and their social graces.[1] No generation of scholars has ever judged its predecessors more ruthlessly, and it would be surprising if these opinions of Gell, written years later, failed to reflect the fact. Gell had belonged to that world, only too obviously; but we have seen how, in its day, the world had sincerely honoured and acclaimed him.

1. L. Wickert, *Theodor Mommsen, Eine Biographie*, vol. ii, p. 80.

Letters from Sir William Gell
to William Hamilton Esq.,
The Society of Dilettanti
1831–1835

Naples, April 8th 1831

My dear Sir,
    You desire me to continue my communications to the Society of
Dilettanti & therefore at the risque of repetition I will give You
some account of whatever may have occurred in the way of
Antiquities or the Arts since I last addressed You & first I will
mention the new house at Pompeii[1] which perhaps was named in

1. The famous House of the Faun, excavated in October 1830. The mosaics,
including the famous Alexander Mosaic to which Gell frequently alluded later,
are now in the Naples Museum. For other accounts of the finds, *Bullettino*,
1831, 18 ff.; *PAH*, ii, 240 ff.

39

my letters to Mr. Sotheby.[1] This mansion differs from all others yet discovered by having two doors between the street & the Vestibule. You descend by two very shallow steps from the first threshold to a pavement only 3ft 8 wide whence two more steps & a second door are passed before You enter the inner vestibule the pavement of which in the length of 9 feet rises 12 inches, & consists of perfect & beautiful little triangles of black, white, yellow & red marbles. The outer door is 10 feet 7 wide & about 20 high. It was hung between 2 Corinthian pilasters, & was trivalve as may be seen by 3 holes for bolts in the step. The inner door was 6 feet 10 wide & about 12 high. On each side of the vestibule, at the height of 8 feet 10 are two temples or shrines placed on what may be called brackets projecting from the Wall, the whole so singular, that a sketch will be the best way of giving an idea of it to our Learned Society.

Opposite to this were other ornaments exactly similar. The cell of the temple or shrine was painted red, the pillars & architecture were of white plaster. The lacunaria both of the pronaos and under the Brackets, on consols were red with heads of deities with gilt diadems & ear rings. The Consols were supported by alternate Sphinxes & Lions, which could be represented on so small a scale

thus, but these were nearly destroyed by the workmen & the shrines themselves are quickly disappearing. The pillars project about 18 inches before the wall. I am not without hope that You will be able from this little sketch to understand the effect intended to be produced, & that the Society will think the house interesting from its novelty. Several beautiful mosaics have been found in this mansion. Fish finely done, Bacchus on a Tiger, Ducks & Masks, with an obscene subject, all well executed & in smaller tesserae than usual decorated the pavements. It is singular that as yet no painting has been discovered except vile imitations of imaginary marbles which cover the walls in glaring colours. The Atrium is 51 feet long by 33 with the usual Compluvium in the centre, & it is not easy to say how so great a space could have been covered

1. Sotheby, William (1757–1833). Scholar, poet and translator of classical texts. F.R.S., F.S.A. Elected to the Society of Dilettanti 1792.

without any sort of pillar. Two more courts are becoming visible. I mentioned before the great number of bronze Vases and the spades[1] which I saw taken up: since that time a skeleton with several gold rings and one with an engraved stone have been found, & a golden bracelet in the form of a twisted serpent & weighing one pound is now added to the list. A Fete at which all the inhabitants of the country assemble in Pompeii, when more than usual liberty is allowed, procured me the means of drawing & measuring many things usually watched with much jealousy till they are destroyed by the weather. I will add to this an account of a singular discovery at Calvi;[2] the ancient Cales near Capua the medals of which are common. A man by excavating seems to have alighted on the shop of a vendor of Votive offerings in Terra Cotta. 300 Pigs, 1,200 Heads, 500 feet, priapi without number, 800 small statues, 12 large figures & a variety of other objects have already been produced. Everything seems to have been painted red or white. Many are rough & cast, some are beautiful & evidently modelled by an artist. I am not certain whether it be worth the trouble or rather whether it would enter into the plans of the Society to take any means of giving information to the public on the subject of Etruscan architecture. If the Members should think it of consequence to publish in England the tombs which cut in the rock, line the whole Valley of Castell d' Asso[3] near Viterbo an entire new species of ornament would for the first time be made known in England, for nothing really Etruscan has yet appeared. The valley of Biban el Malouk near Thebes is the spot most resembling that of Castell d' Asso. I think I saw about 30 with inscriptions and among them VSA > Ǝ several times over the doors. Dodwell[4] who I am sorry to say has had a slight paralytic attack, has made a number of interesting discoveries in

1. Below p. 49; cf. *Bullettino*, 1831, 27.
2. The site of the ancient Latin colony of Cales. Many similar terracottas have been found there since, see G. Novi, *Iscrizioni Monumenti e Vico* etc., pp. 38–9; M. Ruggiero, *Scavi di antichità nelle provincie di Terraferma* 268 ff.; W. Johannowsky, *Boll. d Arte* 1961, 258 ff. Some terracottas from Cales were later presented by Miss Auldjo to the British Museum and are perhaps some of these finds, see Walters, *Catalogue of the British Museum* D 193 ff.
3. See now G. Rosi in the *Journal of Roman Studies* vol. xv (1925) and xvii (1927). The inscription mentioned is that published in *Corpus Inscriptionum Italicarum* of A. Fabretti (1867) no. 2089.
4. Dodwell, Edward (1767–1832). Classical scholar, archaeologist and traveller. Only son of Edward Dodwell of Moulsey. Travelled in Greece in 1801, and 1805–6, part of the time with Gell. From 1806 lived in Rome. Married Theresa

the country of the Equicoli near Ciccolani between Rieti & the Fucine Lake. The whole of the interior is yet unknown and a most interesting district for researches would be the ancient Samnium[1] & the cities of Bovianum, Alife, Isernia & Saepinum round mount Matese, but I am too infirm to undertake these investigations without more assistances & conveniences than I can afford at present. A map with details would really be a most desirable acquisition but I think it too late in life for me to undertake it. It has only been known a few years that a City called Samnium existed near the source of the Vulturnus. Certain brass ornaments & leather & brazen helmets have lately been found there, probably of very ancient date. Mr. Craven[2] has been to Melfi & Mount Vultur[3] which Horace mentions & which seems an insulated Volcano. In the Crater amidst shady forests is a lake and a picturesque Convent, & I believe He will publish his tour. Believe me ever most truly yours

W.G.

M.R.P.D.S.

[Minister Resident Plenipotentiary Dilettanti Society]

---

d. of Count Giraud, who was 30 years his junior and a noted beauty. She m. secondly Count de Spaur in 1833. Dodwell was the author of many works, but is best known for *A Classical and Topographical Tour Through Greece*, 2 vols, London 1819 and *Views in Greece*, illustrated with his own drawings and coloured Plates, 2 vols, London 1821. Madden (*op. cit.*, vol. i, p. 427) relates that on one occasion when Dodwell was animatedly discoursing on the rare perfections of an Egyptian mummy, Lady Blessington, who was of the party, could not help giving a glance at Dodwell's beautiful young wife 'offering in her own person one of the most faultless models of loveliness ever beheld, while the arch smile that played around her lips seemed to say that living beauties might be found to compete with dead ones'.

An entertaining account is given by Capt. Gronow of Pope Pius IX's escape to Gaeta in 1848, which was organised by Countess Spaur whose husband was then the Bavarian Minister. See *Reminiscences and Recollections of Count Gronow*, abridged by John Raymond, London, 1964, pp. 283–85.

Gell wrote a brief account of Dodwell's tour among the Aequicoli in a letter to Bunsen. *Bullettino*, 1831, pp. 43–8.

1. The site of the medieval Abbey of San Vincenzo al Volturno, where an ancient city called Samnium was once thought to have stood; in fact the ancient remains there were brought there by the medieval builders. See K. Craven, *Excursions in the Abruzzi and the Northern Provinces of Naples* (1838) ii, 63–6.

2. Craven, Hon. Richard Keppel, see *Introduction*, pp. 6–8.

3. Monte Vulture is an extinct volcano—the 2 small lakes in its crater are known as the Lakes of Monticchio: by the upper lake is the former Capuchin monastery of St. Michael. There is now a good road to, and hotel near, these lakes. Published in Craven's *Excursions op. cit.*, 11, 286 ff.

Dear Sir,
I am much flattered by the interest that Dil. Soc. seems to have
taken in the letters already sent, & much obliged by the resolutions
taken with regard to the Map.[1] My first care shall be to add to the
original drawing any observations which may occur for its improvement & when that is finished I will send it by the first safe
opportunity to the Society with a copy of the Roman plate, whence
the names will be more easily taken by the Engraver & he will
observe the faults to be avoided. I will send also instructions to the
Engraver himself. The Plate engraved at Rome is in my possession
but being the first attempt of Sig. Trojani[2] in geography, it is
roughly executed. I beg moreover, to state that such a map ought to
be accompanied by a book, perhaps an octavo of explanation
description etc. & perhaps by some particular plans, or eye sketches
of the more interesting points. With regard to the Book I had agreed
with Professor Nibby[3] to give him half the map on condition that He
should write the accompanying Volume & in the Latin Title to the
Roman Plate I have announced that such a book would be added—
The book however never has been nor ever will be written, nor
even begun, & in fact as Nibby has never been over a considerable
part of the Country it would be useless for him to undertake it
nor does he any longer pretend to interest himself about it. I am so
used to this sort of literary trick that I shall leave his name &
promise upon the Roman Plate & let him take the half of the few
dollars it may produce at Rome though he has not (as indeed no
Roman ever does) fulfilled any part of his agreement. But a book
to be sold with the map should be written for the use of Travellers,
Schools & historians & I believe I could write it while the new
copy was engraving. Now to state clearly my own wishes on the

1. The first edition of Gell's map of the Campagna, privately produced in
Rome in 1827; the engraver was the person mentioned below, Signor Filippo
Troiani. See further *Introduction*, pp. 25–29.
2. Filippo Troiani, Roman engraver, who produced the first edition of Gell's
map of Rome and its neighbourhood in 1827; it appeared in a limited edition
called *Tentamen Geographicum* in 1827, financed by Lord Blessington (see p. 57,
n. 1). It was later used as a basis for the studies of Antonio Nibby, *Analisi storico-
topografico-antiquario della Carta de' Dintorni di Roma*, 1st ed. 1837, repr.
1848.
3. Antonio Nibby (1792–1839), young and brilliant professor of archaeology at
Rome University. Already author of *Viaggio antiquario nei contorni di Roma*
(Rome 1819) and the *Itinerario di Roma* (2 vols, Rome 1826) and many other

subject, I will begin by observing that the Dilettanti have usually in their publications only put forth such works as were got up at their own expense, & that their custom is, to suppress the names of the bona fide authors, publishing each work as the production of the Society in a Body. Now I should prefer selling the drawing at once to the Society who would then publish it in their usual manner. I am not at all afraid that they should not be satisfied with the Map but They might doubt my execution of the Book, which I should propose to make in Alphabetical order like a dictionary of the places mentioned. This would take some time to compile, & I should like to have a power of drawing for a sum not exceeding £50 if I wanted it to visit more accurately some points which may be interesting. I cannot however at this moment say I want any information, as of course I have notes & separate sketches without number. I would not engage however to complete the book before next June in order that I might make the thing more perfect during the ensuing spring at Rome. I propose that the Society take the Map with its accompanying Book at Their own price & make it Their own property taking to themselves the merit which will be Theirs of presenting the public with such information as it contains. The Map to be paid for on delivery just what They think fit & the Book on the same terms not before They receive it. Of course it is always understood that I engage to assist in every way possible to render it perfect during the engraving & publication. Were I richer I should be ashamed of making such stipulations but as I leave the price entirely to the Society I imagine I am not doing wrong. I have thus explained my own wishes but I am by no means wedded to them. I am exceedingly anxious that the Thing should not be left in the wretched state to which it is reduced by Roman engraving, & only beg that the Dilettanti will act in any way concerning it which may suit Them & please Them best. We will now proceed to the other parts of Your letter. Does the Society think the country of the Caudine

---

works and dissertations, he and Gell began to collaborate in the 1820's in producing Gell's map and the accompanying volume. Gell's impatience with the young scholar's delays, reflected at various points in these letters, seem in retrospect rather extravagant; Nibby himself was in poor health at this time, and throughout his short life was remarkably prolific. His concern with original sources, and his diligent search for documents, he describes in the 'Discorso preliminare' of his *Analisi*.

For Gell's affectionate relationship with this young and brilliant man, see *Introduction*, pp. 27–9.

Forks[1] an object worthy of examination? The plan of it should include Calatia North of the Vulturnus[2] and the Other Calatia on the south with the two passes by Arrienzo & St. Agata dei Goti & as far as Beneventum where the Roman army was going. This is one of the most, if not the most, interesting scenes mentioned in Roman History & I think in the month of September I might be able to accomplish a map views etc. & obtain information which would be worthy of the Society. I think £50 would go very far in the acquirement of all that would be satisfactory on the subject, which has been one of much dispute but like most in Italy conducted from the closets of the combatants without visiting the Spot. Next, Would not the Country of the Hernici make a most beautiful work? Of the 4 cities Anagni, Alatri, Ferentino & Veroli[3] the Three last have stupendous walls of unknown antiquity & nobody has ever taken the pains to examine them thoroughly. The Country is small & consequently to be surveyed without much difficulty. Thirdly. Samnium[4] is in England an unknown country. The lofty Mt. Matese formed its nucleus. The Cities of Telesia, Alife, Saepinum or [Sepino], Bovianum & Isernia surrounded it & the City of Samnium itself stood at the Fountain of the Vulturnus. It will be observed that in examining one of These districts, much knowledge of the nearer Provinces must be obtained. Thus in observing the country of Caudium much will be seen of the Samnites & among the Hernici of the Volscians. I beg if the Society do me the honor to employ me that I may be favoured with instructions if They should not feel satisfied without. I take the liberty to recommend that the Etruscan Tombs of the Valley of Castell d' Asso the Castellum Axii Norcia[5] etc. be examined & drawn in detail. There is so much to be done that I must have the help of an Architect for the elevations there, for I am unable to climb myself to measure but I would take a Roman at a very

1. Name of a valley through which the Via Appia passes, the scene of a famous Roman disaster at the hands of the Samnites in 321 B.C.
2. Gell means the modern Caiazzo, whose ancient name *Caiatia* was often confused with another *Calatia*, that lay near Maddaloni on the Via Appia: cp. Craven's *Excursions* ii, 120–2.
3. All ancient towns in the territory south of Rome, with considerable traces of ancient walls and buildings. Gell knew these from his earlier trip there of 1826.
4. Recently made known through the travels of Dodwell and Craven, and especially the drawings of Fox: see *Memorie*, vol. I, 77.
5. For these spectacular tombs, see now Dennis, *Cities and Cemeteries of Etruria* I, 175 ff.

small expense. The Tarquinian Tombs[1] and the paintings they contain are objects of great curiosity & I shall try to send you by Mr. Laing Meason[2] a few absolute scratches which may suffice to give You & the Society an idea of what they are like, as also of some other Etruscan sepulchres. Please when You have cast Your eye over them & shewn them to any of the Dil. Soc. who choose, to return them to me by Mr. Laing Meason. Remember They are only such notes as I could steal in a short time for it was forbidden to draw when I was there.

The next thing I could propose to the Society might be the illustration of Virgil with maps views etc. both in Greece & Italy. Running over the index to letter A, I find 38 names of places of which 12 are Greek & the rest Italian & this proportion may be nearly preserved through the Work. It would make a magnificent Thing & the Geography Topography & certain specimens of painting & sculpture relating to the subject might be introduced. I think this might be worthy of the Society. I could illustrate Homer having a great collection for this purpose. Pausanias also would be extremely interesting given in Greek & Latin with ample notes in English with plans maps & views of which I am possessed without number.[3] I think of sending to England by Mr. Laing Meason half a dozen specimens of a work I am preparing on the paintings of Pompeii[4] not yet published. I have some 70 or 80 ready & will desire You to look at them & carry them with You to the Dilettanti to shew the Members, for such a thing would be exactly in Their way. Call it 80 drawings of the size You will see & suppose some little description to each. The Plates must be coloured without which the intention of the Painter is frustrated. I intended this to be offered to the Booksellers, but it may suit the plans of the Society & assists much towards the understanding of Antiquity & the ancient way of treating ancient subjects. In case They like it I am ready to do anything according to Their wishes. A sort of (Transactions of the Society) might not be an unpopular Work. If any of my propositions are approved pray let me know as I would

1. The Cemeteries of the Etruscan site of Tarquinia had recently been the object of excavations by Lord Kinnaird in 1825 and especially by Kestner and Stackelberg in 1827. See *Bullettino*, 1829, 1–5; 1830, 231; 1831, 81; etc.
2. Laing Meason, Gilbert of Lindertis, Angus, who published anonymously *On the landscape architecture of the great painters of Italy*, London 1828. Died at Rome 1832.
3. Examples of how Gell's fertile mind was always dwelling on further publications.
4. Later incorporated into the second series of *Pompeiana* (publ. 1832).

begin in September when the heats diminish. I shall immediately prepare the map & send it, but I must get it brought from Rome to Naples first. With profound respect & Veneration to the Learned & Illustrious Society, I remain Dear Sir,

Yours most truly,

W. Gell.   R.P.   D.S.

I find my letter already so full that it is better to enclose it so I will add what some of your Members may think Curious. Sir Charles Monck[1] who is fond of Etymology had among other things frequently asked me why I did not go & see Avella the ancient Abella. Virgil says *Et quis maliferae despectant moenia Abellae Teutonico situ soliti* etc.[2] Abella said Sir Charles coupled with Teutonic shews that the people were of German descent & that the word Abella meant apples. The other day I went with Lord De Ros[3] to Avellino & as we joked so much with Sir Chas. about his derivations we took Avella in our way. It is very remarkable that the best productions of the country are yet apples, & the rents consist in that fruit chiefly. But what is more singular is that the populace attracted by the sight of a Great Lord from a fine English carriage & so lame a person as myself climbing to the top of a house to look at the place flocked about us in great numbers never having seen any strangers before—and *all* of Them had yellow or light hair of the *true German colour* not at all like the universal black which marks the Neapolitan race. At all events this is curious & Dr. Edwards says the distinguishing marks of a race never change.

June 16 1831.

My dear Sir,

I have delayed in answering Your letter of May 5th because having already written to You & sent you other communications by Mr. Laing Meason who I also took the liberty of introducing to You. I had already answered to the greater part of the questions & proposals Your last contained. With regard to the map it was

1. Monck, Sir Charles. Gell records that Monck had given him an organ for his house at Naples in 1832. Monck employed Wilkins and Gell to design his 'grim mansion' of Belsay Castle in Northumberland; the hall being the work of Gell.
2. Virgil, *Aeneid* 7, 740.
3. De Ros, Henry William, 22nd Baron (1793–1839). Eldest s. of Charlotte, Baroness De Ros and Lord Henry Fitzgerald.

at Rome but I have since had it sent to Naples & I am now employed, till I shall find a good opportunity of transferring it to You, in putting it into better order & in repairing the damages which were unavoidable after so many journies & having been in the hands of an engraver. All these defects as You are aware disappear in the Copper plate. I perceive that the book which should accompany the map would be very much increased in value if it contained sketches or eye plans of the places which are the most interesting. For instance of Alba Longa, of Lavinium of Veii etc. If I was. allowed one page for a more detailed plan, which might even be executed in Lithography the thing would be more satisfactory & the book more valuable. This however I will not undertake without the sanction of the Soc. Dil. & as it will cost a good deal more time though of course I have almost everything in my note book. I am not rich enough to undertake without being sure of profit. I hope you recd. the order for the new *Pompeiana*[1] & which I sent You in a letter. If not pray let me know as also if You find any difficulty in getting the book from Messrs. Jennings.[2] You speak of the Materials for Judging, on the subject of Castel d' Asso, They are as You must be aware only to be had on the spot, but there is no chance of their ever being published by the Roman Archaeologians[3] who do not undertake anything in the way of expense & are entirely supported by voluntary contributions necessarily of less importance & no cost whatever. I have just sent to that work a survey of Veii[4] which I should propose to put in the book accompanying the map but with a short instead of a long dissertation, but such communications of course cannot be frequent. I wrote to Chev. Bunsen[5] the Prussian Minister at Rome to state Rodwell's[6] complaint about the publication. I hope they will be ready to remedy the irregulari-

1. 2nd Series, see *Bibliography*, p. 175.
2. Messrs. Jennings and Chaplin, Booksellers of 'Cheapside or Poultry', London.
3. The *Instituto di Corrispondenza*, see *Introduction*, pp. 26–27.
4. Published in *Memorie* I, 1832, 1–29, with a map and additional remarks by Ed. Gerhard.
5. Bunsen, Christian Karl Josias (1791–1860). Diplomat, archaeologist and theologian. Prussian resident Minister at Rome 1827, Ambassador to Court of St. James's 1842–54. See *Memoirs of Baron Bunsen* by Frances Baroness Bunsen, 2 vols, London 1868. Founder of the German Archaeological Institute at Rome. Greville (*Memoirs*, ed. H. Reeve, vol. 1, pp. 322, 397) records visiting Bunsen in April 1830 and said, 'He is really luminous, and his conversation equally amusing and instructive—a man of very considerable information, learned, very obliging and communicative, sensible, moderate, but rather prejudiced.'
6. Messrs. Rodwell and Martin. Publishers.

ties. The select specimens[1] which you mention, of course I have never heard of. If not well published already it would certainly be of consequence to publish the Didymaean statues[2] on the seat of one of which is a Boustrophedon inscription, for the originals are certainly burnt into lime. I shall send with the drawing of the Map an impression of the Rough engraving made at Rome from it as the names will probably be better understood by the engraver from a printed copy than from a M.S. I should recommend however that the Engraver in London see not the Roman print till he has finished or nearly so his own copy. The Roman Engraver had never attempted a map before & consequently did not know how to represent mountains properly. The Word You cannot decypher must I think mean *Zappa*[3] [drawing] which is a species of spade not [drawing] which is, & probably was anciently unknown, but which is yet common & indeed the only spade in use except [drawing] la pala with which gardens are usually dug in Italy. The new house where I saw these dug up was at Pompeii not Portici. I hope you will not have answered my last communications by Mr. Laing Meason till You receive this, as You will then have an idea of the tombs of Corneto on Tarquinii. I have nothing of Castell d' Asso that could give any idea of the tombs, except this little bit

1. Hamilton had mentioned to Gell the Society's decision to publish the second volume of *Select Specimens of Ancient Sculpture preserved in the several collections of Great Britain*; it appeared, 26 years after the first volume, in 1835, and was clearly a major item in the Society's expenditures.
2. From Didyma in Asia Minor. They were first noted in 1764 by R. Chandler in the first expedition to Ionia sponsored by the Dilettanti (publ. 1769), and later by Gell in 1812: see *Ionian Antiquities* (second edn.) vol. I, 47. Some of the statues were brought to London by C. T. Newton in 1857–8, and are now in the British Museum; Gell's description does not enable us to identify the statue he has in mind. See F. N. Pryce, *Catalogue of Sculpture*, vol. I, 103 ff.
3. For the finds in the House of the Faun, see above p. 39.

which I have among my notes. You are to imagine a valley worn away by torrents in a nearly flat plain. The *peperino* precipices have been assisted by the Etruscans & formed into a great Necropolis. No Etruscan Architecture being known & probably never having existed even the mouldings of those tombs are curious. I copied the outline of a few. Here are 4

All these are new architecture. L^d [Drawing, source given Lord B, presumably Beverley] as the cornice of a rock Tomb at Falleri & a door with Doric Triglyphs thus [sketch] One of the tombs at Norcia has a tolerably regular Doric frieze with a curious Tympanum coloured pink & forming the ground to a *basso rilievo* yet remaining. About the expense of these, I conceive it would be trifling with the help of a Roman Architect, but I cannot enter into their investigation before next Spring. I don't know if You ever saw the gate of the ancient Arpinum. My theory[1] is that it is the copy of the Gate of the Lions at Mycenae & only wants 4 stones to be precisely the same thing. If you meet with Sir Chas. Monck ask him to shew You a book I gave him with that gate among other Italian walls. A sketch is worth more than a long description.

1. Gell reverts to this theme on other occasions in these *Letters*.

As a gate could not easily be made of this shape [drawing] to open & shut I have no doubt that the triangle & the jambs & architrave of the door existed. The two gates are I suspect of equal dimensions & the same number or very nearly so of blocks. My paper is ended so I must take my leave as I believe I have proposed both Samnium & the Hernici to the notice of the Society in my last. Mr. Craven[1] has another four nearly ready for the press & is gone on an excursion to the Fucine Lake to finish his work.

Ever most truly Yours

W. Gell

What do You say of Aquinum[2]—an Amphitheatre of Brick, everything else of great blocks. Two Temples, 2 sepulchres, a gateway entire & a Triumphal Arch Corinthian or Ionic. Walls & the Cathedral on the site of a large temple of which much remains etc.

If you could assist me in getting No [blank] of my new work as well as all which may be published after 2,3 & 4 which I have, You would oblige me, as well as the map of Greece which the University writes to me is published. Could they not come to Mr. Hill.[3]

Naples July 12 1831.

Dear Hamilton,

The last resolutions of the Society by which it seems They have unresolved all They had not resolved before & resolutely dissolved

1. Craven, see *Introduction*, pp. 6–10.
2. Gell speaks from personal knowledge of the site of Aquinum; see the modern study of M. Caggiano de Azevedo, *Aquino* (Rome 1949).
3. Hill, William Noel (1773–1842) who suc. his bro. as 3rd Lord Berwick 1832. M.P. for Shrewsbury. British Envoy at Court of Sardinia 1807–24. Envoy Extraordinary and Minister Plenipotentiary at Court of Naples 1824–33.

all connexion with unhappy Latium would have been sufficient to operate as a dissolution to all my resolutions had I not entered too far to recede so that I resolve to continue the Book—though an unprotected orphan. *'La razon de la sinrazon que a mi razon se hace, de tal manera mi razon enflaquer? que con razon me—de vuestras razones.'*[1] So *I shall send you the Map by the first opportunity* & the Book to accompany it by the second, & take my chance, only observing that a Map of Latium can never be measured by its direct utility in lowering the price of corn or finding employment for superfluous population though it might be highly interesting to history and science & worthy the protection of a Society which rejoiceth in publications not tangible by the common bookseller. You say "correct my map"—I know not how, for in the original is all I know & in most places all that can be known, but I have filled up the page with the neighbouring Towns which I have seen, tho' not thoroughly examined, by way of shewing the connexion of my map with the surrounding country. As to the names, some of them are too small & rather too indistinct, but it should be recollected that my map is the Topography of the country & not an essay made in *the house as almost all maps are*; that mine is made on each spot & that where the natural disposition of the ground is what Mr. Walker the Engraver calls "busy" a name written in large characters, puts an end to my delicacy of detail of facts I hope you will comprehend & make others understand that a large name is very well in a map full of imaginary mountains or destitute of facts but that where the detail is really known it must be sacrificed if over large characters be used. In this case my map a great part of which is as I pretend (more than any yet published, except that of Eleusis) a real representation of the country would in the end be little better than any body elses map. The writing however may be somewhat larger. I will now speak of the Greek map which I daresay has been bungled & the detail which was immense half omitted, for a purpose which I will not now mention. You say Acarnania &

1. The Spanish quotation, according to Dr. C. A. Jones of the Spanish Department, Oxford, comes from Cervantes *Don Quijote* Pt. i, ch. i, to illustrate the artificial style of the chivalresque romances, and was taken by him from Feliciano de Silva, the author of several such romances. It should run: 'La razón de la sinrazón que a mi razón se hace, de tal manera mi razón enflaquece, que con razón me quejo de la vuestra fermosura.' (The reason for the non-reason which is being done to my reason in such weakens my reason, that with reason I complain of your beauty.) Gell is here making a play on words and he misquotes the last word to make it fit better with his opening paragraph.

AEtolia are wanting in detail—Whose fault is that—Did I not do the whole of the rest, on condition that Leake[1] should do those 2 provinces from the Acheloũs & a bit of Laconia. Did I not perform my promise. Now open before You Leakes map of the Morea. I ask whether at first sight, it may not be visible on that map, where I W.G. have travelled, or where I have *not*. *Is* or *is not* the line of detail (that is of personal & accurate knowledge planned & drawn on the spot) bounded by those portions of the country by me visited & planned. I only ask of You & this only between ourselves to spread out that map & satisfy Yourself because it is only in that manner that I can prove to You & cause You to [word illegible] where it ought to be useful the difference between my maps & my neighbours. These observations may go as a comment on the wish of the D.S. to aid me & the present re-vocation of the Edict. When I did, as a private individual, un-protected even by a good firman *topographier* & lay down all Graecia proper, for my own pleasure as far as Pausanias had rendered it interesting, do You think I should not have also ex-amined Acarnania, & AEtolia if I had found the slightest assistance from Government Dilettanti or others. Now as to Expense, I stated that I would finish all the borders of my map I mean the details of it the mountains if £50 were allowed me and I don't believe any surveyor could do it cheaper, besides which one can take angles, & another can draw in details, & a third is an Antiquary & a fourth is, an historian, but these make a Commission & would require funds, whereas all these requisites I unite in a degree sufficient for the purpose. That is unless competent Judges think otherwise. I will make one more remark. When I have sent You the book of illustrations of the Map & it has been kept 15 years like that of Greece everyone will of course know its contents & all will cry out there is nothing new. But answer me now, what do you know of AEfula of Falerii Caere even of Alba Longa: "*de Verulis et Bovillis pudet sed ignoravimus.*" Look at Mr. Cruttwell[2] or some such name of Oxford, he does not know even where was Bovillae, though his book was published only 3 years ago and people think it very fine. Know ye where are Medullia Caenina Cameria Corniculum Tellene or Politorium etc. etc. If I cannot say positively

1. Leake, William Martin (1777–1860). Classical topographer and numismatist. Author of many works on Greece, the Levant etc.
2. Cruttwell, John Antony (1793–1848). Regius Professor of Ancient History, Oxford. Author of *Description of Ancient Italy*, 1826, 2 vols, and a similar work on Greece, 1828, 3 vols.

which is which, at least I can point out where the ruins of 6 corresponding cities may be found, & they will no longer pass for romance. Can any boy by any whipping learn from any thing now existing in England the situation even of Antemnae[1] only 30 stadia from Rome. I expect 3 or 400 £ from my map & the Book together and believe that when 200 £ be expended on engraving no School could ever be without it & the money could very quickly be repaid. Here we will leave the Map for the moment in despair—I conclude You have neither seen nor heard of Mr. Laing Meason whom I sent You in a letter with some things to see. I conclude there is no use in thinking any more about the Dilettanti etc. Castell d'Asso etc. or indeed anything else, as could I show You what there is it would be useless to think of drawing it. In the same way Your elections prove that the reform is useless, for when the people think it worth their while to have a majority of votes on any subject it is plain they can have it even as things now stand. How then can reform be necessary if when they want a thing they can get it without any change. Cannot they look on the french side of the Channel & see what is going on there & how they are gone to the devil & will go still further by following theories instead of experience. I hear however with pleasure that the Revolutionists are d—nably frightened at their own works—d— their bloods. What saith Terrick [Hamilton] to it? I wish you could manage to send me my copies of Greece—the map to Mr. Hill & reiterate to Jennings that I have yet never seen No 1 of *Pompeiana* having only 2, 3 & 4 & that all the rest are due to make even one copy. I fear he is a Reformer also. I sigh for Tom Hopes new Book[2] & a new map of the Moon value 3 or 4 £, which said Mr. Jennings if he had any charity would procure & send. Craven has got a new four ready or nearly so. I don't know whether you know Ld Hertford[3], if not I desired him to introduce Himself to You should You ever meet. We hear of another row

1. The site is mentioned in Gell's book, and his view was later confirmed by excavation, see T. Ashby, *Papers of the British School at Rome*, vol. III, 1906, 14 f.

2. Presumably *An Essay on the Origin and Prospects of Man*, 1831.

3. Hertford, Francis Seymour-Conway, 3rd Marquis of (1777–1842). Was caricatured by Disraeli as Lord Monmouth in *Coningsby* and Marquis of Steyne in Thackeray's *Vanity Fair*. The Duke of Buckingham (*op. cit.*, vol. iii, p. 101) remarked, 'Lord Hertford is come here (Rome), with Lady Strachan (n. 211), travelling with him, in a doubtful and double capacity.'

in the Roman States[1] which indeed everybody knew would take place. Our troops are sent to prevent any of their morbus from entering here where we go on well & quietly. They say Ld Ponsonby[2] is coming here if we must change. I shall pray to have Him & that he may remain, but I am content without any reform. I thank you. Kind regards to Mrs. Hamilton & l'aimable Julie & believe me most truly & sincerely Yours W.G. I am happy to inform You that all the little boys in America will be whipped if they don't know what I say on some subjects for there is a new Lempriere[3] full of me published there so that tho' the Prophet have no honour in his own country he may be revenged in the other or next world.

I cannot conclude without a lick at those fools of County Squires who imagine they don't make a part of the Aristocracy, as if Their manors & rights did not annoy the Mob more than the parliamentary privileges of the peers. They don't see that their Courts Leet & Court Baron make them privileged and that they are really nobles tho' not peers of Parliament. I have preached this with some success this winter. Of course They are Baron of all other countries.

Naples Aug. 9 1831

My dear Sir,

Though I am working night and day in order to send my map & the greater part of the articles under the letter A (not the schedule A I hope) by Sir Richd Acton[4] who sets out soon for England; yet I know that in England such is the desire for information, that I cannot be doing wrong in sending you what is known of the New

1. In January and February, 1831, there were Bonapartist uprisings in nearly all the northernmost Papal states; which were suppressed by the Austrians, who actually occupied Bologna and Ancona for some months. Their withdrawal led to fresh disorders in July in many states. By 'our troops' Gell clearly means those of Naples.
2. Ponsonby, John, 2nd Baron of Imokilly (1772–1855). Diplomat. Eldest s. of William Brabazon Ponsonby, suc. father 1806, m. Elizabeth Frances Villiers (1803–1868), 5th d. of George, 4th Earl of Jersey. H.B.M. Minister in Ionian Islands: Buenos Ayres 1826–28; Rio de Janeiro 1828–30; at Court of Naples June–November 1832; Constantinople 1833, Vienna 1846–50. See *Appendix A*.
3. Lemprière's Classical Dictionary was a schoolbook of the time and went through many editions.
4. Acton, Sir Ferdinand-Richard-Edward, 7th Bart. (1801–1837) m. 1832 Marie Luisa Pelline, only child of duc de Dalberg and assumed that name. Chamberlain to the King of Naples.

55

Volcano[1] or rather the 5 new Volcanos off the coast of Sicily as the D.S. would probably like to be informed of the real state of the case which is shortly this.

The Volcano No 3 is behind the others. Above the fire is seen an immense column of water spouted from each Crater. This was the case on July 30th 1831. An Englishman got as near as 250 feet to the shore. At 500 feet from the land was deep water. The whole was on July 29 only 30 palms high as it was supposed, but its height now is probably doubled. The three islands together were about one mile in diameter, that is taken together, they were 3 miles in circumference. The position is in a direct line between Cape Bianco near Sciacca & Pantellaria. Menfi in Sicily is only 25 miles distant. Mazzara 50—Marsala 65—30 miles to Pantellaria—33 to Cape Bianco. The sea is said to have been almost boiling at first & the fish dead. The *Asia*[2] has sailed over the precise spot in the course of the last year & fears are entertained for a very small English Trader which has not yet been heard of. The Volcano or system of Volcanos must have broken through a ridge of coral rock, as it

1. This singular volcano was preceded by a series of earth tremors between June 29 and July 11 of this year. It is described briefly in *Giornale del Regno delle Due Sicilie* no. 167, July 1831, p. 678.
2. *Asia* was a 2nd rate ship of 84 guns—saw action as Sir Edward Codrington's flagship at Navarino on 19/20 Oct. 1827 and was in the Syrian operation of 1840. In 1830 was stationed in the Mediterranean, her commander being Christopher Wyvill and her captain, W. J. H. Johnstone.

is supposed, & they say the King[1] is to be requested to send a commission of Naturalists & Geologists to make observations, which will probably throw new light on the subject. You will say that Arts & Antiquities have nothing to do with this but generally speaking you are all eager for information & can only blame my judgement & not my zeal if I have not succeeded in sending you what you want. You could if you like lithographize the sketch as the Geological world will certainly have pleasure in seeing it.

Believe me most truly,
Yours ever,
William Gell.

Naples, Sept. 4th 1831.

My dear Sir,
I send to the Foreign Office directed to You. The map of the country about Rome. A copy of the rough engraving of it with many defects & many omissions which was made at Rome at the expense of the late Lord Blessington,[2] & to which Nibby was to have made a book as You will see in the Title but of which He has never written a single word & never will. I have no scruple in saying that it is all the better, for He, not having been at half the places could have only copied from other books what had been written before, & I am sure that he has saved himself a great deal of trouble, for never did I undertake any thing so disagreeable as writing a number of treatises in alphabetical order, some of them as You will see long, and all upon subjects which if not correct would be easily contradicted. Not but that I have it all in my head, but that authorities might be constantly looked out in stating facts, & the authors cited. I send You now only the letter A leaving out the words Aborigines, AEqui & AEquicoli, because there is a great deal of new matter quite unknown with regard to the AEquicoli now Ciccolani which I must have time to arrange shortly yet tangibly so as to make it admissible in such a work, as only my rivers run into that country, & my map does not go so far as the most interesting valley. The articles in A are about 75 & they are much more likely to be interesting to You who know something

1. Ferdinand II, b. 1810, reigned 1830–59, d. 1859 who m. (1) 1832 Maria Cristina di Savoia who d. 1836 (2) 1837 Maria Teresa Isabella d'Austria.
2. Blessington, Charles John Gardiner, Earl of, 2nd Viscount Mountjoy (1782–1829): created Earl of Blessington 1816.

of the country than to one who neither knows nor cares about it. You will see I have put S^t. Angelo rather than Corniculum, & the Angelo first, rather than S^t., on purpose to give You one or two things which are absolutely new under the A's. Of course in writing these, I have partly written a great portion of the remainder of the Book, & I am enabled to state that the whole number of articles, ending with Zagarolo, will be as nearly as possible 666, which You will say is the real number of the beast. The M's are very numerous with the mountains 99, the P's with the ponte's 62 & the S's with their Saints 71. I have sent You, Festoi, Fossae Cluiliae, in the F's, to enable You to understand more thoroughly the country 5 miles on the Via Appia, & its ancient importance, & all that from no one having taken the pains to map the country, has not been hitherto observed. I have sent You Falerii[1] also as totally unknown in England, for which Vide Oxford edition of Strabo which is all wrong beyond belief, & I have sent You a disquisition upon Veii[2] the great Rival of Rome & as large as Athens, which Antiquaries have hitherto placed at Civita Castellana, Baccano, Scrofano etc., etc., & which much wiser people had crammed into the little knoll of Isola Farnese till I took the pains to search out the walls round its real situation. I send You a separate map of Veii, because if any knowledge of the kind is worth having, that is, & the vestiges of so important a place in the early history of Italy are fast wearing out on the spots. Do not imagine that because I originally wrote that dissertation for the Roman Archaeologia, that can be any reason why a work in Italian should ever be seen or be of the slightest use to those who in England study Roman history, as boys or even grown up children are never likely to meet with such a work, & which moreover from its ill distribution is as You say very likely to fail. I have sent You therefore Veii, which is one out of 57 V's. Of course you will recollect that a great many of those articles require only a few lines, & others must be treated thus—"Corniculum Vide S^t. Angelo"—or "Roma Vecchia vide Festi & Fossa Cluilia"—Now my pretensions are these.[3] First I have given a faithful representation of the country in which high mountains, being deeply shaded, maintain in a great degree their pre-eminence, permitting

1. For Gell's map and description, see *Topography*.
2. Gell's identification of the site of this ancient Etruscan city was immediately accepted by all scholars of the day. His account of the site (first published in the *Memorie* in 1831) was incorporated with few changes into *The Topography*.
3. An important passage for Gell's view of his patient and laborious cartography.

at the same time the lesser elevations which are infinitely numerous to appear in their proper proportion, & which if the great hills were faintly touched, must have been entirely omitted. Secondly— every turn of every mountain or eminence has been inserted from actual drawing & observation on the spot, & not invented as is the common & usual custom in map making in the closet, so that a student reading the account of any battle may be certain that here stood such a height & there ran such a brook. Thirdly where I have not been, I have left the place blank instead of imagining anything to make the map look prettier—as yet give me leave to say an unheard of piece of honesty, & what is more I have put a "desideration" on the spot. Should I ever go over these parts, than which nothing is easier, the word "desideration" etc. is affected on the plate, & the new facts inserted which makes what is called a new edition. Fourthly all the places are laid down by innumerable triangles taken with a Sextant & fifthly & lastly whether schoolboys or others read Roman history they will now be enabled to understand & clearly perceive how much of the early conquests of the Romans, of which so confused an idea existed, are really reducible to the test of locality, and are no longer Romances. If ruins of Lavinium, Lanuvium, Corniculum, Caenina, Cameria, Medullia, Collatia, Gabii, & Alba really exist, somebody must have built them, & somebody must have destroyed them, and untill another account equally probable in all its bearings with those of Livy & Dionysius, can be offered, it cannot be denied that a great step is gained by proving that as many Cities & Towns did exist as names can be found for in the most authentic history. In short I cannot help thinking You will perceive the value of the Map & its accompanying book, &, I am certain that the rising generation, if classical education be encouraged, will be much in-debted to whoever shall promulgate them to the world. You will perceive that the I is purposely left out in all descriptions that the Dilettanti may be the propriator in a body of the work. You will perceive also that in the article "Artena Volscorum" I have run into a little digression: not however long upon certain walls, which I am persuaded contains remarks new & not uninteresting. I should have liked much to have given 2 little views of the gates of Mycenae & Arpinum but I feared You would say neither of these places are in the map—They are as like as these I now draw.

When any fact or custom of antiquity is mentioned it is usual, & even required, that an authority should be cited—on this principle

I wish, & most earnestly recommend, that the vignettes of the walls which I have introduced with a very sparing hand, should be inserted in their places in the work. They are the vouchers that

in such & such places the walls of an ancient city, & of such a style exist, & add great authenticity to the declaration of the fact. I cannot but think that all my judges will concur in this opinion, & I only beg that Cluver, Cellarius, & the Oxford Strabo, & a new Oxford work by Mr. Cramer[1] (Mr. Strangeways[2] says & I forget the name) may be compared on any article with mine say Ardea, Veii, Alba, Allia or any other before You tell me I am good for nothing as I can assure You they are. I see many defects of style in my own work, such as the perpetual recurrance of the same words which in description is perhaps unavoidable, & I see that the information is sometimes introduced without much order but in a dictionary this is of no consequence. I imagine that A in bulk will be about $1/3^d$ of the Volume.

Ever yours,

William Gell.

I cannot suppose that, undertaking as I hereby promise, to finish the whole of the text in the best manner my knowledge & notes permit, more than these A's will be required as a specimen of the work, which shall be finished before the Map can possibly be engraved, & of which a very great proportion is now lying by me I recommend that the Roman engraving which I send with this be kept by Yourself and *not* shewn to the English engraver till he has nearly finished & then he may have it to examine the names by when he is in doubt with the MS map. Many of the names even in that engraving are ill spelt though Nibby who is as

1. Cramer, John Antony (1793–1848). Regius Professor of Modern History at Oxford, later Dean of Carlisle. Author of *A Geographical and Historical description of ancient Italy with a map and atlas of Rome*, Oxford 1826, 2 vols.
2. Fox-Strangways, Hon. John George Charles (1803–1859), y.s. of Henry Thomas, 2nd Earl of Ilchester. Diplomat. Was *en poste* at Naples, Florence and Vienna.

idle as a pig was consulted. The faults consist in such things as 2 C^s where only one should be, or 2 L^s which by the bye it is impossible to correct as Vallerano from the Valley or Valerano from Valerius unless one knew the history from the time of Valerius to the present. Many names are also omitted. So I will say no more about the map. I sent You by Post a picture of our new Volcanic Island. It is now said to be another mile (i.e.) 4 in circumference altogether. The throwing out of the water & the burst of fire have either ceased or they have been very much exaggerated. The first view I sent You, was neverless from Monticelli's.[1] They now say—no fire bursts out but only a dense smoke. The water very muddy flows from one of the craters and is not spouted, it seems heaved up from a depth. A Captain Swinburne[2] in a Brig of war from Corfu has taken possession in the name of England & the people here remonstrated. Pray get the appointment of Governor for one of Your friends before it cools. I think Mr. Hunt or Cobbet[3] might be appointed with advantage or that

1. Presumably a publication of the famous vulcanologist of the name, Teodoro Monticelli. Born at Brindisi in 1759 he studied at Lecce, Rome and Naples, where he finally became Professor of Ethics in 1792. He was imprisoned for his views under the Parthenopean Republic, but on his return was warmly supported by Pope Pius VII and made a titular abbot. From 1808 he was the permanent secretary of the Academy of Sciences and recovered his chair. He was especially known for his studies of Vesuvius. His collection of volcanic minerals was famous; it was praised among others by Sir Humphry Davy, who accompanied him on many expeditions. He died at Pozzuoli in 1845. See the 'Discorso' by Grimaldi in *Rendiconti della Reale Accademia delle Scienze Della Società Reale Borbonica*, IV (1845).
2. Swinburne, Capt. (later Admiral) Charles Henry (1797–1877), 2nd s. of Sir John Swinburne, Bart. of Capheaton, Northumberland. Was in command of the brig *Rapid*—she carried 10 guns and was stationed in the Mediterranean at the time of the eruption of the volcanos—was finally wrecked off the coast of Crete 1838. Capt. Swinburne's eldest s. was the poet, Algernon Charles. *The Dictionary of Naval Biography* records, 'The *Rapid*, in July 1831, discovered a volcanic island on the south-west coast of Sicily, which has since subsided into a dangerous shoal', and the *Mediterranean Pilot*, vol. I (9th ed., 1963) indicates that the remains of the volcanic island still exists and is known as Graham Shoal and lies about 25 miles southward of Capo Granitola.
3. Cobbett, William (1762–1835). Essayist, political reformer and agriculturalist. 1802 started publication of his *Weekly Political Register*. Supporter of Queen Caroline. 1821 undertook political rides on horseback resulting in publication of *Rural Rides*. Writing on 10 November 1830, Mrs. Arbuthnot remarks, 'It is a great scandal, but Hunt and Cobbett have opened a meeting house they call the Rotunda near Blackfriars Bridge, there they assemble and harangue crowds of the lower orders in the most seditious manner, and from that place they issue in large bodies and come and alarm peaceable people in the West End

Mr. Taylor[1] whom they call the Devil's Chaplain. You seem now even to make Kings who find reigning rather hot work. *Nolo Episcopare & Nolo regnari* as things are I thank you. What a piece of work You are all making by way of improving Your liberties it is like setting the house on fire because the parlour chimney smokes. I suppose if France does not go quite upside down to stand for a scarecrow soon, it looks as if You must be upset Yourselves, but to cut your own throats is the most curious thing. L^d De Ros has built me a portico to my house which is so much improved it can scarcely be recognised & Sir Chas Monck has given me a great Organ from London which makes when all out a noise enough to tear it down. We have many sojourners here even in Summer & I am going to see the Talbots[2] at Cast 'a Mare & with the Lushingtons[3] to Miss Whytes[4] at La Cava. Our first rain has just fallen & the climate is quite heavenly. Kind regards to Mrs. Hamilton & believe me most truly yours.

W.G.

Naples, Jan. 3, 1832.

My dear Sir,

I send You the rest of my book except perhaps the articles on Tarquinii, Rome, Campagna, Etruria, Siculi, Languages and Latium. The article History is so nearly finished, that I shall try to send it if in time for Mr. Ashley's[5] departure this evening, & I think you will find it interesting. The others are so far advanced that you shall have them by the next safe conveyance.

I will now begin with the map. Whatever is done to it to change it must ruin it. A new drawing of it would reduce it to the level

---

of the town. I can't understand why it is allowed.' (*Journal*, vol. ii, p. 400). Hunt, Henry (1773–1835). Politician who shared rooms with Cobbett in gaol in 1810.

1. John Edward Taylor (1791–1844), a well-known radical and Quaker. He is best known as founder of the *Manchester Guardian* in 1821. The origin of the unflattering *sobriquet* is unknown.

2. Talbot, Sir George, 3rd Bart. (1761–1850). Gell remarked that Sir George and his daughter Marianne gave 'great and good dinners' at Naples.

3. Lushington, Sir Henry, 2nd Bart. (1775–1863) m. 1799 Fanny Maria, d. of Matthew Lewis, Under-Secretary of State for War. She d. 1862. Lushington was H.B.M. Consul at Naples 1815–32.

4. Whyte or White, Anna Baptista to whom Gell rented his house at Naples in 1828. She d. 1833 at S. Iorio near Portici and was buried at Naples.

5. Ashley, Hon. William (1803–1877), 2nd s. of Cropley, 6th Earl Shaftesbury.

of other maps *not executed in detail on the spot*. The map has *trees marked where trees exist*. The mountains at first sight shew which are high & which are mere eminences. The villages where known are inserted in their real forms. A town upon a rock cannot be made clear but by a sacrifice of its identity. It is not clear in nature. Where the map is black the mountains are high & rugged. Mr. Strangeways who was in my room when your letter arrived, immediately exclaimed that the Map would be no longer identical. If it were to be drawn again it would become a common map "from the best authorities drawn by Thomas Kitchiner[1] geographer to the King" in his own room and not a fiftieth part so good as the rough Roman copy of it. Let the engraver take a magnifying glass & assure himself that every turn of mountain etc. is found there, because it is so on the spot, & is not placed *ad libitum* like the maps He is undoubtedly used to. Every deviation will be so much done wrong, except in writing names clearer & here & there making the rivers less ragged my blue ink being greatly defective. The watching will be necessary to prevent the engraver from altering or leaving out facts, which doubtless will be very troublesome to him but immensely add to the Value of the map. It is the detail, & the facts, which he pretends to want, which makes this map so different to any other. I conclude You understand & that You will be able to convince the Engraver.

I am glad You like my M.S.S. from the little You have got of it, & I am quite certain that the whole with the little historical account over which You must have patience, will set things in a clearer light, & will establish the very ancient state of Italy, better than anything that has yet appeared, & that the work whatever be its present reception will prove eventually of great service to literature. Mr. Austin's[2] remark on the subject of Niebuhr[3] arrived here the very day after I had written the preface which You must also look at & which refers to that Author.

1. Thomas Kitchin (d. 1784). Engraver, publisher and Hydrographer to the King. As well as maps, plans, and charts he engraved bookplates and portraits. See Thomas Chubb, *The Printed Maps in the Atlases of Great Britain and Ireland, a Bibliography*, 1579–80 (London 1927). (We are indebted to Mrs. Laurence Middleton for this information.)
2. Austin, John (1790–1859). Celebrated jurist. Appointed to Chair of Jurisprudence at newly-founded University College, London 1820, but went to Bonn to perfect his studies and did not return to take up his Chair till 1828. Frequented circle of scholars, including Niebuhr, at Bonn.
3. The famous historian, and author of *Roman History*. For Gell's views on Neibuhr, see the *Introduction*, pp. 25–26.

I have consulted Mr. Laing Meeson as to the form in which it would be most adviseable to print the book & I send You His letter on the subject. He having great experience in such matters, & agreeing with me, that living here, not one penny could I even expect to receive from a London Bookseller. Of course I can have no right to dictate to the Society, and what is more, being in want of the money on which I have calculated, I must accede to any proposition, therefore I leave it in Your hands entirely, but as unasked on my part they did me the honour to desire to be informed how my literary undertakings could be assisted by Them, I really believe 500£ would be a very moderate remuneration for the work Map & Copyright for ever. You know my last work on Pompeii which is got up by simply paying two dollars for a carriage, a third to a *Custode* at Pompeii & spending a morning every now & then very agreeably on the spot. My work was presented to Messrs. Jennings—my demand was 500 £ & it was immediately given. But the trouble & the expense of the Roman Map admits of no comparison being 100 fold that of *Pompeiana*, & though I have in my head all that is contained in the M.S. you will immediately, even from what You have read of it, perceive that the alphabetical arrangements of so much detached matter yet all referring to the same subject & the authorities to be hunted up for my assertions, are most bewildering & disagreeable duties which I have done my best to perform. Now, I am told that—owing to the unsettled state of the public mind in England the Booksellers are not equally inclined to enter into speculations, but of this not having offered my work I cannot judge, but I know that before any profit could come to Jennings, 500 £ to me & 2,000 £ for engravers was the least sum He could expend The Society would have little more than 200 £ to lay out in the Map & printing, & a good deal of this would be recovered in the Copy of the work to each member. The Society being on the spot would be able to adopt Mr. L. Meeson's suggestions by which He has himself profitted & which Sir Walter Scott[1] has always followed with very considerable success, but nothing could ever come to me from a Bookseller while I reside here. My first *Pompeiana* produced much more than 500 £, perhaps 8 or 900 in the way of sharing with the Bookseller & 900 more to Mr. Gandy[1] to whom I gave half my

1. Scott, Sir Walter (1771–1832). For further reference to Scott's association with Gell, see J. C. Corson, *op. cit.* (below, p. 177).
2. Gandy, John Peter (1787–1850). Architect and R.A. Assumed the name of Deering 1827. M.P. for Aylesbury 1832. Travelled with Gell on the second

profits on condition that He should get up the work & oversee the engravers & Booksellers. He being used to such matters examined the books & though he had half my profits I was probably, living here a very miserable gainer by my bargain with Him. The work neither being all Latium nor Etruria nor all the country of the Volsci nor AEqui but having much of all included in the map & Agro Romano not being an English expression we have called a Council & decided upon Roman Topography if that pleases You, but put more or alter or change, to a descriptive title page, just as You like & just as You may think it will suit the public or the Society best. I beg over again to state, that as I cannot but be convinced that the Society intended to confer a benefit upon one of Their members by that very honourable & unexpected offer of assistance, so I should be delighted to receive 500 £ for my work at their hands, instead of from a Bookseller, believing that that sum would speedily be recovered by the sale of the Work which Mr. Austin finds now & You already say gives You much information. For this I cede all right & title to every future profit, (except the 20 copies which the Author always has) either from the first or any after edition, the Society if they judged favourably might print it if they pleased as their own work or as their Act, or as their undertaking as having bought it it would be. That is what I wish but I *must* take what They will give having stated my thorough conviction that it is cheap at that rate & given You I think good reasons for my opinion. I leave the settlement to You so pray do what You think right & let me know the result & how I am to apply it to the extinction of my debt to Torlonia[1]—Mr. Meeson's idea is I think just as to the two

Dilettanti expedition to Ionia and Greece 1811. Elected to the Society of Dilettanti 1830.

1. Torlonia, Giovanni, duca di Bracciano. Well-known Banker. He d. 1829 and was suc. by s. Alessandro, who was head of the Bank at the time when Gell was writing these Letters. The Duke of Buckingham (*op. cit.*, vol. iii, pp. 16, 94) writes 'Torlonia, the banker, now transmogrified into the duca di Bracciano, was a porter, and his father a *lacquais de place*; his wife, a vulgar, old, red-faced woman, a sadler's daughter, acted Duchess ridiculously.' The Duke went to a ball at Torlonias and remarked, 'He had got some King of Naples, or some other petty sovereign, to make him a Chambellan (*sic*) and he went about with a huge gold key to his pocket-hole, which I told everybody was the key to the till...the old man is, however, sometimes good-natured.' Writing on March 1 1829 after Torlonia's death, the Duke says, 'Torlonia has been lying-in-state, as it is the fashion for all Roman dukes and princes to do, dressed in a full court dress, his hair well-powdered, white gloves on his hands, his *chapeau* or

columns being unadvisable, for the vignettes & plans will render the work pretty if only decently executed & books sell when they are fit for a drawing room table.[1] The Map cut into 3 pieces in height by 4 in length thus [sketch] would make an exceedingly pretty 2^d Volume to the small Quarto of the same size, it would be large enough yet portable—The truth is that 8^{vos} are now made even larger than that. This however is all as You like. I must give another vignette of the gate of Falerii when I send You the 4 or 5 remaining articles & I now send You a little map to add to the account of that City. I have seen Cramer[2] some years ago, & his book only proved to me the necessity of a new publication, being a *risarcimento* of the old errors without looking at the place. Put in therefore what You like, & please to correct what You find wrong or incongruous. Before I had myself arranged the history I had not so clear an idea as afterwards so pray read the article History, which I am persuaded You will like as soon as You get it. I think You will forgive the insertion of a bit of Grecian wall of Lycosura & see the use of it. You will not also object to Palatium which I think of the first consequence to Rome, that being evidently the mother of the Palatine & quite forgotten or treated as a romance. I shall write as little as possible upon Rome that being so often done. I send You the index or list of places which I think will surprise You.

We have few people of note here but the Town is full. Ld Hertford wrote to me to say he should be here immediately. Vesuvius runs over on both sides from a Cone which is risen out of the old Crater—[sketch] It is a fine sight but the vineyards are beginning to suffer on the Resina side. The battle of Issus or Granicus at Pompeii[3] about 18 palms long by 10 in mosaic is the finest thing ever seen. I cannot get any sort of copy yet. They are so jealous, if I can or when I can I shall let the Society see it. The Sciacca Volcano is either washed away or very much reduced. Sir Grenville Temple[4] spent 25 hours in finding it in vain. I got Your

---

plumes upon his head, his sword by his side and the hand grasping the hilt. The body being laid upon the carpet of the floor of the room, with a cushion under the head.'

1. Now referred to as a 'coffee-table' book.
2. Author of the work referred to above, p. 60.
3. The famous Alexander Mosaic, found the year before in the House of the Faun and now in the Naples Museum. The Mosaic depicts Alexander of Macedon in a battle against the Persians, but it is not clear which of his battles is meant to be represented, if any at all.
4. Temple, Sir Grenville, 10th Bart. (1799–1847). The baronetcy is now extinct.

10 Nos of *Pompeiana* thank You. Do try to get me a Greek map even if cut in bits. I cannot even tell if Mr. Gandy or Wilkins[1] ever got their copies of Pompeii. I hope I have written what will satisfy You. My object is to do what will be most agreeable to my friends. Pray act for me as You think right & believe me ever Yours

W. GELL.

Naples. Feb. 20 & 22 1832.

My dear Sir,

I have this day finished the Work descriptive of the Map of the Vicinity of Rome, & You will receive it by the first safe person who leaves Naples for London. We have no Courier ready at present, but the Work is positively finished. The articles You are to receive are Campagna, Etruria, Language, Latium, Rome & Siculi, perhaps Pelasgi, & a little addition to Tibur which I must get You to apply where it will come in best. I think that the two articles Language & Etruria, which I nevertheless shortened as much as possible so as not to omit the pith of the subjects, contain a great deal which has never been thought of in England, but which people ought to know. I have been forced to give a good deal of Tarquinii which is a little out of the map, but it was necessary to explain Etruria & set some of Niebuhr's errors right.[2]—such as his only 3 games which I have shewn to be 8 from positive evidence now existing. I have given You a touch also of Castell d' Asso as one of the most curious Etruscan burial places and please to recollect that a good portion of my map is Etruria which wanted examples, in a case of such extreme curiosity. I sent You in my last packet by Hon[ble.] Mr. Ashley a sketch of the plan of Falerii. I would send the gate of Jupiter at Falerii, also if I thought it was wished for. It is a pity I did not enlarge my boundaries & survey the line of country from Viterbo to Graviscae, but

1. Wilkins, William (1778–1839). Architect and R.A. Edited *The Unedited Antiquities of Attica* for Society of Dilettanti and was elected to the Society 1809. Wilkins acknowledges Gell's assistance in his Antiquities of *Magna Graecia* (1807), and in a copy at Downing College, Cambridge are pasted 2 designs for Greek Revival buildings in the hand of Gell. See also p. 47, n. 1.
2. Niebuhr had said that the Etruscans practised only two sports, chariot-racing and boxing. For Gell's discussion of the point, see *Topography*, i, 392.

infirmity, which doubles the expense of going about and the expenses simply for one who has barely enough for existence and is totally unassisted in any way, with as You see the extreme uncertainty of remuneration, rendered even what I have done a ruinous task. Cast. d' Asso, Norchia, Tarquinia, Graviscae & now the treasure of Vulchi [sic][1] would make a most interesting addition to our Etrurian knowledge. You have certain specimens of my work on the paintings of Pompeii and a little sketch book of Etruscan tombs which when You have an opportunity free of Cholera I shall request You to send back to me as I must now get on with that work, the Roman being finished. I think I shall publish about 80 of the paintings if I can get the bookseller to undertake the work. We have here L^d. Hertford who has a great mind to have the plates done at Paris by a person He knows, but I am fearful of getting Him into expense as I believe without a Bookseller there is nothing to be gained by any book whatever, & these plates must cost something—Vesuvius was gone out since I wrote by Mr. Ashley but has since become more active, & with the snow on the top looks magnificent. The lava ran out on the T[orre] della Annunziata side next Naples, so the whole crater is filled up & is become a sort of sea of black scoriae, with a core at the north end of it whence smoke & stones yet come occasionally. The newest wonder is that certain salt water in the interior is so infernally hot that contrary to the usual custom the salt itself is held in solution in the steam & it deposits itself in such quantities & is so pure at certain orifices that the poor people are able to collect a quantity worth gathering. I have not seen Your friend Monticelli for several months, but I hear of him from Mr. Auldjo[2] of Mt. Blanc who is now making a work on this & all other eruptions which I have little doubt will be good, & the only real drawings on the spot ever published! We have here Sir Walter Scott who is by no means in an unenjoyable state but very chatty

1. The rich cemeteries of Vulci were being opened up in these years, see *Bulletino*, 1829, 2 f., 49 f.; *Annali*, 1839.
2. Auldjo, John (1805–1886). Author of *Narrative of an ascent to the summit of Mont Blanc on the 8th and 9th August, 1827*. London 1828. Gell refers to him as 'wet-nurse to volcanos'. Writing to Lady Blessington from Naples on 25 September 1835 about Sir Walter Scott, whom Auldjo and Gell had accompanied to Pompeii, he says, 'However, poor Sir Walter, takes little notice of anything, being buried in his own past dreams, and was as one called from the grave, and only kept with them by the enchanting smiles of the beautiful genius who being upon his, the delighted author's arm'. Lord Lytton dedicated *Devereux* to Auldjo. See *Appendix* A.

& amiable. I conclude much improved in health. I see a great deal of him & am going on Friday to betray him into the hands of Miss Whyte at La Cava in his way to Paestum. He gave us all great pleasure the other day by the information that he had paid every shilling of his debts & received a letter to say he had 3,000 £ in hand, all his rents his own, & all he made in future—He has already got a Malta romance[1] in hand & almost finished & a poem & other things in view. He thinks he is now going to Greece, which considering how little he cares for Greece & Rome is certainly not worth the trouble to him. But he seems to like sailing & so Greece is very well for that in a good Kings Ship.

I wish You could finish Your Reforms & other novelties for the nation is in the mean time looked upon in these parts as completely done up particularly as You are retrenching, which they consider as a sign of coming Bankruptcy. I wish You would finish it on one side or the other, for both sides have good arguments but is arguing it looks as if the whole risked going upside down. We expect an American fleet to bombard us as they now say our Court won't pay. The affair was supposed settled—St. Angelo[2] is called from the Country & made Minister of the Interior. He is a very clever person, & in short hopes are entertained that we are likely to go on well. Certainly for the present there are no symptoms of disorder in our country—I have given good reasons for not writing more on the subject of Rome which would require a whole volume but which may be bought in many other publications. I hope You will succeed in settling for my 500 £ for my book in fee simple & 20 copies. It gave me an immense deal of trouble & I am sure it is well worth the sum with the map, & I am not at all afraid that You will find the rest unequal to the articles in A. Mr. Strangeways who is here in my room sends love & Compliments to You—his expression is a little of both—on which Mr. Ramsay[3] remarks—an excellent man he deserves both. I shall

1. *The Siege of Malta* is still unpublished.
2. Marchese Nicola Santangelo (1785–1851), the much disliked and powerful Minister of the Interior to Ferdinand II from 1831 to his dismissal along with Del Carretto in 1847. He began as a lawyer, was 'intendente' of Basilicata and Reggio Calabria, judge in the High Court, and finally King's Commissioner in 1824. His policy was thought to be reactionary. He was a great (if unscrupulous) collector of pictures, which were housed in his splendid *palazzo* in the Forcella, the house formerly that of the Carafa of Maddaloni and one of the finest Renaissance *palazzi* in Naples.
3. Ramsay, James. A Scottish merchant of 'elegant taste and classic law' who had lived at Mordaunt College, Blackheath before taking up residence at Naples. See *Appendix B*.

hope to see You in Italy again on some of these fine days. The last news from Rome is that they *are* to have a Carnival. Please to have a person to take care of spelling in my work for my room is always like a Café so full of people that I wonder how I write at all—Ever my dear Sir with Compliments to Mrs. Hamilton & l'aimable Miss Julie

Yours most truly

W. GELL.

23 Feb. Vesuvius has ourst out again & the Lava runs this way.

Naples. March 5, 1832.

My dear Sir,

I had already finished my work when Mr. Strangeways who overlooked its progress & comes almost every day to read what is written, insisted upon an article upon the Pelasgi. I believe he was right, & thinks that the Roman walls etc. are traced from the Pelasgi, & the whole set in a clearer light, as well as the Cyclopeian question more decidedly settled than You will ever have seen it in any other shape. I maintain that nobody ever saw Lycosura[1] except myself which is the original City of all Cities, & Pelasgissima —I am certain things are put in a new light & am persuaded that History will profit much by researches made in so many spots, from Arcadia, down the Valley of the Velinus to the neighbourhood of Rome, which has never been thought of. I believe I must retire to Mount Lycaeus myself if the Dilettanti do not think as I do for I thought myself sure of Their illustrious protection after the pains I had taken in searching out the materials, & the laborious work I had to write & compress them all into so small a compass. Major Scott,[2] Sir Walter's son, is to take this to

1. The town in Arcadia in Greece from which the Pelasgians are supposed to have originated, see *Topography* ii, 141 and 367. Gell visited the site and gave a brief description of it in *Itinerary* 93 and 101, but the identification was not made until later by Dodwell (*A Classical and Topographical Tour through Greece*, London 1819).
2. Scott, Major Walter, later Lt. Col. Sir Walter who m. 1825 Miss Jane Jobson. Sir Walter Scott writing to Lady Davy from Edinburgh on 24 January, 1825 remarks that his son 'has acquired him the affection and hand of a very sweet and pretty Mrs Anne Page, known here as Miss Jobson of Lochore, which

England or at least to Mr. Seymour[1] at Florence to transmit it to You. I have got the 10 numbers of *Pompeiana* which You sent me & only those. If You can ever get the rest so as to send me one copy complete I shall beg of You to do. I must write to Jennings about my work on the paintings of which I sent You some 12 or 14 to look at. Should You chance to go to Jenningshire & would consult him & persuade him to undertake the work You may do me a service. There will be an appropriate description to each & there must be an introduction on anc[ient] painting & all these were half written when I left off to write the Roman Topography. I shall recommence tomorrow. I hope You will approve of what I have written on Language & Etruria. Certainly in England no one knows anything about the subject, & I set Mr. Laing Meeson to enquire of the learned & he found them all ignorant of the facts. My articles will at least open the eyes of people & of travellers to the subjects. I have given You as much of Tarquinia as I dare in Etruria, & I am sure it could not be shorter without being too imperfect. I have not time at present for Major Scott goes tomorrow to send You the new picture which I have got & mean to publish in my Ancient Paintings.[2] It is magnificent, I mean Alexander's battle with Darius. I must now stop as I am going to dine at Sir Walter's to carry my packet. I trust to You for shewing to the Dilettanti the propriety of acceading [sic] to my proposition of letting them have the fee simple of my Map & Topography for 500 £ of which (from the disappointments incident on Railways which have superseded my shares in Canals etc. etc. etc.) I am really in want & so is poor Torlonia who is the Victim of my circumstances.

Vesuvius still continues running in 2 streams. They pretend there is a new Volcano at the Arco Felice. I believe it is a humbug. An earthquake at Pozzuoli is true. No trace of the Sicilian Volcano remains, only a shallow & a rumbling. The earthquake at Foligno was disastrous, & with kind regards to all Your family believe me ever Your

W. Gell

---

she exchanges next week for that of Mrs Scott of Abbotsford'. (Lockhart's *Life of Sir Walter Scott*, Edinburgh ed., vol. vii, p. 318.) Gell's reference to Anne Page is an allusion to *The Merry Wives of Windsor*.

1. Seymour, Rt. Hon. Sir George Hamilton (1797–1880). P.C., G.C.B., G.C.H. British Minister at Florence and later Envoy Extraordinary and Minister Plenipotentiary at Vienna.
2. See above, p. 46.

Mr. Hill is at Persano shooting. Mr. Strangeways went there yesterday. I have not determined whether the cold will permit me to go. Sir Grenville Temple last night told me there was, a cry of wolf at 2 in the morning. He got up, awakened all the family & they contrived to kill the poor devil. The Royal servants rushed out into the woods with each a couple of wax candles in their hands.

Ramsay, Lushington, Craven & all Your friends here desire *mille amicizie*.

Naples, March 16, 1832.

My dear Sir,

There are a few things which I must get You to insert. One where the *perisculacismos* or dog sacrifice[1] is mentioned in the article Language. "This sacrifice of the dog is mentioned by Lycophron as practised to Hecate in the Cave of Zerynthos[2] in Samothrace [Greek given], which island was the holy place of the Pelasgic mysteries & particularly connected with Umbria by the flight of Dardanus from Cortona to it."

There is another little sentence also I want inserting, but I cannot find it in Virgil where it certainly is. It is a Counsel given to AEneas not to land in Magna Graecia where are so many Greek settlements.[3] He lands in fact at Laurentum only a few miles above Ardea, the same Laurentum being the most southern Pelasgicco Sabina establishment on the coast & Ardea the last Argive colony to the north. If You have time to consider this argument & to write a sentence in the article Pelasgi it would be very kind of You—

I do not remember whether I sent a map of Veii with the article, please let me know if I did not that I may send one directly. I wish to send a view of the site of Alba Longa also.

I once thought of sending a view of the Gate of Jupiter at

1. See *Topography*, ii, 383.
2. The exact location of the Zerynthian Cave does not seem ever to have been discovered. It is referred to several times in ancient texts. 'A long monster of a serpent, dappled with horny scales' is supposed to have inhabited it according to one authority, another says it is 'the cave of the goddess to whom dogs are slain, that is a grotto to Hecate', while another associates the cave with Aphrodite. (N. Lewis, *Samothrace Excavations*, Vol. I, nos 152, 153, 155, 156. We are indebted to Mr. Peter Fraser for this reference.)
3. See Virgil, *Aeneid* 3, 396–8.

Falerii, but having sent a plan I was fearful of overdoing that place. If permitted I should like to send a bit of the wall under the *Tabularium* of the *intermontium* or the Capitol, as the date of it seems decided & it is the best specimen of Roman walling at Rome. If You wish for it pray direct to me at Rome where I shall be in the month of April. If You can get me the money for the Book and Map which I made so sure of that I am in debt to the full value & expect to go to the *Vicaria*[1] here unless quickly & efficaciously relieved. I have just been driving out Mount Stuart Elphinstone[2] who is a friend of Yours & Who has been suffering from rheumatism. He is better & thinks of a Tour in Sicily. Your house of Pollio[3] at the end of Pausilypo is in great fashion. Mr. Laing Meeson has made plans & elevations of it, & I have been there with Sir Walter for whom a Ghost story & the name *Casa degli Spiriti*[4] (Pls. VI, VII) has been got up. Somebody attempted to open an old chest in a room there which having done out of the Well arose a tall white Ghost in a Toga & the money is let fall so as to strew the floor. Perhaps this is new to You, we intended to get a ghost for Sir Walter but the stairs are so dangerous it was thought unwise for him to go up. I have just been with him to Paestum sleeping 3 nights at Miss Whytes at La Cava.[5] He was much pleased with the Convent at La Cava & the M.S.S. & with the Laws of the Lombards with pictures of Lotharius, Ataulfus & such Kings, to which he is more addicted than to Greeks & Romans.

1. Castel Capuano, known as *La Vicaria*—constructed in the 12th century and at one time was a royal residence. In 1540, was restored by order of the Spanish Viceroy, Don Pedro di Toledo, and became the *palazzo di giustizia* and prison. Gell is jokingly implying that he will be imprisoned here for debt.
2. Elphinstone, Hon. Mountstuart (1779–1859), 4th s. of John, 11th Baron Elphinstone. Indian Civil Service, Envoy to Afghanistan and Governor of Bombay. Travelled in Greece 1827–29. Elected to the Society of Dilettanti 1831.
3. The villa of Roman date called Pausilypon, situated above the modern Gaiola, which gives its name to the modern cape, Posillipo. It was built by the wealthy friend of the emperor Augustus, Vedius Pollio, who was said to have fed slaves to his pet lampreys. For a description, see R. T. Gunther, *Pausilypon* (Oxford 1913).
4. Or *Palazzo degli Spiriti*. The name given to a prominent three-storeyed villa of Roman date at Marechiaro. It can now only be reached by sea; see R. T. Gunther, *op. cit.*, 173 ff. The visit of Sir Walter Scott is described by Hamilton, basing himself presumably on Gell's letters, in *Transactions of the R. Soc. of Literature*, 1837. For a photograph of the ruin, see *Storia di Napoli* 475; cp. also below, p. 94.
5. The Benedictine Abbey of La Trinità della Cava dei Terreni, founded in the 11th century, and famed for its collection of MSS which happily survived intact during the Second World War.

This being the case I hope I shall persuade him not to go to Greece for which He is quite unprepared to take any interest & for which his health is quite unequal. He has an idea of a poem on Rhodes when he has finished a Romance on Malta, but as I go about a good deal with him & observe how he sees things, I can tell him more about Rhodes,[1] than he will ever learn if he goes & am now making him a little collection of notes, sketches & hints which I trust will render the voyage useless. The fact is that though he is very well & much better since he has been here, a case might arise when he might be lost in a few minutes for want of a Doctor which as He is now quite free from all debt, if he will go, he will I hope take with him. He is very agreeable & a very benevolent person & a great resource here. I daresay He will come to Rome when I go & return for the summer here—We have fewer great people than usual but I see no difference as to balls & dinners for I dine out every day & go to a ball half the nights in the week though Lent has begun. Vesuvius blazes & becomes extinct by turns, but Auldjo of Mt. Blanc is writing and drawing & lithographing all it does. L^d. Hertford says that the people in London will attend no longer to the arts, & that Ackerman[2] bowed him out of his shop when he found his L^{d}ship came to sell & not to buy. Nevertheless I wish when You have contrived my Roman map & Book You would see what You can do with Jennings for my Pompeiana paintings—Say 60 paintings & among them the new mosaic all in colours—80 are ready if He likes it better.

We have got Mr. Philips[3] of Trin. Coll. Cam. & Mr. Wordsworth[4] both the greatest of scholars here & they are sent me in a letter. They seem much interested in the Roman map & work &

1. Gell's *Notes on Rhodes* have hitherto remained as an unpublished MS in the Library at Abbotsford, but these have now been edited by Edith Clay and appear in the *Journal of the Warburg and Courtauld Institutes*, Vol. XXXIII, November, 1970.
2. Ackerman, Rudolph, Senior (1764–1834) who at that time was carrying on business at 101 Strand.
3. Phillips, Thomas Jodrell, afterwards Thomas Jodrell Phillips-Jodrell, s. of Shakespear Phillips of Manchester. Pensioner of Trinity College, Cambridge 1822, Fellow 1830, M.A. 1832. We are indebted to Dr. R. Robson for this information.
4. Wordsworth, Christopher (1807–1885), later Bishop of Lincoln and 3rd s. of Christopher Wordsworth, Master of Trinity College, Cambridge. Travelled in Greece 1832–33 and was the first Englishman to be presented to King Otto of Greece. He m. Susanna Hatley Frere. Headmaster of Harrow School 1836 and Canon of Westminster 1844. Author of a monumental commentary on the

particularly in the article Language. I have just had them to Breakfast. L^d. Hertford is going to hire the omnibus carrying 24 inside to go to Pompeii tomorrow week. I expect to be overturned & killed in the fray. If You do not get a little tracing of the mosaic of the battle of Issus in this You are to think only that I would not get it ready for young Mr. Garnier[1] to carry off by the steam vessel. You must give no copy of it as it will contribute to ruin my next work in pictures. I trust entirely to You & Your influence in the learned world for my 500 £ with which to pacify the bank of Torlonia & Co. in return for the fee simple of my work on Latium etc. Believe me ever most truly yours

W. Gell.

Pray try & get me from Mr. Jennings the other nos after No. 10 which You sent me of the New Pompeiana.

Could You not contrive to get me one copy of my Greek Map at my own expense by saying it was for me. You might cut it in pieces if You could not get it carried whole.

Dr. Goodall[2] & Dr. Arnold[3] would both protect my Roman work & Sir Walter is going to puff it. Pray send & seal my letter to Messrs. Jennings & shew him my pictures if You can.

Rome. April 26, May 2,6,8,11,14, 1832.

My dear Sir,

Your letter dated Grafton Street March 5,1832 reached me while I was yet at Naples doubting whether my finances would possibly

Bible and *A Journal of a Residence in Athens and Attica*, but better known for his *Greece, Pictorial, Descriptive and Historical*. London 1839.

1. Possibly Charles Garnier, author of *Journal of Siège de Gaète*. Brussels 1861.
2. Goodall, Joseph (1760–1840). King's College, Cambridge, assistant-master Eton College 1783, Canon of Windsor 1808 and Provost of Eton until his death. Was one of the first housemasters at Eton and of whom it was said, 'a pleasant joyousness overflowed his face'—William IV was sitting beside him at Speeches in 1834 and remarked to Keate (another master), who was on the King's other side, 'When he goes I'll make you him'—Then Goodall piped up. 'Sire, I would never think of going before your Majesty.' We are indebted to the late Mr. G. A. D. Tait for this information.
   Gell writing to Lady Blessington from Rome on 7 June 1827 says, 'Dr Goodall, the Provost of Eton, is here—we are such friends that he sends me Latin verses on myself, which I shall put I don't know where to be seen, they are so flattering.'
3. Arnold, Dr. Thomas (1795–1842). Headmaster of Rugby 1824–42.

allow me to venture on a trip to the Holy City with Sir Walter, & its arrival was very opportune as on the 13th I set out for this place, where by the bye I have been laid up by a most painful fit of gout in my hand ever since, & am only This day, now the 26th getting out again & taking Sir Walter to dinner at Bunsens the Prussian Ministers in the Capitol. It is now May 2nd when I continue this letter having been prevented by illness again & also by the wish to send You certain little paragraphs & illustrations of the work & particularly the tablet of Nemi[1] the preservation of which is of consequence. But first I will say that I thank You very much for the trouble You have taken & the difficulties which You have encountered & finally vanquished in regard to the Map, Book, & the Society. I feel that they have been great & I beg to say that I am most grateful to You for assistance without which my pains & researches would have yielded no fruits. I did as You desired in drawing 200 £ upon the D.S. in favour of Torlonia, & I have promised him the rest when it comes, which will set me about right in his books—thanks to You—You are quite right in what You say about inaccuracies & contradictions on my work, I have here & there discovered & corrected them myself but if a work be written in the shape of a Dictionary, the subjects are treated of at so many different times & so totally without connexion that it is very difficult to avoid both saying & thinking at one time that which may not be found correct at another. Added to this I became myself, so much more knowing in my subject as it came towards its close that I may have contradicted things in the later articles which I have said before my materials were well put together. I hope & trust that You have not found the finishing of the work less interesting than the beginning which Your Judge Mr. ——[sic] of King's College confessed was in a great measure new. I have recollected a passage which I intended to insert in the Article Pelasgi: & which I omitted because I could not find the lines in Virgil but which I daresay You could remember. "AEneas is advised not to land in the South of Italy which was so much occupied by his enemies the Greeks, & he accordingly continued his Voyage towards

---

1. Mentioned below (p. 77) as a 'basso rilievo'. Present whereabouts unknown; for a sketch, see *Topography*, ii, 117. Excavation was conducted at Aricia, on the site of the shrine of Diana of Nemi, by Cardinal D'Antonio Despuij y Dameto, Archbishop of Valencia, in the years 1787–96. The stone does not appear in his collection, which is now in Palma; see E. Hübner, *Antike Bildwerke in Madrid* (Berlin 1862), 292 ff.

the North 'till he arrived at the first Pelasgic territory"[1]—Can You
be so good to contrive this for me & insert something with that
meaning where You think it would be proper. Next in speaking
of the Etrurian Vases of Vulci, I only knew of 2,000 but 4,000[2] have
now been found & more are expected—I send You some sentences
to insert & some Vignettes. The *basso relievo* of Nemi I think
invaluable & I hope it will not be objected to, as it is the only
way of preserving the memory of it. I saw Nibby & asked him
what he knew about it as he had mentioned it in his book. He told
me he knew nothing of it but from me & quoted it from my
engraving, the stone being gone to Spain & lost. You did not
answer me about the Map of Veii, thereupon I conclude that I sent
it to You with the first Packet. If not, it is of great consequence
to have it, & I find here that my dissertation has produced much
effect upon the Antiquaries. I wish to add to the account of
Farfa.[3] "The buildings of this once famous Monastery are now
reduced to a Church with a high belfry tower, & an ordinary
building, serving for the lodging of four Monks, but the revenues
are yet valued at 9,000 Scudi annually, which are enjoyed by a
Titular Abbott who resides at Rome"—The rest of the explana-
tions and additions which You were kind enough to say You would
overlook & regulate, I have written in such a manner that You
need only cut the pieces out & join them on to the articles,
without the trouble of rewriting. It is possible some of the later
articles, or those last sent may be omitted in the index, as I remember writing one or two at the instigation of Father Strangeways, as Mr. Hill calls him. What trouble I give You and how
You must hate the sight of a letter from me, though You are
always so good & so effective a Protector. I shall remain in a
fright till Torlonia gets Rodwells 300 £, though I am sure You
will do everything that can be done to keep all right. The hiati
in my map are only such as if I did not tell You, You would
never perceive, for the borders to the right & left are as I state
in the book merely to give information as to the places by which my
map is surrounded, not being regularly surveyed. As to undertaking more at my own expense it is impossible in the present state
of my rents from my Chateaux en Espagne. I have a strong
hankering after the Valley of the Equicoli, the Fucine Lake, the

1. See above, p. 72.
2. Compare *Bullettino*, 1831, 161 (Gerhard was obviously Gell's source for this
figure).
3. A former Benedictine monastery founded in A.D. 681.

Valley of the Hernici & the country about Rieti for which last I made many observations & collected the details, but the completion of the project is beyond my means or hopes. It is absolutely *Terra incognita* & will still continue so though Craven[1] has got a tour ready for printing, through some part of the country. You know that Vesuvius has erupted during the whole Winter. The Crater became full of Lava & overflowed on both sides, towards Pompeii & Naples, without doing any damage to the country. Auldjo of Montblanc has written & drawn & engraved its history—We have Sir Walter rather in a better state & he has this morning been to breakfast in my Garden May 2nd. I am going to take him to the Castle of Bracciano on the 9th, after which He is going home by Venice & Innsbruck to see certain statues of 13 Emperors in Bronze[2] about which he raves. The Cloaca Maxima & the Colosseum seem to have taken his fancy, but except these objects nothing except that relates to the Stewarts seems to have any charm for him in this Country, & it is amusing to observe the ingenious contrivances by which he changes the conversation from any other subject to the history of Prince Charles & the Stewarts in general. He is a most aimable benevolent person & I find him extremely amusing on all subjects connected with his own line of thought or observation. This I hope will reach You safe through Messrs. Aubyn & Seymour whose residence here does not seem at present likely to terminate speedily at least if success is to attend the negociations for I fancy we are more obstinate than 50 mules in not performing our promises or executing our treatises, so that we only exist by a miraculous want of Concord among the Allies. I can go no further without stating that I forgot as I wrote at Naples who wrote 2 volumes on the Fratelli Arvali, but I find here it was Marini which pray insert. On the whole I am as well pleased that my Roman books were not at Naples for I could not copy them & what I wrote ought to be new. I fear in one place I have made a mistake in the article Rome & said that the wall of the Intermontium was built about 400 U.C. Evidently it was the wall of the Capitol I mean, the style of which is the same. The only *intermontium* wall is that under the *Tabularium* which I now send.

1. This was published as *Excursion in the Abruzzi* etc.
2. Evidently the reference is to the Tomb of the Emperor Maximilian of Austria in the Imperial Palace at Innsbruck, on which are depicted the bronze statues of his ancestors and relatives. Sir Walter's interest in 'the last Knight' was quite natural to him. There are 28 statues round the Tomb, some of which are illustrated in Eduard Heyck, *Kaiser Maximilian I*, Bielefeld, 1898.

I believe it is now the 6th but I cannot get well. May 8 my right hand is in so wretched a state & in so painful a fit of gout that I am reduced to write with the left & I don't know how I shall ever get to Bracciano[1] with Sir Walter who goes there two days hence & we have already got the Castle lent to us to receive Him. You remember our subscription for excavating the Forum.[2] It has been going on ever since by means of The Galley Slaves, but so slowly that two years have scarcely made any visible difference. The Temple of Concord is however clearly made out & the *Tabularium* cleared to the bottom. It corresponds perfectly with the marble plan. It appears that till the space was filled up by buildings there really was a little ravine between the two tops of the Capitol that is between the Arx & the Capitol. Bunsen has been trying to place the Arx at the Ara Coeli & the Temple of Jupiter on the western summit but I think he fails & the excavations seem to contradict him.[3] The Tarpeian rock and the circumstances that till the time of Trajan the eastern top was not fairly detached from the Quirinal & ergo not a good place for a Citadel are against Bunsen & for Nibby. They are both grown tremendously fat over it & Bunsen has had twins. Lady Charlotte[4] writes that Ld Dudley's[5]

1. The expedition to Bracciano took place on either May 9th or 10th.
2. The forum excavations at this time were directed by D. Carlo Fea, director of the Capitoline Museum. For an account of them see Bunsen's reports in the *Bullettino*, 1829, 26 ff.; 1835, 65 ff. The marble plan referred to is the fragmentary map of ancient Rome prepared under the emperor Septimius Severus, of which some parts survive.
3. Bunsen's view has been confirmed by subsequent finds, which make it clear that the Capitolium or Temple of Jupiter lies under the *Palazzo dei Conservatori*, and the ancient *arx* on the site of S. Maria in Aracoeli. But Gell's view was common at the time, being shared by Nibby, Canina, Braun and other authorities. See H. Jordan, *Topographie der Stadt Rom im Alterthum* (1871–1901), I, etc.
4. Most probably Lady Charlotte Bury. She was Lady Charlotte Susan Maria Campbell (1775–1861) d. of John 5th Duke of Argyll and the famous beauty Elizabeth Gunning. She m. (1) John Campbell of Shawfield in 1796 and (2) Rev. Edward John Bury in 1809. On being first widowed, she became a lady-in-waiting to Princess Caroline of Wales, but in 1814 went to live abroad. She continued to correspond with the Princess and her suite, and in April 1815 rejoined H.R.H. in her frigate *Clorinda* at Genoa remaining in attendance for some weeks until she finally left the Princess's service. Lady Charlotte and Gell kept up a lively correspondence over many years. See *Introduction*, pp. 3–4.
5. Ward, John William, 4th Viscount Dudley and 9th Baron Ward (1781–1833) who suc. his father 1823 and was created Earl of Dudley 1827. Secretary for Foreign Affairs. Elected to the Society of Dilettanti 1826. Lord Dudley frequented the circle of Princess Caroline of Wales who rather indelicately remarked of him that 'he eats like a hog with his snout sucking in a trough'.

. case is not without hopes of cure, which I sincerely hope may be true. Poor Dodwell, who as soon as he became rich had something like an apoplexy, has either been so much neglected or has so much neglected himself that his case will soon become desperate & he will not see Dr. Jenks[1] only the lemonade D^{rs} of the country. His wife writes this morning that She was much alarmed in the night. I wish Lady Chrichton[2] or Crichton who I know he has made his heir were here to see that what can be done is done for water on the chest seems now to be apprehended by the Roman Physicians such as they are. It is a melancholy case but he goes on drawing & hunting out walls & calling all of them cities as merrily as ever every time he gets a little better. Pray with regard to my work & map expunge & add what You like as I am no judge of what the public like, & the not having had books at hand at Naples, tho' it forced me to write what I knew myself only, may have been a disadvantage. I will not end without thanking You once more for all Your goodness & support. Believe me Yours much obliged.

William Gell.

May 11: Mr. Seymours Courier not being dispatched it seems, that my interminable letter is likely to be continued, sine fine, to torment You. I am come back from the Scott expedition to Bracciano which considering I went ill & returned no better seemed to answer Sir Walter's expectations well. I have this morning parked them, the Scotts, off for Venice & England. He has no care of himself & really one cannot say how a long journey will suit him. On my return I found Dodwell worse & reported dying, but he seemed cheerful last night & is better today but Mrs.

1. It appears that Dr. Jenks was an English doctor at Rome. Henry Fox (*op. cit.*, pp. 237, 250, 292) says that on his arrival in Rome in March 1827 he called on Lady Westmorland. 'She I found in a pink bonnet, fur cloak, and numberless costly shawls, haranguing her servant at the foot of the palace (Rospigliosi).' Fox and Lady Westmorland conversed about the 'respective merits of Dr Jenks and Dr Peebles', and on 19 April 1828 Fox wrote that 'Jenks ordered me to stay at home'. Lord Malmesbury also refers to a 'Dr. Jenks, ex-surgeon of the 10th Hussars' in his *Memoirs of an Ex-Minister*. London, 1884, 2 vols, v. i, p. 21.
2. Crichton, Sir Alexander (1763–1856), 2nd s. of Alexander Crichton of Woodhouselee and Newington, Midlothian. Physician to the Duke of Cambridge—1804 was offered appointment to Alexander I of Russia—knighted by George IV 1821. He m. 1800 Frances, sister of Edward Dodwell (p. 41). Lady Crichton d. 1857.

Dodwell has written to D^r. Crichton. The Roman D^{rs} seem to think there is an organic defect in the heart & he will not see Dr. Jenks. If so I fear he has not long to live. He has had extreme unction which he told me this morning was his passport & the absolution he calls his clean boots. Mrs. Dodwell who is considered to have cared little for him has been most exemplarily attentive.

14 of May. Mr. Seymour has been here & says he will take charge of all this packet. Poor Dodwell expired yesterday very quietly & I found all the house weeping when I went to see him at 5 p.m. Mr. Mills[1] & Luigi Chiaveri[2] are the executors but they are now reading the Will so nothing is known. *Later in the same day*. Dodwell's will being read Mr. Mills and myself are made Trustees to a very unjust will. He leaves 12,500 Scudi to

1. Mills, Charles Andrew (1760–1846), 3rd s. of Peter Matthew Mills of St. Kitts in the West Indies who d. 1792 leaving his son £10,000 and certain sugar plantations. Mills first came to Rome in 1817; the next year he and Gell acquired jointly a property on the Palatine Hill known as the Villa Mattei or Villa Spada, which was situated in the ruins of Domitian's Palace. Later Mills became the sole owner, although Gell continued to share house with him when in Rome. Mills rebuilt the villa in Gothic style imitating Strawberry Hill at Twickenham and Fonthill Abbey. He lived there until his death and is buried in the Protestant Cemetery at Rome. On Mill's death the Villa passed into private possession, but in 1856 became the Convent of the Order of the Visitation; a new wing was added which now forms the Palatine Museum. In July 1923 an English newspaper reporting on the excavations on the Palatine by Com. Boni stated that he 'will preserve the "Scotch Gothic" architecture of the quaint Villa Mills where Charles Mills and Sir William Gell once lived together and he will cover the picturesque ruin with ivy. He had cleared out the fountain at the back of the Villa and will provide it with water. He also removed a large bank of earth from the front so that it is easy to look down into the halls of the Imperial palace below'. No vestige now remains of this strange and fascinating home of Mills and Gell. Some 30 years ago the Italian archaeological authorities decided to pull the whole edifice down in order to reveal the remains of Domitian's Palace. See H. V. Morton, *A Traveller in Rome*, Methuen, London, 1957, pp. 156, 246–7 and Appendix.
    Before Mills took up residence at Rome, he was living in London and frequented the circle surrounding the Princess of Wales. On 4 September 1813 Lady Charlotte Campbell wrote (*op. cit.*, vol. i, p. 172), 'I dined at Kensington. A Mr. Mills dined with her Royal Highness. I never saw him before, and I could not discover who he is, or anything else about him, except that he has very white teeth and very festooned lips!' As we see in correspondence between Gell and Lady Blessington, Mills was something of a botanist.
2. Chiavari, Luigi. Lord Houghton in his *Memoir of Edward Cheney* remarked that Chiavari had taken Gell to the house at Rome where Benvenuto Cellini said he slew the Constable of Bourbon with a bullet fired from the Castel Sant'Angelo.

his wife which would only produce 60 Scudi per month. The house & furniture which is only a lease go to her, but the museum & books are doubtful. We intend to accept the trust in hopes of being useful to Mrs. Dodwell who ought at least to have had 400 a year. The estate is left to Lady Crichton & all the personalty, but I fancy a claimant will appear to a part which is entailed. We are in hopes however Lady Crichton will give the Widow an allowance. He has left his servants handsomely but indiscriminately. He leaves me 500 Scudi but says not a word of 500 £ which he borrowed of me. Yet with all this his will was deliberately made, & before he went crazy. I don't know how much You may be interested in hearing all this, but You have I believe known him for many years. What a long letter & what a terrible bore for You, but believe me ever Yours

W. Gell

Rome May 14, 1832.

[Rome] May, 1832 [but written at various later dates: received in London 6 July]

My dear Hamilton,
   I ought to have prefaced my last request to the D.S. by an humble supplication that they would accede to it but in my haste to send off my packet by Mr. Seymour prevented me. I am sorry to trouble You again on the subject of the Work itself but You are so good as to say You would protect it & I think You will perceive that my new discoveries are such as deserve Your attention. You remember what I have said of the likeness between the gates of Arpino & Mycenae but I always wished to find a Roman or Italian building like the treasury of Atreus to shew as far as buildings could shew the connexion of the two countries. In fact I have found a Tomb among those of Vulci [sketch] roofed in the Mycenae style & what is better I have established that the real original prisons of Servius & Ancus at Rome were roofed in the same manner. What is more the circular part is like that of Mycenae; a horizontal arch so that the plan of the building is [sketch] though its section be [sketch] Its top has been cut off by the Restorers because it was two peaked for their upper story. With all that has been written about Rome I trust You will give me some credit for this discovery, but as I have been ever since my arrival too ill to examine this satisfactorily myself and besides that might have been

led away by my hopes I have been forced to employ Canina[1] the Architect to draw the place & its section for me & it is his drawing I send You which accounts for its being better done than usual, & I have little doubt if he comprehends the interest of the discovery he will have the modesty to take it to himself. What I send must I think be added to the article Rome. I must have another bit to the article Riano which though I had seen & triangled I had not visited. I call it the Ara Jani,[2] & I believe I found there the

altar itself of Janus in white marble substituted by the Romans for the Etruscan one of stone. The rocks are full of caves. I suppose Tombs & it is one of the prettiest places I ever saw. The fact is a bad sketch is worth 50 descriptions & as Mrs. Dodwell, Petre[3] & General Resta[4] are all talking to me. I have sent You this likeness of the place which will enable You to understand it & perhaps assist in persuading You to add a few words to the article.

(seen through trees)

1. Luigi Canina (1795–1856), famous architect and scholar. He laid out the gardens of the Villa Borghese, and was the author of many learned works on Roman topography and ruins. Gell's allusion to the man seems unduly slighting.
2. Gell supposes that this was the origin of the name Riano. Several inscriptions are mentioned *in situ* in G. Tomasetti, *La Campagna Romana*, iv, 282 ff., but we cannot identify the one Gell has in mind.
3. Petre, William Henry Francis, 11th Baron Petre (1793–1850) who m. Frances Charlotte, eld. d. of Sir Richard Bedingfield, 5th Bart. in 1815.
4. We have been quite unable to identify this person.

This letter was so far written about a week ago & since that time I have been so ill with the gout, only more or less in 12 places, that I have been unable to attend to work. It is now June 2nd or 3rd, & I positively had a fire to dress by for the Comet or the approach of the end of the World have so changed the seasons that it has lately snowed hard at Naples, & they pretend was two palms deep—which I conclude means 2 inches. All yesterday we have had at Rome the most fearful thunder & lightning which lasted above 12 hours with torrents of rain & now after 12 other hours seems ready to begin again. All the prisoners to the number of 300 at Spoleto have broken out & are gone to Ancona[1]—the devil to pay—What a horrid state combined with Cholera the world is in, & You in England are at length arrived at a point at which get out of it how You may every sort of mischief must be apprehended. I hope Your great Duke [of Wellington] is really coming to take a trip in this country for amusement for after all he is the greatest man of the age who beat Buonaparte. All this might be very well, for down to that sentence I thought the book was going on well, but last Friday, 7th, on my return from the Tre Fontane with the two Cheneys,[2] Mr. Laing Meeson & Young Wordsworth, Your ugly letter arrived with the funniest news that nothing could be done for the work, which I once thought settled, than rather deranged, & which I now find in a hopeless state. As to Jennings, He is not at all deeply engaged with me for I sent him my work & he sent me the 500 £ I asked for it long ago, before it was in the press, so I am quite free with him. Mr. Laing Meeson to whom I read the passage of your letter about the 5 or 600 £ which the work ought to cost in printing, says that 200 £ would be an ample sum for it provided that the vignettes are either done on wood or stone, for an edition of 500 copies. The worst of all propositions is that of publishing the Book jointly between myself & a Bookseller for not one shilling could I possibly gain by it in that manner I being here & the Bookseller in London.

1. One of the few allusions that Gell makes to the deep disorder that afflicted the Papal States in 1832. Ancona had been seized by the French troops in February of that year in order to pressure the government of Rome into liberal reforms. Gell is evidently concerned for the political implications of the desertion of prisoners to the French.

2. Cheney, Edward (1803–1884), 2nd s. of Lt. General Robert Cheney of Badger Hall, Shropshire. Cheney lived in Italy for many years. His elder bro. was Henry (1801–1866), who was elected to the Society of Dilettanti in 1854. See *Memoir of Edward Cheney* by Lord Houghton. *Philobiblon Miscellanies*, Vol. XV, 1877–84, pp. 1–18; also *Appendix C*.

I feel sorry that I gave in to the plan of writing an account of the Map which has been a most troublesome undertaking in itself & has taken a great deal of time, & ends by giving You so much Annoyance that I have long been heartily ashamed of it. For Your sins, You must be so good as to submit to this last letter of improvement for the unhappy book & then You shall be tormented no more. As to the Peutingerian Table[1] which refers to that part of Italy detailed in my map, I have rendered it as human & as little distorted as I could to make it intelligible, & I believe it would be well to add it, but if You don't think so it may be left out. The plan & section of the Prisons at Rome[2] I think so curious & it is so new that I should be sorry if You did not protect it. However I will do no more—I will plague You no more after this time—In my two last I begged the D.S. to advance the money to me & to take all the profits to whatever sum they might ever amount, & whenever they might arise. In a work like Pompeii, the Society for the diffusion of Knowledge & the confusion of states, undersell the Author in a five shilling duodecimo, but in such an unornamented Book as the present Roman Topography that would be impossible, particularly if it were printed in two columns on whity brown paper as one proposed. In short one is in a monstrous scrape & I know not how to get out of it, though for one's consolation as I am reading Croker & Boswells Johnson it is evident that even the great Goliath himself was always in an *embroglio* on the same subject of money matters. I shall retire in disgust to Naples about the 15th of this month of June, there to await the Cholera with Patience. I have only got the gout at this moment in 12 places which if they should unite & coalesce in one would probably save me the trouble of thinking any more about sales of Books or other speculations. Looking over Dodwells papers we see what incredible sums he threw away on his Cyclopean Walls.[3] I think there are a dozen payments to Hulmandell[4] of 200 £ each & one of 360 £ & one of 400 £ & the Work in Lithography not much advanced. It was his sole object during his last years & he gave half a crown to any one who could shew him any bit of

1. A copy made in medieval times of a map of the world as known in the third century A.D. It came into the possession of a scholar named Peutinger, and is called after him.
2. Surely the Tullianum.
3. *Views and Descriptions of Cyclopian or Pelasgic Remains in Greece and Italy* ... by Edward Dodwell (London 1834: with French text and title, 1834).
4. Hulmandel, Charles. Lithographic printer of Great Marlborough Street.

polygonal Wall so that he had imagined 20 Cities in the space of 5 miles square which were really Roman Villas. Your houses by the bye at Pompeii are I fear imaginary. The house of the Fauno in which is the fine Mosaic is really very large & occupies an entire Insula but it is not of so superior a class to those already discovered. This

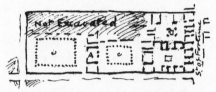

will give You an idea of the whole house of the Fauno as far as it is known. It will occupy the whole Insula and is in fact the family house joined into another of the Servants side by side. It differs from that of Pansa in having a second peristyle instead of a garden but is perhaps but little larger. A is the great Mosaic— Speaking of which I have no doubt L^d. Hertford would undertake to set right all our affair of the Book if it were not for the peculiar pressure & troublesome state of the Times which make wise people hoard their money to be prepared for the worst. I conclude He is at the Bains d' Aix at this moment but that when he has finished that he will return to England. If You meet Him or get near Him do either renew, continue or make His acquaintance for You will at least have the pleasure of meeting a person who thinks as You do. When You make me a Peer I shall leave it on record that I voted for the Bill to avoid worse immediate mischief but that I was threatened & not a free agent. If each party when it takes to making Peers for convenience You are likely to have a large house in a few years. You have nothing left now but to leave on record that You were bullied out of it. We are in a nice state here for we have neither men, arms nor money, two foreign armies & five or 6 rebellions in our provinces yet we go on or rather creep on to our grand finale, each Sovereign only anxious in his turn to keep things together during his own time.

I believe it is now the 13th, & I was in hopes to have sent You the view of Alba Longa, to have dined at the Torlonias at Castel Gandolfo, slept at Mr. Cheneys at Frascati, ascended to Tusculum & examined whether the houses excavated were ancient or modern, but it always rains so Mr. Laing Meeson & I come home at night re infecta in every branch. The Tusculum therefore as I am out of spirits about the work, I fear will never be done as I am too ill to

86

ride a jack ass if no good is to come of it. The Alba I can do in a carriage.

I have done all that can be done to ruin Your eyesight by way of getting all my communications into this sheet which I find at last I cannot do. The drawings which You have got of mine Craven can bring back for he will be by this time in London but where I know not, at L^d. Cravens,[1] or L^d. Seftons[2] he may I conclude be heard of but he is gone round by ——[sic] to avoid the Cholera. (Evening of the same day) I have just seen Bunsen the Prussian Minister who says there really is a house at Tusculum with the imitation of mockery of an *Atrium* & *impluvium*. It is very curious & would shew that ancient & modern worlds separated in Italy about anno 1180 or a little before that time. The said Bunsen says that the Library & Museum of the Roman Archaeology[3] is to be open to students & that the French Government is to give it the great Work on Egypt & other Governments are sending other works. They have now 500 volumes besides casts & Marbles & they insinuate that any of the Works of the D.S. will be highly acceptable & useful to their collection for Students of all Nations.[4] I believe I am now arrived at the 19th of June & I have in obedience to Your orders made another Tour of Alba Longa & taken a view of the place with Camera Lucida which I am quite incapable from illness of rendering pretty but which with the

1. Craven, William, 8th Baron and 2nd Earl of (1809–1866): nephew of Keppel Craven.
2. Sefton, William Philip Molyneux, 2nd Earl of (1772–1838) who m. 1792 Hon. Maria Margaret Craven (1769–1851) sister of Keppel Craven.
3. Compare the announcement in *Bullettino*. 1832, p. ix (May 1832). This was the beginning of the famous library that was to become the German Institute in Rome. At the time it was housed in the Palazzo Caffarelli and opened every day at 5 p.m. in summer and at 3 p.m. in winter. See *Introduction* for Gell's relations with the Institute.
4. There is no record at the German Archaeological Institute in Rome of this suggestion being carried out, but their records show that they possessed none of the Society's publications in 1835, and did do so in 1839. However, a Minute of the Society of Dilettanti on 14 April 1833 recorded that on consideration of Gell's request that copies of the Society's publications be sent to the Archaeological Institute at Rome, 'the Secretary was directed to write to Mr. Bunsen to learn the state of that Society, and particularly to draw his attention to the Irregularity with which publications are behind to Subscribers'—Later on 2 April 1837, on a suggestion made by Mr. Gally Knight 'it was resolved that copies of such works of the Society as are in their possession, and at their disposal be presented to the Instituto Archaeologico at Rome in the name of the Society, and that the Secretary should write to that effect to Mr. Bunsen, Prussian Minister at Rome, to announce the same'.

description must be I think very satisfactory. I was resolved to do this job so I took Mr. Laing Meeson & told him where to look for the ruins in the Bushes while I drew. Thence I went & dined at Torlonias at Castel Gandolfo & since that have never been able to stir. The first day I am better I shall return to Naples where I suppose I am better in health than at Rome. I intended to make another attack upon Empulum,[1] Saxula[2] & Siciliano[3] beyond Tivoli before my departure but between poverty & illness I must give that up. Gherard[4] the Secretary of the Instituto came back from Vulci yesterday. He says a sort of Tripod of Bronze[5] has been found. I believe it is a sort of tree which stands on 3 roots, to the branches of which 6 or 7 vases were found suspended. The Vases small & not good. The whole was found in a Tomb. We have just heard You have passed Your Bill—I only wish it may be followed by some sort of quiet. It would have been better if the Peers had at first considered whether the thing must be passed or not—if it must pass, it would have been more dignified to have had nothing to do with it. Let up hope headlong Democracy will not be the necessary consequence.

I intended to have gone to Tusculum the other day to have examined if at that place destroyed in 1180 any vestiges of an ancient house with *atrium* or *impluvium* remain. You know in the

1. Empulum. Fosso D'Empiglione, the ruins south of the modern Castel Madama. Since Nibby's time this has been identified with Empulum, an ancient town of the Aequi.

2. Saxula, another walled site nearby.

3. Ciciliano; in the modern town traces of polygonal walling show the presence of an ancient town, recently identified with Trebula Suffenas, see L. R. Taylor, *Memoirs of the American Academy in Rome*, 1956.

4. Gerhard, Dr. Edward (1795–1867). Baroness Bunsen (*op. cit.*, vol. i, pp. 342–3) states that in 1828 the Crown Prince of Prussia, afterwards King Frederick William IV, wrote to Niebuhr relating to the final effort to establish the still subsidised and flourishing Institute for Archaeological Correspondence at Rome which he 'had been led to consider a necessity by the experience of his invaluable friend, Edward Gerhard, then an early pioneer, and long an honoured centre of antiquarian studies in Germany, who had been wandering for years throughout Italy, exploring in all directions its unnoticed treasures and historical inscriptions and relics of the past'. In 1828, as a result of the patronage of the Crown Prince, the Archaeological Institute was founded and Gell was one of the first to give his 'cordial adhesion' to the plan. For a detailed biography see 'E. Gerhard', by Otto Jahn in *Gesammelte Akademische Abhandlungen*, Berlin, 1866–68.

5. Mentioned also in *Bullettino*, 1832, 194; it is probably that which passed to the Duc de Luynes and is now in the Bibliothèque Nationale; Giglioli, *Arte Etrusca* tav. ci.

work I have of this & Bunsen now swears there is either an ancient or a mock ancient house among the excavated ruins in the street going towards the Theatre. Our Roman Forum will I think sometime or other be cleared. The *clivus*[1] between the temples of Jupiter & Fortune is creeping up the hill but slowly. It seems narrow & ill paved. The Arch of Constantine is quite clear, & all the great fountain[2] & Colosseum are now standing on their original pavements or nearly so. The Venus of Rome[3] stood on a tremendous *podium* opposite the Colosseum all of which has been cleared since You saw it. They are now cutting so as to unite the hole of Phocas[4] with that of the *Grecostasis*. In the hole of Phocus are found 5 other pedestals, & behind Phocas I see[5] [sketch] a little cell of brick which must have been awkward for the arch of Septimus Severus. Bunsen is straining heaven & earth to place Jupiter Capitolinus on the western top of the Capitol instead of at the Ara Coli, & in spite of Nibby the Forum is going to be turned toward the Arch of Titus again instead of between the Palatine & Capitol. The excavations may in the end clear up this point. In the meantime I see near Phocas buildings of brick of the middle ages buried up to the second story. Thus far had I got in this days work while waiting for Countess Ludoff,[6] the Neapolitan Ministress, to breakfast with both my feet tied up in a red silk handkerchief & in considerable pain. However she never came but in rushed in young Wordsworth, son of the Master of Trinity, & young Milner[7] of Yorkshire instead. Wordsworth is going to Greece immediately & is here learning Greek. I have sent them to see

1. The *Clivus Capitolinus*, running between the temples of Divus Vespasianus and Saturn. Gell follows Nibby's identifications of these two temples (cp. his *Del Foro della Sacra Via* etc., Rome, 1819).
2. The Old fountain called the *Meta Sudans*, a Roman landmark destroyed in 1936: Lugli, *Roma Antica*, 312 ff.
3. The temple of Venus and Rome.
4. Excavations near the column of Phocas, begun in 1817, had dug right down to the ancient pavement-level through the deep soil that then covered the Roman forum. The excavations were directed by the tireless De Fea, and financed by the Duchess of Devonshire.
5. The area excavated near the temple of Divus Julius in 1780–89.
6. Ludolf. Countess Ludolf was the wife of Count Guglielmo Costantino Ludolf (1758–1839), a Neapolitan diplomat. Count Ludolf was later appointed to the Court of St. James's where on 2 August 1837 he and his wife were guests at one of the first dinner parties to be given at Buckingham Palace by Queen Victoria after her Accession. See *The Gascoyne Heiress*, by C. Oman. London, Hodder and Stoughton, 1968, p. 252.
7. Lady Blessington refers twice to 'Mr. Milner of Yorkshire' in her journals, but with no indication of who he was.

about Gherards Vases[1] which Wordsworth swears he got in his late tour & have Etruscan inscriptions. I shall know tonight all about them & tell You before I close this. You know the 4000 Canino or Vulci vases are Greek with Greek inscriptions[2] but 2 were found of black real Etruscan earth & the letters which were Etruscan were painted on with red paint. I hope Gherards are of the same kind for at present the case seems clear that all the fine vases are Greek & those of black earth Etruscan. I must get You to scratch out the scale or measure at Falerium which was a bad approximation. The additions I have written so that You need not copy them, only cut the piece of paper off with scissors & with a wafer stick it onto the MS. I promise You that after this which I hope will go with Sir Charles Greville,[3] who says he will take it, You shall have no more adjuncts to the M.S. about which I am indeed now so out of spirits that I shall give up Archaeology & write Novels for the short remainder of my existence. It is impossible to imagine how pretty my Roman garden is become in 10 years nor what a *Boschetto* of Cypresses I have got now I have neither health nor riches to enjoy it. The damp & heat of the climate produce wonders. And now my dear Sir You are relieved by the end of the paper from the longest & most troublesome letter You ever did or ever will receive. I am certain You will do what You can to dispose of my work, always recollecting that going halves with a Bookseller while I am abroad is throwing it away though by no means so to a resident in Town. It is very unpleasant to beg of the Society through a Member, but it should be recollected that the original propositions come from them for I never should have presumed to ask assistance had I not been requested to name my wants. Pray remember me most kindly to Mrs. Hamilton & believe me ever most truly & sincerely obliged.

W.G.　　　　　　June 19 1832.

I intend to go to Naples in 4 or 5 days. Wordsworth came back to tell that Gherards Etruscan upon the Vases was nothing more than a few Etruscan letters scratched with a nail on the bottom of some Greek Vases. As Gherard says *Krattato sobra il vondo telle Fasi*[4] which You will perceive is German Italian. I hope by cutting

1. This must be Gerhard's great *Antike Bildwerke* in 4 volumes, Munich, 1828.
2. See also *Annali*, 1831. 67 f.
3. Greville, Major-General Sir Charles John, K.C.B. M.P. for Warwick Borough 1812–30 who d. unmarried 1836.
4. 'grattato sopra il fondo delli vasi' meaning scratched on the bottom of vases—Gell writes it as if pronounced with a German accent.

out the additions & wafering them with 9 wafers to the M.S. You will not have so much trouble.

Naples Nov. 12 1832.

My dear Hamilton,

Your last letter to introduce Your Nephew who I suppose to be the Son of the Revd Anthony[1] was sent to me yesterday by Lord Ponsonby, so that I conclude Your friends are yet to arrive at Naples in the course of the Winter. Depend upon me for doing all that I can to set them agoing both in the world and among the curiosities, & I will among other things make them go to Your Villa of Pollio,[2] to which by the bye I took poor Sir Walter, where Miss Scott[3] proposed to give a fete though the Police will no longer permit it to be inhabited for fear of its falling. I shall send You with this a coloured drawing of the Grand Mosaic of Pompeii which is beyond doubt "The *Battles* of Alexander"[4] for it represents the facts both of Granicus & Issus. Darius was not at Granicus & Alexander did not lose his helmet at Issus. On the Persian standard was a cock. Some silly people here have set up an opinion that the Romans and Gauls are represented, because of the Cock as if the Gauls were likely to pun in Latin. Both Hesychius & Suidas say the Cock was the Persian Bird. You will be pleased to take the drawing to the Dilettanti with my profound respects. One sketch among so many is useless, but they may Lithograph it if they think proper & if You can retain it for Yourself. At all events they will be able perfectly to judge of the scene & the colouring. Please to remember one error in the colour of the horse in the centre with his back to You. I had made it Black from memory whereas I have since been many times & got the details perfect, but in water colors I could not change the horse from black to yellow or what we call cream colour with very deep shades which deceived me till it was well washed. Everything else You may depend upon as exact. I think it will be admired. I shall I hope publish a drawing of it when I finish the book of which I sent You some of the plates to work at. When You find a good opportunity &

1. Hamilton, Rev. Anthony, father of W. R. Hamilton, see *Introduction*, p. 1.
2. See above, p. 73.
3. Scott, Miss Anne (1803–1833) d. of Sir Walter Scott.
4. Modern scholars also think that the mosaic does not represent the battle of Issus but a composite scene with elements from several battles. E.g. G. Mansuelli, *Enciclopedia di Arte Antica*, s.v. Alessandro Macedone.

without Cholera You may be so kind as to send back my drawings of the new work on the pictures of Pompeii etc. not that I am in immediate want of them having copies sufficient to describe them. We are in hopes of a new discovery on the subject of Pompeii which at present bids fair to gratify curiosity in a line hitherto unknown. Colonel Robinson[1] the great Engineer has been employed in boring with the instrument used by the French to make what they call the Artesian Well, which nevertheless has been used in England as long as I can remember to examine the ground for coal. The Society will probably be interested in the communication. First the Colonel found a copious spring of mineral water more highly impregnated with the same airs & gases than the Seltzer Water and very agreeable to the taste, with which already many cures have been performed, so that the King is now constructing baths on the spot. In excavating for these an ancient Cypress tree or rather the trunk of one was discovered which was preserved almost entire by the Volcanic matters. This was on the shore nearby at the West end of Torre della Annunziata. The last account however is of the ancient port of Pompeii situated at the original mouth of the River Sarno, not very far from the Amphitheatre and near the place called Il Valle. It may also be called near Scafati the Village on the great road to Nocera where the Sarno is now passed. In digging it seems that the top of a mast was discovered which some one recognized to be such. Soon afterwards another & another appeared & it is now said, (for I only give the first vague account) that 30 masts have been found which give the hope of finding all the Vessels stranded by the earthquake & convulsion and covered by the Volcanic materials. This discovery is so recent that I have not yet been able to visit the Spot but the Society shall have the earliest information when any thing precise is known. With regard to the accounts in the Papers of other discoveries of Cities by Professor Zahn[2] which He put in Himself, so little is true that He learned the names of them from me in my house, & was so ignorant that I was obliged to write them down myself in his book. Judge my surprize when I saw the week after that he had found the site of these Cities himself & the history has been repeated in every Paper in Europe. Count Lebzeltern,[3] the Austrian Minister, did

1. It has not been possible to identify Col. Robinson.
2. Professor Wilhelm Zahn, corresponding member of the Institute at this time, had evidently exploited the discoveries; on him see also *Introduction*, p. 24. For the sad story of the supposed Roman fleet, see below, pp. 102, 110, 125, 131.
3. Lebzeltern, Count Ludwig von (1774–1854) who m. Zenaïde, Countess Laval

indeed publish in the Roman Archaeologia that He had employed Zahn to dig & instead of all these wonders had found nothing worthy of notice in the single hole which he had made bear Bosco Tre Case. So far with my respects to Your Learned Body. I know not what to do with my unhappy account at Torlonias since You are unable to send me a more favourable account of the Booksellers. It is a cruel thing the Dilettanti at whose instigation the work was written which hindered me from writing other things cannot take the risk of loss or gain & let the work come out, without which their Map will be by no means so Valuable. It was impossible for me to guess how much matter I had till I came near the end of the Work, & You say that it is interesting & new though so much had been written before on the country by men who did not examine the localities. Major Fancourt who is to be M.P. for Barnstaple writes to engage me for a new Periodical. *This he says is a secret*. If He should come to You to see my Latium, will You be so good as to receive him. Perhaps he is now Colonel Fancourt.[1] I do not exactly see how it could be so disposed of. I have received the last two Nos. of *Pompeiana* which are good & I thank You, also the Map of Greece of which I will not say all I think. It is but a middling sort of a job & I have lost by it all the credit & all the pains I took to possess myself of the facts during the four most active years of my life which with many years passed in putting the said materials together is really provoking. However I am glad that the thing is finished and got rid of at any rate. I will publish the parts of most consequence in some other way if I live & can work.

I am sorry to say I could not get the picture into the state of forwardness which I wished before the Courier is to set out, so You must take it as it was intended for I have not a moment to lose or to revise what I have written. I will only add that the Ships in the Port of Pompeii are said to have fallen on their sides, & to lean from the Mountain towards Castelmare [Castellammare], & that I am with many thanks for Your protection most truly & sincerely yours

W. Gell.

in 1823 in Russia where he was *en poste* before being accredited to Naples. Mrs. Arbuthnot refers to him as 'the most famous spy in Europe'. See *Journal of Mrs. Arbuthnot*, edited by F. Bamford and the Duke of Wellington. London, Macmillan, 1950, vol. ii, p. 14.
1. Fancourt, Charles St. John, M.P. for Barnstaple 1832–35.

You might perhaps expect that I should have something of more consequence to communicate before I wrote to You again but I find that the excavation of the boats or ships at the ancient mouth of the Sarno is put off till the days get longer and a days work will produce more effect. Colonel Robinson has got possession of the land & has the necessary powers for carrying on. The research & You shall be informed whether the Vessels are clinker built & all the peculiarities of their construction as soon as they are visible. The place is much nearer to the bridge on the great road going to Castell à 'Mare than to Scafati, & consequently the sea has not receded so much as was supposed. I have I believe also persuaded them to bore, in a line from the marina gate of Pompeii to this spot & we shall in time know more about it. As to Your *Casa degli Spiriti* at the end of Pausilipo, poor Laing Meeson who died last summer at Rome, had taken a great deal of pains with it & had got it regularly surveyed by an Architect & himself, & his family have of course got the result. It is by no means in such imminent danger of falling but without repair, they say the police will not permit anyone to inhabit it. I don't know where the story of the Ghost which comes out of the well is to be had, but I remember that Miss Talbot who was a great protector of the Roman house had a painting of the Spectre & the place. Miss Scott had the intention of giving a festa there, which would probably have pulled the house down—You said nothing in Your last about the offer Colonel Howard Vyse[1] had made to subscribe 100 £ to the printing of my book which only wants 200 more. I have rec^d a letter from Lady Blessington[2] who heard that I wanted to publish something about the Alhambra & mentioned it to a Bookseller. He writes to Her thus—New Burlington Street, Dec.13, 1832.—"Mr. Bentley[3] presents his respects to Lady Blessington & feels ex-

1. Howard-Vyse, Major-General Richard William Howard, D.L., J.P. of Stoke Place, Bucks who m. 1810 Frances, 2nd d. of Henry Hesketh. M.P. for Beverley 1812 and Honiton 1816-20.
2. Blessington, Marguerite, Countess of (1789–1848) d. of Edmund Power. She m. the Earl of Blessington (p. 57) in 1818 and they resided at Naples between July 1823 and February 1826. See *The Idler in Italy* by the Countess of Blessington. Paris, Baudry's European Library, 1839. Also see *Introduction*, p. 13.
3. Bentley, Richard (1794–1871). Publisher and printer of note. In 1829 joined with Henry Colburn, a publisher of fashionable novels, and who had just published editions of Evelyn and Pepys. Colburn retired in 1832 and Bentley moved to New Burlington Street.

ceedingly obliged to Her for the offer She has been so good as to make him of a work by Sir Wm. Gell on Spain. Should Sir Wm. put his design into execution it will give Mr. Bentley much pleasure to enter into arrangements with him for its publication. Do You happen to know Mr. Bentley & could You manage to consult him. If he is so ready for Spain he would probably be as eager after Italy? I see in the literary Gazette You have read some more of the work to the R.L.S. & with success. I see also that I am made a member of the french National Institute[1] which is a great honour, but all these are of the genus "Molto onore e poco contante"[2]—How does the Map of Latium go on as to engraving— Dr. Goodall would I am sure lend us a helping hand in regard to the book if he could. The difficulties about that quite deter me from writing more at present. Messrs. Jennings & Co. send word that Pompeians goes on very well. There is news of a fresh discovery at Tarquinii.[3] I have not as yet a detailed account but it is in the land of Sig. Manzi[4] & has more & larger paintings & several etruscan inscriptions longer than any except the (so called Etruscan) of the Eugubian [sic] tables, I have sent to procure the inscriptions if it be possible to obtain them. I don't know if You have well examined Cumae. The largest temple of Apollo was evidently Ionic[5] if one may judge by the bases which I found in the bushes nearly 3 feet in diameter. Col. Vyse, Strangeways & Auldjo are going to discover a passage from the Temple to the Sybils grotto through what seems to be the mouth of a well or cistern at that Temple. I send you Auldjo & Colonel Robinson's history of the Acqua Vesuviana with a view of the place. The Water is like that of Seltzer but as the analysis says stronger. It is said to have cured a great many diseases & baths & other conveniences are to be erected forthwith on the spot. Among the curiosities discovered at the place was & is a large ancient Cypress tree[6] many palms

1. ? Academie des Inscriptions.
2. Gell quotes Figaro's aria 'Non più andrai' from Mozart's *Marriage of Figaro*.
3. Gell's information came through his friends in the Institute: see *Bullettino* 1832, 213 ff.
4. Possibly Pietro Manzi, author of *Lettera a S. E. Donna Teresa de Rossi Caetani sopra le ultime scoperte fatte lungo il litorale dell' antica Etruria nello Stato Pontificio*, Prato, 1836.
5. One of the column-bases of the Roman reconstruction of the modern 'Temple of Apollo'.
6. For the details here and in the following letters about the Roman baths, see the *Introduction*, p. 32. In Liberatore's account the tree is called a pine, but Gell's observation is closer.

below the tufa of the eruption, supposed of Roman times. Since that 6 trees & a garden have been found which only want to be cleared from the superincumbent mass. The wood is quite perfect & not charred in the interior. Auldjo is making walls to protect these curiosities as the Tree was given to him. His work on Vesuvius he says is before this time printed in London. I must get You to insert my dissertation on the Lake of Albano, the information which I have lately collected from the fragments of Dionysius of Halicarnassus[1] with regard to it. These fragments are published by Monsig. Mai[2] from the Palimpsests at Milan. The subject is so curious that I am persuaded You will think that I now send a worthy addition. Stick it in therefore with a wafer into the M.S.S. if You please & forgive the trouble I give You. I wish You would also be so good as to attach the Caesar fragment to the Article Veii which I put on another paper not to give You the trouble of anything more than a Wafer. I find You at the head of all the learned & literary institutions so You must have enough to do besides the trouble I give You.

You will probably have heard of the projected voyage to Greece,[3] the archipelago and Constantinople of one of our Neapolitan steam boats, but I hear they have no Agent in England, though Hammersleys[4] have said they will give the necessary information. The Vessel goes to Messina, Corfu, Nicopolis, Zante, Patras & so round by Navarino to Nauplia allowing time to see the places & indeed for passing by land from Patras to Nauplia—Hydra, AEgina, Corinth, Athens & then across towards Mytilene & the Dardanelles, Constantinople, a day in the Black Sea & then to return. I think they are not above 22 days on the Water and the rest out of three months are to be passed ashore. It is certainly a very good opportunity for any one who wishes to see much in a short time. Provisions & beds on board. Price about 80 £ for best places. If You send any one it should be quickly as from 1st to 10th of April is fixed for departure. It seems there is a number sufficient to make the Voyage practicable but not above 5 have yet put down their names on account of the doubts people entertain of the cer-

1. A selection of excerpts, from a poor fifteenth-century manuscript, had recently been published by Cardinal Mai, see E. Kiessling's edition (Teubner 1860–70), p. xxv.
2. Mai, Cardinal Angelo (1782–1854). Philologist and Librarian at the Vatican.
3. See *Appendix* A.
4. Probably Messrs. Greenwood, Cox and Hammersley, Bankers of Pall Mall, and Army Agents.

tainty of the Voyage. However yesterday the Prince of Butera[1] informed me it was certain & that he was going. If You don't find accommodation on shore You may always return to the Ship & as to eating while in port You may also have that on board by paying a small fixed sum. The Ship only finds You in eatables while at sea. However 80 £ in 3 months & so much seen is not considered dear. We have now Ld Ponsonby & Ld Berwick as ministers here & we expect Mr. Temple[2] shortly as the third. As to going to Constantinople it seems quite a joke at present as there will probably be no government at all there. I have caught a Maronite Monk who says that the whole of Syria is so committed to Ibrahim & so satisfied with him that it is impossible it can ever return to the Porte without extermination. Pray remember me kindly to Mrs. Hamilton & all the Santa familia including Don Tarick and believe me ever Yours most truly

W.G.

Naples 14 & 18 March 1833.

My dear Sir,

Mr. Temple arrived here a few days ago & I took him last night to the Vomero to dine with his Ancestor Ld Berwick at the Villa Belvedere. His Father, Ld Ponsonby, yet lingers in Naples so we have three generations of Ministers at once, besides Father Strangways who is supposed to be going to Vienna. The people here pretend that the reason of Ld Ponsonbys delay, the frigate having been here above a month, is that he intends to be promoted to Petersburgh. Others say he has already refused that situation & thus You have our diplomatic Lewes disposed of. Mr. Temple brought me the Etruscan Tombs & the Pompeian paintings quite

1. Stefania Branciforte (1788–1852), Princess of Butera, Radali etc. m. (1) Giuseppe Lanza, Prince of Trabia and (2) Georg Wilding (d. 1842), a Hanoverian mercenary usually known in Sicily as Prince of Radali. Henry Fox (*op. cit.*, p. 238) maliciously says 'he was a German adventurer of the name of Wilding, and though no beauty yet he so continued to enamour Princess Butera, that sooner than not be gratified unlawfully (which she went on her knees in vain to sue) she at length consented to acquire a lawful right of him, and by marrying him made him one of the richest and most powerful subjects in Naples.'
2. Temple, Hon. Sir William, K.C.B. (1788–1856) s. of Henry Temple, 2nd Viscount Palmerston. Envoy Extraordinary and Minister Plenipotentiary at the Court of Naples.

safe. He seems a most aimable good natured person. I will now recur to our unhappy Roman Topography. If You can make nothing of Major or Colonel Fancourt nor of the Bookseller I sent You the name of from Lady Blessington, nor of any other such person we have nothing left but to agree with Murray, for the engraving of the map has already advanced far. As to the names there is a vast collection of horrors which I sent You an impression of the Roman map to serve as a rule to correct. Now if You are close with Murray, I must take the 100 £ from Colonel Vyse which will only put off the sale of my Roman Villa a little, & stop the mouth of Torlonia, or rather my own conscience for he encourages me to get still further in debt to him. I really think being ordered to write the Book by the Dilettanti & the said book being approved by the Big Wigs in London I had a right to calculate on its producing 300 £, giving up for ever the fees simple of profit of said Book & Map to the Dillys who I think must eventually be paid & who are rich enough not to feel the bad effects of waiting for it which I do grievously. I still think the Society treat me unkindly in this respect, & one proof is that Col. Vyse, a perfect stranger, having read the book advances a third of the sum to further the publication. He is to have the first profits if You agree finally with Murray though he says he is indifferent even as to that. It is I think at all events of consequence to publish the Work even if I lose all the profit except the 100 £ which Col. Vyse will advance to me when the Work begins to be printed or the agreement made. So much would transpire that though no one knows most of the facts detailed in my Book somebody will be beforehand with something like it. Therefore I will conclude that in one way or other You will dispose of my child speedily. We have by the bye Hare and his Brother Julius[1] who translates Niebuhr here & very agreeable people. I have lent Hare the new inscriptions from a Tomb at Tarquinii[2] but if they come back

1. Hare, Rev. Augustus William (1792–1834) and his bro. Rev. Julius Charles (1795–1855), sons of Francis Hare-Naylor of Hurstmonceaux. Augustus was ordained in 1825, m. Maria Leycester d. of Rector of Stoke-upon-Trent, appointed to living of Alton-Barnes 1829, but failing health caused him to go to Italy and he died at Rome. His guide-books to Rome, Florence and other parts of Italy are still invaluable today. Julius was ordained 1826 and appointed to family living at Hurstmonceaux, became Archdeacon of Lewes 1840 and translated Niebuhr's *History of Rome*. He edited it with fresh notes in 2 vols 1828–32, but was met with charges of scepticism and in 1829 published *Vindications of Niebuhr*.
2. Now known as the *Tomba del Tifone*. The inscriptions were first reported

before I close this I will send You one or two of them. Some are Etruscan & some Latin, one has the word F. AMEN out of which they have invented that it is christian, but the word is no doubt FLAMEN ill copied & the same with the Etruscan part which the copier did not understand. I imagine [inscription] Larthial Lumpus to be one of the personages. We shall soon know more about it but it is the first Tarquinian Tomb with Latin. I think the Tullii are the Roman family—Here comes in Mr. Ramsay & sends You his most respectful compliments. Mr. Strangways who is also here says he tried to make Your Nephew get the prints of the Museo Borbornico for You but he was too active for him & went off without. Ld Chelsea[1] late Cadogan is to meet Your Nephew or rather take him up at Civita Vecchia & between them they are to bring You a Packet containing Notes for the Life of Sir Walter Scott which Mr. Lockhart is writing. You are to read it if You like it & then sealing it up to convey it to Mr. Lockhart[2] with my Compliments. I think for anyone who wants to know about Sir Walter in Italy it is very interesting & nobody else could have done it for I was his keeper usually. Our King here seeing that his troops opened up to let through a splash of water in a Review was in a fury & went to the Sebeto, got off his horse & passed through the river up to his neck & then went home & dressed himself afresh but sent the troops to Nocera before drying. This gave great disgust but on San Carlo was posted *"Qui se rapresenta il pasaggio del Sebeto,"* which is considered rather a good satire.[3]

18 March since I began this. I see You have some knowledge of the Tomb at Tarquinii in the *Literary Gazette* in a letter from Rome calling it in the Nekropolis of Tarquinia. There is also a letter from Mr. M . . . [sic] at Naples saying he is going to take notes

---

in *Bullettino*. 1832, 213 f and published fully in 1833, 53 ff. The reading should be *Larthial Pumpus*. (For an authoritative text, *Corpus Inscriptionum Etruscarum*, 5407 ff.)

1. Chelsea, George Cadogan, Viscount, later 4th Earl Cadogan (1783–1864).
2. Lockhart, John Gibson (1794–1854). Literary critic and biographer of Sir Walter School who 1820 m. Sir Walter's elder d. Charlotte Sophia (1799–1837).
3. Gell evidently refers to an incident in the military exercises that took place in the 'Campo Marzio', the area outside the walls of Naples on the eastern side, which were sedulously followed by the King. Gell means that the troops broke line when fording the river Sebeto. In disgust the King dismounted and plunged into the stream, to show his contempt for such weakness. The satirical notice posted outside the San Carlo alludes to Rossini's opera *Mosè in Egitto*, first produced in Naples in 1818, and a triumphant success elsewhere in Europe.

on the Roman fleet, but You need not be so precipitate for till June or July Colonel Robinson has no intention of beginning to excavate, being entirely occupied in excavating rocks at La Torre della Annunziata to erect the new baths over the Acqua Vesuviana of which I sent You an account. These baths are to perform miraculous cures & among others upon me. I hope they will be strong enough to work without faith, for as far as drinking the water goes I tried it for 2 months without finding the slightest effect. They say quantities of it have been sent to the King of Spain.[1] It is a pleasant sort of Seltzer & I should think to drink quite innocent of good or evil. They have discovered not only a cypress but several pines and a garden overwhelmed by the tufa. This is supposed to have taken place in Roman times. The wood is not carbonized but quite sound. We have frequent horse racing on the Campo & tomorrow are to pay two ducats each carriage to see Chariot races, *Bigas* & *Corribolas* under the direction of Guerro the leader of the Italian Astleys[2] who has all those things in perfection. A stand is erected for the Court & it is to be all in high order. I rather think Ld Chelsea who is to take my Packet of Scottiana to You is to ride a race & Mr. Bagot,[3] Ld Bagots son, who is considered a most talented jockey is also to mount. Today the Actacon is to take out Prince Charles,[4] our Lord High Admiral, to Capri to show him the open sea, so You see there is every

---

At first it was a failure in Naples, but in the next year it was put on again with the famous prayer. 'Tu che dal cielo stellato' added, and was an overwhelming success. Sensitive young ladies were so overcome as to need medical attention after the sensational change from minor into major key half-way through. (We are indebted to Mr. Michael Cartwright-Sharp for the information.)

For a description of the 'Campo', see H. Acton, *The Last Bourbons* etc. 66 f.

1. Ferdinand VII who m. 1829 as his 4th wife Maria Cristina of Naples d. of Francis I of the Two Sicilies: she was his niece.

2. The reference here seems to be to Astley's Amphitheatre whose famous equestrian performer and manager was Philip Astley. There are portraits of his son John (1761-1821) and his wife by J. Saxon at the Garrick Club. On 5th August 1807, Lady Bessborough writes to Lord Granville Leveson Gower, 'Think of my going to Ashley's last night. There is a battle on the stage, with real horses Galloping full speed and fighting to a beautiful white light like Day dawn.' (*op. cit.*, vol. ii, p. 273). Astley's Theatre (or Circus) in Westminster Bridge Road was famous in the 1830s for its 'equestrian drama', a combination of circus, music-hall and melodrama. There is a description of Astley's in Dickens's first book, *Sketches by Boz* (1836).

3. Bagot, Hon. Sir Charles (1781-1843) 2nd s. of 1st Baron Bagot. Minister to the Netherlands and Governor-General of Canada. Elected to the Society of Dilettanti 1834.

4. Carlo, principe di Capua (1811-1862).

sort of gaiety going on & last night I dined at Ld Hertfords at a splendid dinner of 18 with our new Minister Mr. Temple, & the old one Ld Ponsonby who is in no sort of hurry to go to settle the disputes between Ibrahim Pasha & the Sultan. The Neapolitans already argue from the delay that Ld P. goes to Petersburgh and not to Constantinople. Prince Butera is to go in the steam boat at his own expense on the 10 of April to congratulate King Otho[1] & to carry him a Neapolitan order. It seems when here they have paid him no sort of attention, so are now to make up for it. It is said the Duke of San Teodoro[2] has been offered to go as Ambassador to Paris but at his own expense but has declined the kind offer not being fond of spending money, but You see at least that we are economical here even without a reform Bill. I believe it is impossible to be in a worse way than Your friend the Pope is just now, for even the illumination of St. Peters is doubtful which is the last thing given up, there not being a penny in the Treasury or any hopes of one. The Romagna people[3] are also it is said quite resolved never to submit quietly to the Papal government which is so faithless. The Popes[4] side of the question says that it is better to die by the hands of the enemy & to protest than to cut their own throats, & so we go on. There are reports of Mr. Temple having been robbed near Velletri but he says he is quite innocent of it, but that he saw some peasants with guns in the dusk. Lady Augusta Coventry is decidedly to be married to young Fox, Ld Hollands son.[5] I see my whole sheet is filled & no room for the inscriptions unless on the last fold. You will however be little the wiser for them if I have them in time. Major Fancourt told me they would not consider any price too much to pay me if I would write for His new periodical Work. The *Recollections of Sir Walter Scott*[6] would just do for such a work but I can do no other than given them to Mr. Lockhart as he

1. Otto, 2nd s. of Louis I of Bavaria (1815–1867) who became King of Greece in 1832 but was dethroned 1862. See *Appendix* A.
2. San Teodoro, Carlo Caracciolo, duca di, who was Neapolitan Ambassador in Spain at the time of the marriage of Francis I to the Infanta Maria Isabella.
3. See above, pp. 55, 84.
4. Gregory XVI (1831–1846).
5. Fox, Henry Edward (1802–1859), 4th and last Baron Holland who m. 1833 Lady Mary Augusta Coventry d. of George William, 8th Earl of Coventry. Fox spent many years in Italy both before and after his marriage. In 1835 was appointed Chargé d'Affaires at Vienna, later went to Frankfurt and ended his career at Florence as Minister to Tuscany. He died and was buried at Naples.
6. See *Introduction*, p. 30.

asked for them. If he will not insert them or undervalue them they had better be sold. Believe me most truly & sincerely Yours

W.G.

Naples, April 13, 1833.

My dear Sir,

My letter begins with a date this time as You complain of the want of time & place in my last. I will next inform You that Colonel Howard Vyse is at present resident at Naples, & after thanking You & G. A. Browne for Your care of my unhappy Book which has appeared at so unfortunate a moment & which keeps me in perpetual alarm for my finances, & in default of which I cannot go this year to Rome, I shall give You an account of what is going on in Italy that may interest the Learned & Illustrious Society of Dilettanti.

The Ships or Vessels, the masts of which have been discovered near Pompeii are in *statu quo*. The owner of the Soil had agreed that Colonel Robinson should excavate the place in the month of June, but the said Proprietor being dead the heirs are now to be treated with, so that we are now again in uncertainty though I hope no serious obstacle exists. You have probably a map, by the help of which You may judge of the position of this supposed Port. It is on the left bank of the Sarno, about a quarter of a mile above the Ponte della Persica on the bridge between Torre della Annunziata & Castell' a Mare. When anything is done, I shall not fail to attend & shall duly inform the Society of all that is discovered.

This day the Steam Vessel with 52 passengers on board for Greece & Constantinople was to have departed. The weather is however so tempestuous that the voyage is deferred till tomorrow or till the wind moderates. The Equinoxial gales still continue with fury & from whichever quarter they blow, they seem to annoy us with as much cold as if they had passed over the Appennines which are covered with a fresh coat of snow. The tempestuous weather has equally prevented a Trip to Pompeii in the public omnibus this morning under the patronage of Lord Hertford. This Vehicle conveys 18 persons well provided with provisions & Champagne & several rooms have been left unsearched that the Company might be entertained with a *Scavo*. If You ask what can be done in so great an assemblage of people on this occasion, I can answer that the crowd occupy the attention of those who fancy themselves interested in maintaining a jealous prohibition from drawing & planning, & thus such an expedition answers my purpose, better than if I were alone. I do not know whether You know the situation of the house of the Faun, that in which is the great Mosaic of Darius & Alexander. The Street is that of Fortune or that which runs along the north side of the Temple. After the street of the Mercuries is a *Vicus*, then the house of the Faun which is double & occupies an entire *insula*. Then comes another *Vicus* & as far as this, the Street of Fortuna which occurs as if it would terminate at the *Porta Nolana*, has been cleared. That street has however for the present been abandoned & an opening has been just cut from the House of the Faun to the *Vicus* which runs to the eastward of or behind the Pantheon & the *Chalcidicum*.[1] One of the houses[2] so opened, has after the usual *Atrium* & *Tablinum*, a handsome peristyle of 6 Ionic columns by four, and fortunately the architraves of many have been preserved so that the effect is finer than in any of the preceeding excavations. On the sides of the 4 columns the intercolumnation is at least 3 diameters of the pillars, but on the two other 6 column porticos the arcostyle is doubled, so that timber only could be used for architraves & that being carbonized has now been replaced by new beams, carefully put in so as to preserve the frieze, & thus one is enabled to judge of the effect. I find that the frieze[3] in the house of the Faun in the last court, which had 13 doric columns by 11 & which is really magnificent, was of terra cotta & consisted of figures of Thetis bringing the armour of Achilles and seated on the back of a Marine Monster.

What is curious is that though many remains I could find none perfect. I believe I cited in a letter to You Hesychius & Suidas[4]

1. Now known as the *Vico Storto*, and its continuation in the *Vicolo di Eumachia*. By 'Pantheon' and 'Chalcidicum' Gell means the Macellum and the Eumachia Building. The *vici* mentioned here are, in order, the *Vicolo del Fauno*, the *Vicolo del Labirinto* and the *Vico Storto*.
2. Now known as the *Casa dei Capitelli Figurati*, cp. below p. 105; *Bullettino*, 1833, 2; *PAH*, ii, 255 ff.
3. Not mentioned in the official reports. It is now in the Naples Museum, see G. von Rohden, *Die Terrakotten von Pompeii*, pl. xxii and p. 57 f.; Gell's letter confirms that this pretty piece comes from the House of the Faun.
4. See above, p. 91.

who both say that the Cock is the Persian Bird. The Italians nevertheless who do not know this are calling the great Mosaic, Romans & Gauls, or Greeks & Gauls, because the head of a cook is seen in the Persian standard as if the Gauls punned in Latin. What is curious, is that I no sooner saw the picture, than I was struck with the likeness of the Persian Turbans to those of the Kings of Granada yet remaining in the Alhambra & which I with some difficulty copied there. I send You one or two of them

Now these Moorish Kings came from Damascus, which at once brings them near to the Persian frontier & as Oriental fashions never change, so this War Turban, as it may be called, seems to have been continued from remote times, & was tied under the chin or not according to the circumstances. I suspect that the Saracens at the time of the first Crusades always fought in these war Turbans which had sometimes a steel cap underneath, & though the Rey Chico, Abdallah [sic], the last King of Granada in 1495 wore a helmet of steel, yet it is made of such a size that I suspect his Turban was contained within it. This is its form

You will say I am now wandering far from Pompeii but what I have now stated is I think interesting with regard to the Mosaic and somebody or other in a penny magazine will probably publish it as his own observation. It is pretended by some that the head of Alexander cannot be his, because it is like an Albanian, but was Alexander but an Albanian. It is remarkable that this should have struck Ld Ponsonby, without communication, just as it did me. He by the bye sailed for the East in a gale of Wind in the *Actaeon* a few days since. To return again to the House of the Faun, I found scratched with a pin or nail, upon the coloured plaster of the Faun between the 2nd & 3rd Court what was certainly intended to represent Darius in his Chariot as in the great picture and however ill it may be executed I must examine whether it retains any lines which might serve to establish or to give any idea of what might have been represented in that part of the picture which is wanting on the right. These scratches of the boys & servants, I always look for on walls coloured in black or dark red, & I find not only pictures scratched with sharp points but inscriptions not always particularly modest. I must now quit the House of the Faun & return to the house of the Ionic Portico on the opposite side of the street, *Holconivm Priscum* is written at the door. The Capitals of the Pilastres at the door may be called Corinthian but they contain figures in conversation, little better than those which we often see in Saxon Churches. In one room many bronze vases were found on the floor, and the bits & all the metallic parts of the caparison of a horse in another, besides some very elegant candelabra. Behind the portico is a place not yet cleared but containing three or more little hand mills & a curious oven heated by a furnace from below & with two divisions shewing that some of the things baked required a stronger heat than others. Behind this again are some small chambers well painted in red & yellow, in one of which the panels have the attributes of Mercury, Mars, Apollo & other deities. It is not at present clear what this will turn out to have been—it seems a sort of hidden sanctuary to the house. Parallel with this house & to the east is another fine house opening towards the south.[1] In the *Atrium* is an *Ala* with a shrine but no statue, & the marbles, of which there are only fragments, have been all carried off by the ancients. In an *Ala* from the peristyle of this house is a very pretty landscape, and an almost defaced picture of an old man selling cupids out of a cage to a female which may have been pretty. Where iron has touched the *stucco*, that which was originally red has become black, & that which was yellow red. I think there is nothing more recently discovered at Pompeii. I conclude however that You are all aware that the walls of the house of the Faun, the proprietor of which only liked mosaics, & did not possess a painting, were nevertheless lined with thin plates of lead fastened on by large headed nails over which again was a coat of *stucco* painted with ill executed & unnatural marbles. I am not sure whether this might not be a useful hint for some sort of building inclined to dampness in our

1. The Casa di Arianna: *Bullettino*, 1833, p. 3; *PAH*, ii, 267 ff.

own country, and the expense would not be great. You ask about Cumae. Colonel Vyse has been amusing himself by examining a Cistern situated close to the Temple above the Grotto,[1] thinking that though a Cistern it might have water at the bottom yet side passages might exist towards the Cavern. In effect he has really found two niches, but they seem covered with stucco like the rest of the reservoir, and there the matter rests for the present. There seems to have been a Roman Temple of later times, with marbles and Latin inscriptions on the spot, but the old Temple above the Grotto was of black Volcanic stone and I found some of the bases of the columns which must have been Ionic. The Aqueduct[2] of which a part remains at Ponte Rossi, and which supplied Nisida, Puteoli, Cumae, Baiae etc. is found to have really passed near Sarno, but the springs of that river being on a very much lower level were not included. The real sources were at a place called Serino high in the mountains south of Avellino. The water was kept on the hills on a high level, and crossed the plain on lofty arches from near Sarno towards Vesuvius, & from the nearest part in the plain a branch ran off on the left to Pompeii. Colonel Robinson has found that the springs of Sarno beautiful & copious as they are, but much too low to have been available for any but the lowest of the houses at Pompeii. The Colonel has also made another bore not far from that mentioned in Auldjos paper & another water of stronger properties than the former has appeared, which I have not tasted but which is described as extremely palatable & as frisky as Champagne! Baths are building on the spot & I have just agreed with L[d] Selsey to try the reputed good effects of the water in the summer. Since You quitted Naples, the water, which originally gave the name Bagniuoli to the spot where the Pozzuoli road first touches the Sea has been rediscovered, & two good Bathing houses have been built there. The water was only tepid during the first year but the last time I bathed I found it too hot for pleasure. At this moment enters Mr. Pashley,[3] fellow of Trinity College, Cambridge who has got an Admiralty order to be received on board a Brig which is employed

1. Now called the temple of Apollo.
2. The Serino aqueduct, built by the emperor Augustus to serve the cities of Campania in the 20's B.C. It was repaired in the fifteenth century and served as Naples' chief water supply until quite recent times. I. Sgobbo, *Notizie degli Scavi*, 1938, 75 ff.
3. Pashley, Robert (1805–1859) s. of Robert Pashley of Hull. Barrister and traveller. Under influence of Sir Francis Beaumont travelled in Greece, Asia Minor and Crete. Author of *Travels in Crete*, London, 1837. 2 vols.

in surveying the coast of Asia Minor from the Dardanelles to Rhodes. I have done what I could to persuade him to go to Imbros & Samothrace & at the last place to find out the Zerynthian Cave on the high mountain which was sacred to Cabeiri. I have no doubt much might be found of great interest & antiquity there & no Traveller visits it, being out of the way. I did what was possible to persuade Wordsworth to go there, but he is returned as far as Rome, *re infecta*. One of the most ancient inscriptions known came from Samothrace, & if there be any truth in the very ancient communication between Etruria & that Island some vestige of it will probably be found. You remember that Dardanus came from Cortona in Italy to Samothrace & now we are working so hard at Etrurian Literature of which some 20 words only are known, it would be most interesting if an Etruscan inscription which perhaps might then be identified with Pelasgic could be discovered in this Pelasgic Island. But I forget I am writing to the Society or rather to You for the amusement of the Society. There are several Members who were friends of poor Sir Walter Scott. Should this arrive in time, which as I sent You my M.S. by Lord Chelsea it may, pray let any of the Members who may wish it see the same, for though I thought I had so little to say, when the family desired me to write it, yet it contained at least many things which may be very interesting to Sir Walters personal acquaintances which we are by no means certain Mr. Lockhart will publish. The post is here so irregular & the Couriers so much more so that I do not know how far I shall be able to execute Your wishes as to sending my letters before the 10th of the Month but I will try what can be done. In Sicily some more metopes of a temple at Selinus have been discovered. They are not of that Archaic style of Messrs. Harris & Angell,[1] but I have not yet obtained a sight of the drawings. Millingen[2] is here & has got from Girgenti a very magnificent Vase. There is more news from Etruria from Tarquinii & Vulci but my paper is finished & I have no very detailed account of the discoveries made nor will my finances permit me to go in search of them this year. A sort of mystic chest with *relievos* in bronze[3] was found at the head of

1. William Harris and Samuel Angell, *Sculptured Metopes discovered amongst the Ruins of the Temples of the ancient city of Selinus*...in 1823 (London 1826).
2. Millingen, James (1774–1845), 2nd s. of Michael Millingen, a Dutch merchant who settled in London. James Millingen was a classical archaeologist and lived many years in Rome and Naples.
3. An Etruscan *cista*, mentioned also in *Bullettino*, 1834, 9; now in the Vatican in the Museo Gregoriano, see Giglioli, *Arte Etrusca*, tav. cclxxiv.

one of the skeletons at Vulci; in it were combs of ivory or bone
which are described as falling into dust soon after being disturbed.
The torrents of rain have so deluged the last discovered sepulchral
chamber at Tarquinii that I am told the pictures are washed away
to the height of about 3 feet at which the water stood. They are
said to have been copied. The Etruscan inscriptions are if possible
10 times more obscure than usual. I am in hopes they will be
published in the Roman Institute.[1] You desire to have an account
of Vesuvius, but the eruption has entirely ceased at present, after
having sent up a cone which looks over the side of the Crater &
has vomited both towards Naples & towards La Torre 3 considerable streams of lava. Auldjo, who is considered as wet nurse
to the Volcano sailed in the *Actaeon* for Constantinople the other
day & intends to be absent some 3 months. I have letters from
Egypt which state that Burton[2] is coming home with Dr. Hogg[3]
& Mr. Baillie.[4] Wilkinson is highly disgusted that no bookseller
will undertake to print his discoveries which are of great consequence.[5] Drovetti[6] has just left us for Turin. He is an aimable
well informed person & has been Consul in Egypt 25 years, & is
quite devoted to Mehmed Ali & Ibrahim.[7] I think I have told

1. See *Bullettino*, 1833, 53 ff.
2. Haliburton James (formerly known as Burton (1788–1862)). Egyptologist. Was
engaged by Mohammed 'Ali to take part in geological survey of Egypt and
sailed from Naples 1822. Many of his sketches and maps are in the collection
formed by R. Hay (p. 126). Published *Excerpta Hieroglyphica* consisting of
64 lithographs with no letter-press between 1825–28 in Cairo.
3. Hogg, Dr. Edward who originally came from Cheshire, but lived most of his
life at Naples. Author of *Visit to Alexandria, Damascus and Jerusalem, during
the Successful campaign of Ibrahim Pasha*. London, 1835, 2 vols. Gell said of
him, 'he makes the most wonderful faces and has the strongest action with the
hands you ever saw'.
4. Baillie, Rt. Hon. Henry James (1804–1885) of Redcastle, Ross-shire. M.P. for
Inverness 1840–68. Under-Secretary of State for India 1859. His sister was the
wife of Hon. William Ashley (p. 62).
5. Wilkinson, Sir John Gardner (1797–1875). Explorer and Egyptologist. His
Extracts from several Hieroglyphical Subjects with Remarks on the same, Malta
1830, was dedicated to Gell.
   Compare Gell's report here and his letter to the Institute, that appeared in
Bullettino. 1833, 130.
6. Drovetti, Bernadino (1776–1852). French Consul in Egypt 1803–30, who
formed a collection of Egyptian antiquities which were bought by the King of
Sardinia and housed in the Academy at Turin. The collection was first offered
to England for £16,000 but refused.
7. Mehemet Ali, The accession of this Albanian adventurer to the pashalik in
1805 imparted a galvanic prosperity to Egypt by the merciless destruction of

You what is going on in these Countries at present, but I desire to be informed if this irregular sort of information is just what the Learned & Illustrious Society desire, & to have further instructions if my style can be improved. Most truly Yours,

W. Gell.

Wordsworth was wounded slightly in the shoulder in Greece, but he says the arrival of the Bavarians has much tranquillized the Country.

To Wm. R. Hamilton Esqre as Secretary of
the Dilettanti Society.

Naples May 1st, 4th, 12th, 1833.

My dear Sir,

I shall hope to send this so that it may succeed to one I sent for the use of the Dil-Soc. on the 14th of April. The difficulty of despatching a letter so as to arrive by a certain day, through the Foreign Office, will I fear always be great but I shall try what can be done & suppose that we shall at length contrive to get each letter to Downing Street in time for Your meetings which I conceive to be on the 10th of every month. Since I wrote last, there has been found somewhere in Calabria an inscription,[1] which we

the turbulent Mameluks. In 1816 Mehemet Ali reduced part of Arabia: annexed Nubia and part of the Sudan in 1821–28; his troops under his son Ibrahim occupied parts of the Morea and Crete to aid the Turks in their war against Greece and demanded Syria in return for his help, but did not receive it until in 1832 he declared war on Turkey and overran Syria. The Western Powers came to the aid of Turkey, and in the Treaty of Kutahya, May 1833, Mehemet Ali ceded Syria and Cilicia, but Russia promised to protect the Ottoman Empire and asked for the Straits to be closed to foreign warships (Treaty of Hunkâr Iskelesi 8 July 1833). In 1839 the Turks broke their truce with Mehemet but were beaten. The West intervened again and demanded the restitution of Syria, the British fleet demonstrating before the Syrian ports; finally in Nov. 1840 Mehemet Ali gave up Syria and was made Viceroy of Egypt. He became imbecile in 1848, dying the next year. His son Ibrahim reigned for 2 months only and was succeeded by Abbâs Pasha, Mehemet's grandson. Mehemet presented a Nubian giraffe to George IV which only survived two seasons at Windsor.

1. Clearly the Greek inscription, *Inscriptiones Graecae*, XIV, 636. In fact it had been found earlier (in 1783) at Petelia, but had recently been taken to the Museum of Naples where Gell no doubt heard of 't first. Compare *Topography*, ii, 402.

are in hopes will turn out in the Archaic style, like that of the Sicani OEOM. TVXA (in Greek letters), for it is in the hands of a person as we hear, whose account of it promises high antiquity. If anything curious should be elicited You shall be informed. You all remember the spot formerly known as Stufa di Nerone or Bagni di Tritoli near the Lucrine Lake, where most Travellers have boiled eggs in the spring. You will recollect also a sort of Gallery in the rock, through which the road passed, lighted by occasional windows or openings to the sea. Unfortunately this exists no longer. A certain Marchese Mascara who possesses land on the Mount of Misenum undertook to make a road, with the assistance of the Government & the late Principe di Cardito.[1] The road was made without much difficulty to the Stufa di Nerone where instead of improving the Gallery the section of which was thus [sketch] the centre being worn down while the sides retained their original height, the whole rock from a great height above the Grotta has been cut away, & that interesting remnant of antiquity has completely disappeared, the wall being now like any other exposed to the Sun on the face of the Rock. Little news is yet known of the fleet near Pompeii. I have seen however a piece of wood. It is decidedly cypress & even yet retains the smell towards the centre of the mast, and its nature & elasticity seems but little changed. It seems to have been embedden in a very wet soil. On the top of a mast it seems there was a circular ring of iron, & this was in so sound a state that the man who found it now uses it as a Tripod to set his kettle upon the fire. I hope we shall know more about this in June. At present Colonel Robinson who is to excavate the Ships & who is erecting baths at Torre della Annunziata is amusing himself with Colonel Howard Vyse by an excavation at Bosco Tre Case where they have as yet found nothing of value. The place is perhaps not far from Hoplontis,[2] yet taking the known distance from Naples on one side & from Pompeii on the other it should have stood somewhat more under the mountain, & just in the spot where the great eruption described by Sir William Hamilton ran from the Crater to the Sea. The road which separates from the Street of the Tombs at Pompeii turning rather to the right, points however very fairly to Bosco Tre Case & was probably that which led to Oplontis.[2] Speaking of Sir Wm.

1. Cardito, Ludovico Loffredo, principe di, who suc. marchese Gallo as Neapolitan Minister at Paris 1805.
2. The ancient village which, according to the *Tabula Peutingeriana*, lay three

Hamilton[1] reminds me of a circumstance at the Court of the late King Don Francesco.[2] When Mr. Strangways returned to Naples as Secretary of Legation from Florence, the King asked him on his presentation if he had ever been here before. He replied, yes, with Monsieur Hamilton, "Oh ho" said the King "that was a long time ago indeed, if You were here in the time of Sir William Hamilton You will find it all new to You." The archaic appearance of Strangways put this into His Majestys head, & occasioned much mirth, as Mr. Hill had always called him "Old father Strangways with his icicle nose & mother Shipton hat, looking for daisies & daffodils under a hedge." He is now gone to Vienna & notwithstanding his seeming antiquity we have lost a very aimable & agreeable person. But what has this to do with the arts or antiquities You may say, only You will recollect that You even gave me leave to introduce scandal if I had nothing better to relate. There is somebody here who sometimes writes "extract of a letter from Naples" & sometimes from Rome. He pretends to be intimate with all people of rank & thought he was writing a fine piece of scandal when he noticed the perpetual solitary walks of Mr. A with Lady Diana B. who only happened to be A's sister.

The excavating at Bosco Tre Case has suffered by this episode so I will return to it by relating that a year ago Count Lebzeltern the Austrian Minister dug at the same place & spent 20 dollars but found nothing. Professor Zahn spent 50 more *Scudi* & tells me he found no painting entire yet he found fragments of pictures so well done as to leave little doubt that some Villa or Village of

miles east of Pompeii, and is surely the modern Torre Annunziata: See *Introduction*, p. 32.

1. Hamilton, Sir William (1730-1803). Diplomat and archaeologist. Envoy Extraordinary and Minister Plenipotentiary at Naples 1764–1800. Elected to the Society of Dilettanti 1777. See Brian Fothergill: *Sir William Hamilton. Envoy Extraordinary*. London, Faber 1969.

2. Francis I, King of the Two Sicilies, b. 1777, suc. 1825, d. 1830. He m. (1) Maria Clementine of Austria and (2) Maria Isabella of Spain. The Duke of Buckingham (*op. cit.*, vol. i, p. 247) says of him in 1828, 'The King is very devout, the Queen (Maria Isabella) not so, and is supposed to be *galant*. She is kept up very strictly, and watched, and has no means of gratifying her propensities but with the *employés* about the palace. Whenever the King finds her out, he *beats* her, and sends the man away, and then kisses her, and is friends again. She is very fat, coarse and red-faced, and has had twelve children. The idea is, that she prefers the beating to the kiss.' Harold Acton referring to Maria Isabella after her widowhood in *The Last Bourbons of Naples* says she was 'generous and tender-hearted, the most amiable of women—perhaps too amiable for a Queen Dowager'.

consequence had existed on the spot. I hope You know that by planting the grapes of Champagne at Resina & at the base of Vesuvius, they have succeeded in making a sort of wine of the same kind & only inferior to very good Champagne. I know not whether it will bear exportation—*May 4th.* Our spring has been so tardy that strawberries are only on sale today, but the weather seems to be getting into its usual happy state of this season. I must again mention Father Strangways who is going North to join the Embassy at Vienna. Mr. Strangways has lately been to Orvieto, where beside the curious front of the Cathedral of coloured marbles there is a good deal of painted glass, a thing almost unknown in Italy. He writes to me thus. "There is a Choir with all the stalls good Gothic, & a fine marble font with a Gothic top. There should be a wonderful Gothic tabernacle of silver which holds, God knows, what Saints bones, which they would not shew me because I could not swear I was either a Cardinal or a Principe di sangue. But I made the Canons rout out of the Archives a famous Bull of Gregory IX, granted at the request of Edwd 1st, to cite the Monteforti for having killed his cousin Prince Henry of Viterbo. The first man I sent brought word that all the Archives were burnt in the revolution & the second said it was burnt by a *Canonico pazzo*, who burnt it himself. At last I went & found them in full conclave & the Dean made the *Archivista* bring a box of papers, in which after much searching we found the said Bull very well preserved but with the *Bolla* loose, which we also found & which they promised to fix on again. Prince Henry is buried at Orvieto" You will remember that Simon (I think) de Montfort, son of the Earl of Leicester, stabbed the Prince in the Church of Viterbo.[1] N. B. Craven is just come in & says the Kings of France & Naples were both in the church at the time. Strangways says there is now a good inn at Chiusi (Clusium) and many of the inhabitants have made collections of antiquities. He added "The black jugs with long processions stamped upon them are very curious & seem perfectly Egyptian. One was ornamented

1. Gell is correct. The assassination took place at Viterbo. It was not at the High Altar of the Cathedral of S. Lorenzo, but probably at that of S. Silvestro (now the Jesuit Church) that in 1271, Guy de Montford, son of Simon de Montfort, Earl of Leicester assassinated Henry, nephew of Henry III and son of Richard Plantaganet, Earl of Cornwall, King of the Germans, in order thereby to avenge the death of his father, who had fallen at the Battle of Evesham in 1265 when fighting against Henry III. Dante mentions the deed and puts the assassins in the seventh region of Hell (*Inf.* xii. 120).

with 24 Persepolitanlike Kings all of a row. Some vases just found had a Terra cotta head like a canopus. Every Thing seems to have been stamped or modelled after some fashionable pattern or composition for there are hundreds of replicas. They seem to have been fond of tea, or rather a drink answering to our tea, for they have a very neat sort of Trays, with services of little cups arranged very neatly in black pottery."[1] By the bye I have myself some, out of some dozens of small plates found in a tomb near Vulci or Vulcium which I have no doubt were used at the funereal feast & then placed in the tomb. They are of red earth smooth but not glazed except over a few ornamental touches of black in the border. Many of the Etruscan paintings seem to refer to this supper. Mr. Strangways also says "I went to Porsenas tomb—it is near the lake. I don't think it worthy of him. It had 2 great slabs of stone set upright instead of a door. The inscriptions at Clusium usually have [sketch] in them. Does it mean lapis? The walls I began to draw, but really I think nothing of them. The Lake instead of a mere marsh is very pretty with wooded hills. The Cornelian pillar in the Church is a humbug, it is small & a sort of siliceous pudding stone, though *Il Granduca che morè (pover'uomo) voleva prenderla per la Galleria di Firenze, ed allora i Chiusini vanno a trovare il Granduca che morì e gli dicono, "Maestà, potete fare quel che voi volete; ma sappiate che quando avrete levata questa volonna avrete tolto tutto il valsente della Città"! "Dunque la lasciamo stare"—e così disse il Granduca che morì*[2]—Lord Berwick writes himself in the Inn books, Mr. Hill & family, & flatters himself he travels *incog.* He is said to have bought £2000 of pictures at Rome besides others at Florence". So for Strangways. That murder of Prince Henry at Viterbo in the Church of St. Sylvester was extraordinary. He was son of Richard of Cornwall. Simon de Montforts father had during a contest been slain & indignantely treated by Henry III. As Prince Henry returned from the Holy Land he happened to be at Viterbo when several Sovereigns met to make a new Pope. Hearing who Prince Henry was, de Montfort ran his sword through

1. Gell alludes to the curious relief bucchero ware that was a speciality of ancient Clusium.
2. 'The Grand Duke, who died (poor man) wanted to take it for the Gallery at Florence, so that the Chiusini go to see the Grand Duke who died and they say to him, "Your Majesty, you can do what you like, but you should know that when to have taken away this column you will have taken all of value in the city!" "Well, then, let it remain"—and so said the Grand Duke who died'—meant to imitate peasants' speech.

him in revenge. Some friend standing by observed that the King of England had not only killed his father the Earl but dragged him by the hair of his head. Montfort who had already nearly escaped from the church, hearing this, returned & dragged prince Henry about the pavement while the Kings & Nobles looked on quietly & then mounting his horse escaped. That is the brief statement of the history, but it would have been a most excellent subject for Sir Walter Scott. It must I think be interesting to the English. Antiquary & some of the Society may not be displeased to hear the Popes Bull to try the murderer yet exists. If ever it be possible I shall procure a copy of it for the sake of English History.

A man brought to me yesterday for sale a golden chain about 3 feet long, found in a Tomb in Calabria.[1] The workmanship was bad. He asked 250 ducats for it, each link was formed by a double ring of this size & shape, united by fillagree [sic]

The rings have been cut out of a thin plate of gold. None are truly circular, but just as here represented. The general effect is better than might be imagined but the execution is bad. It can scarcely be of a good time, but I never saw any thing like it before. It weighs almost as much as the sum asked for it, & therefore will probably be melted. I have sent it to Lord Hertford & Lady Strachan[2] who both told me last night they never saw anything

1. Most likely a forgery.
2. Strachan, Louisa (d. 1867), d. of a Mr. Dillon, who m. 1812 Admiral Sir Richard Strachan (1760–1828), naval commander of the ill-fated Walcheren expedition. After his death, his widow m. an Italian, Picalillo, and went with him to live at Naples. The King of Naples created her marchesa di Salza. Mrs. Arbuthnot (*The Journal of Mrs. Arbuthnot*, ed. by F. Bamford and the Duke of Wellington, London, 1950, vol. i, p. 431) relates when staying at Lord Hertford's seat of Sudbourne in November 1825, '...we have a pleasanter party than usual, tho' Lady Strachan is one of them and is odious. She is one of the most vulgar women I have ever met with, having all the pretensions of a fine lady. The terms she is on with Lord Hertford are most extraordinary; one cannot look at him, crippled with the gout and looking like an octogenarian, and imagine there can be any real impropriety and yet she is the depository of all his secrets. He appears to tell her things that a woman never speaks of but to her husband, and not always that (such as building water closets in the house),

so ugly. I beg to know whether a small marble, light & thin, with this inscription, would not be a very pretty present from the Dilettanti who have done so much for the Architecture to Sir John Soanes Architectural Museum.[1]

If so, I will send it through the Society. A stone with the name of the Great Architect whether Vitruvio Pollioni or not, seems to me a valuable acquisition to such a Museum. There can be no doubt that this inscription concerns some one of the Vitruvian family if not Vitruvius himself. Arch. may mean *Architectus* or it might mean *Archigubernates* of the fleet, perhaps Architect of the buildings for the fleet at the Port of Misenum where I found the Marble & bought it for a few carlines in honour of the Art. If the Society think as I do that the curiosity of the thing merits their notice pray let me know to whom it is to be directed & I will send it. The Marble is less than a foot square & scarcely one inch thick. Before I conclude I will ask whether it be known in England to those who are interested in such subjects that somewhere on the side of AEtna has been discovered in consequence of an earthquake a stratum of snow lying under one of ashes & this again covered by a bed of Lava. This is accounted for by the knowledge that these ashes are very slow conductors of heat & being of a certain thickness the hot Lava has produced no effect on the snow but that of covering up for ages. How far this may be true I cannot say, but the report may awaken curiosity if the Learned Members of the Dil. Soc. think fit to mention it.

I have just got the account of the Excavations & dinner of the two Queens at Pompeii on April 25 last.[2] They found two Herms

---

and she seems complete mistress of the house. She has been staying months there this year, with three children, two governesses and her whole establishment, and always talks as if she was at home. She wears her clothes off her shoulders, short petticoats, and crosses her legs so as to show her knees. She makes me blush often to be in the room with her.' Later at Naples, Lady Strachan is reported as giving 'plays once a week'. See Lord Hertford, p. 54, n. 3.

1. *Corpus Inscriptionum Latinarum*, X 3393, still in Sir John Soane's Museum, London.

2. The two Queens were in all probability, Maria Cristina, wife of Ferdinand II,

or double faced Busts of Bronze. One was the head of Bacchus crowned with Ivy. A Silenus also with an ivy garland. A gladiator with a shield. A Mercury. A head of Minerva—crowned Juno. A boar's head, a fine Eagle, a tiger, 2 rams heads, the heads of several oxen, a Hippogrif, a duck dressing its plumes, a fish which threw out water from its mouth & an Elephants head all in small bronze. A very pretty & well preserved Tripod of Bronze, many articles of less consequence, & a pavement representing Fish in Mosaic were discovered in one of the rooms. All these things were found in two houses situated between the House called that of the Faun or the great Mosaic & the building known as the Pantheon at Pompeii. This is the last circumstance worthy of note which has come to my knowledge up to this 12th day of May 1833. I have the honour to be the humble Servant & by their appointment the Resident Plenipotentiary of the Society.

William Gell.

N.B. Having the Gout in my hand I can write no better, so hope to be excused if a little illegible.

PRIVATE

(May 12 1833 (Naples))

For Wm. Hamilton Esqre

My dear Sir,
It is now I think May 12th, & I have just received a letter from You I believe through Mr. Temple some three days ago which I now answer though I have so bad an attack of Rheumatic Gout in my right arm that I can scarcely hold my pen. I am glad You approve of my Scottiana,[1] though You will not read it to

and the Queen Mother, Maria Isabella. *Pompeianarum Antiquitatum Historia*, edited by Giuseppe Fiorelli (Vol. II, p. 270), Napoli, 1862, indicates that at some date between 21st and 27th April 1833, the Queen Mother, the Queen and the entire Royal Family visited the *Scavi*, where at twelve o'clock French time, they had luncheon, and then visited the *Termae del Foro* (VII, v. 2/7, 8, 10, 12, 24), and witnessed the excavation of a *Taberna* (VII, iv, 60/61) on the south side of the *Strada della Fortuna*. This little shop is just east of the *Casa delle Forme di Creta* (VII, iv, 62) which is the immediate neighbour of the *Tempio della Fortuna* (Vii, iv, I). We are indebted to Mr. Halsted B. Vanderpoel for kindly supplying this information. For another account of the *Casa di Arianna* see *PAH*, ii, 270 ff.

1. See *Introduction*, p. 32.

the Dil. Soc., not having my request to do so or rather my consent. I keep a copy not being sure that Mr. Lockhart will print what I wrote. Sir Walter would never have become Classical had he even resided in Greece. Some of his writings both in prose & Verse will however I think remain to posterity. The Map You have sent for inspection if You mean the engraving will be the death of the Dons at Cambridge if any of them chance to know any thing. Such spelling I never beheld. It could not have happened by chance & must have been done either through wickedness or for fun. I wrote till I was tired, & till I was convinced that it was useless to proceed—corrections of the names. It must to be tolerable be thoroughly reviewed with the help of the book & the Roman copy which I sent You on purpose, for it is absolutely ridiculous & cannot be sent forth either as a production of mine or the Dil. Soc. for the world will think we are gone crazy. If in the University of Thebes as Clarke[1] used to call it there should chance at the moment to be one man of letters what a scrape the poor map will be in. I send a sheet of observations & two new pieces for the engraver, one is only a word or two & a place, & the other the new road to Cora which may easily be inserted & which was made only last year. There can be no difficulty as I conclude the engraver is not paid, & will not be till the work is satisfactorily finished. It ought to go to Santa Marinella on the coast to the right.

Somebody sent me a Mr. Pashley, fellow of Trinity from the University, to travel for a tour in Asia Minor where He is to join a surveying ship. I have given him some hints as to what may be possibly be done, & he agrees with me that the University will give no money & I shall really be surprized if it does. Some big Wig will say Rome never existed till 3 centuries before X^e, that it is all a folly & my map a dream, the book wilful perjury & that will put an end to it. The difference between my Book & Cramers is that mine is original & his Compilation & I fear my Rom. Top. & his do not often agree. You have underlined the word "*cannot incur expense etc.*" so as to put an end to hopes in that quarter, so there is an end to them. I will only observe that the book was written at the desire of the Dil. Soc. & would never have existed but for that desire, & we should all have been wiser to have

1. Clarke, Edward Daniel LL.D. (1769–1822). Traveller, antiquary and mineralogist. His *Travels* appeared in 6 vols between 1810 and 1833, and *Greek Marbles brought from the Shores of the Euxine, Archipelago, and Mediterranean*, Cambridge, 1809 contains a sketch of Eleusis by Gell. Gell, a Cambridge man, here is referring to Oxford. The Boeotians were renowned for their stupidity.

adjusted our works to our pockets before we undertook them. The same reason must prevent any pecuniary results from the letters You propose. I must here beg leave to state that I make no complaint, & that I only state to You in private my feelings, fully sensible that I have no demand to make on the Society, whose favour & protection I fully appreciate with regard to fame, & who have a right to bestow their favours wherever their general sense of propriety leads them. You seem to think that the Antiquaries would be the more proper society for my Archaeology as the Dil. Soc. have only to do with the fine arts. One seems to me to be parent & necessary to the understanding of the other, but at all events I was not the person who proposed myself to the Society, but the Society proposed out of its great acknowledged goodness the whole thing to me. The Antiquaries alarmed by threatened reform might for all I know choose to undertake the work if properly proposed, but all this in England depends on jobs influences & a thousand other chances which cannot be commanded. You mistake me about Col. Vyse he never insisted on any return for his 100£, the repaying it from the profits is or was only suggested by myself. He is the only person here who has seen the work & if it creates in him so strong an interest I suppose in England others might feel the same. I have now answered all Your letter except the Fancourt whose periodical made such fine offers but which appears not. I know nothing more of Him. As to Sir Alex Crichton, it is impossible to say what they would be at for we the Executors gave up to them the Trust as soon as possible & got a regular act for legalizing it, that they might have the full power over their own property, having seen packed up the books left to them sent to England & having got their confession of receipt & a letter of thanks. What disputes they have afterwards with the Widow they must settle with her. They seem to me to have no claim on any other books & she will dispute their title to them. They are of very little value scarcely worth removing—Now for Your note or Word to the wise—I really have so indistinct an idea of who are now Dilettanti that I can scarcely imagine who there may be who are yet kind enough to be my protectors there. Do tell me who are those who are so aimably disposed. You say I may think You very exigeant, not at all, I am sure You are goodness personified and do all You can to be of use to me. Now Your last letter prohibits all subjects except such as are worthy of a Learned Body, but as Your first encouraged scandal etc. so You may already have had one letter loosely Written & this may not be more correct but

118

II Sir William Gell, c. 1814. Artist unknown

III (a) and (b) Sketches by Gell of his and Keppel Craven's house at Naples

III (c) Church of S. Maria a Cappella Nuova, Naples

IV La Chiaia, Naples, by Antonio Senape

V (a) Craven - Gell tomb in Protestant Cemetery, Naples

V (b) Villa Mills on the Palatine, Rome

VI Casa degli Spiriti, Posillipo, by Marianne Talbot

VII Approach to the Casa degli Spiriti, Posillipo,
by Giacinto Gigante

VIII Palazzo Reale, Naples, by Antonio Senape

IX Sketch by Gell of visit to Tusculum showing him hobbling on two sticks

POMPEIANA BY SIR WILLIAM GELL AND JOHN P. GANDY ARCHITECT

Engraved by Henry Moses

X Frontispiece to *Pompeiana*, 1824 edition

XI (a) Mount Vesuvius over the plain and city of Pompeii,
from *Pompeiana*, 1824 edition

XI (b) Restoration of the Atrium in the house of Pansa,
from *Pompeiana*, 1824 edition

XII A plate from *Pompeiana*, 1824 edition

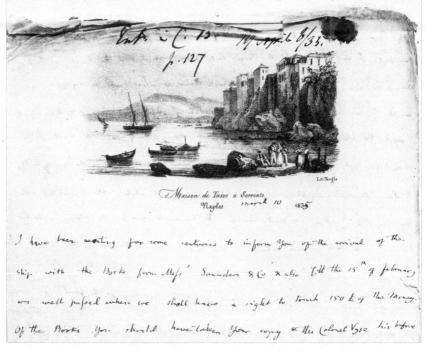

XIII (a) Letter from Sir William Gell, March 10th 1835

XIII (b) Three decorations from *Pompeiana*, 1824 edition

if I address all to You You may read or scratch out what You choose & say it was only private business. I have mentioned Father Strangways at Court which is as much scandal as I dare venture upon but You may scratch out all You don't like. I will in future stick only to the proper material & I should think perhaps some genius & all the documents I may possess for future works must be expended in the making a monthly letter entirely in the serious mood. Formerly the Dil. Soc. was always understood to everything half a joke & half in earnest, from the initiation downwards. I shall send the letter therefore which I have already written for I cannot make one better except in the shape of a solemn dissertation on something which nobody would read. I very much doubt my ability to satisfy a large Society by any thing. I can pick up monthly in Italy. I am however willing to proceed though without much hope.

The Lushingtons have left us. Miss Whyte I dined with at Torre del Greco yesterday. She returns on the 16th to La Cava, but will soon settle on the Vomero. The Ricciardis[1] are well, but the loss of the good old Mother they have not recovered. All along the Chiaja next to the rails of the Villa we have now a broad & beautiful macadamized road for horse & foot passengers. Ld de Tabley[2] has taken the Pavillion of the Villa Salicetti for the summer just above me. All the houses at Castell a Mare are full of strangers. Picnics are much in fashion to Cumae, Baiae, Fusaro etc. & Astruni. I go to most of these though I am mostly half dead with pain & fatigue, but everybody is kind to me & I get on tolerably well. I hope You will be able to read what I can scarcely write & that You will believe me even most gratefully

                    Yours   W.G.

To William Hamilton Esqre
    for the use of the Dilettanti Society.   Naples May 20 1833.

By finishing this letter on the 20th of May I shall hope it may reach You so as to become presentable by the 10th of June. I

1. Ricciardi, Giuseppe, created Conte di Camaldoli by Murat. He owned the Villa Regina on the Vomero at Naples famed for its gardens. The Villa is now a Home for the Blind.
2. de Tabley, George Fleming Leicester, 2nd Baron (1811–1887) who took the name of Warren in lieu of Leicester 1832.

shall be glad to hear if it do so. Since I wrote last, about the first of this Month, several new discoveries interesting to the Arts & Antiquities have been made. Of these one of the most curious is a great Mosaic of Rome.[1] Near the Bastion of Sangallo, one of the external & modern fortifications of the City between the Gates of St. Sebastian—San Paulo, has been found in a vineyard, a mosaic, nearly 16 feet square, situated in the centre of a room more than 40 feet long, decorated with pillars of brickwork, which have originally been coated with fine marbles. The rest of the pavement is finely varied with every species of porphyry & Serpentine, Oriental Alabaster, & other rare Marblés. Round the entire picture is a slightly elevated border of Parian marble intended to preserve it from rough treatment. Round the picture is again another red frame, consisting of *Lacunaria* or panels containing alternate garlands & *bucranii* or Bull's heads. This border is about 6 inches wide. Within this again is a second frame, two feet from the edge, and this is chiefly black, but varied with other colours. The space between the two borders is occupied by every object which might have been supposed to drop from a supper table at which many guests had been eating. Many sorts of Bones are represented. Some of Fowls. Many of Fishes. Lobsters & Shrimps in abundance. Shells of many kinds of fish. Peelings of Apples & husks & shells of nuts with grapes sometimes half sucked & many other such relics of a feast. Among these a Mouse is seen eating up crumbs & fragments, & strange to say the whole is so well arranged & so well executed that the effect is elegant though produced by such ordinary materials. Within this border of House sweepings was yet another space, & at the distance of one foot 6 inches was a third frame parts of which remain, but the foundation of a Wall which has in modern times crossed the centre has destroyed that portion of the picture that is the central group whatever it may have been. Between the second and third frames are several Egyptian figures, Male & Female. The ground is here black, & in colours upon this are represented plants, animals & generally the productions of the Nile, as between the pillars of the *Triclinium* of Darius & Alexander at Pompeii. The border of fragments is only continued round 3 sides of the Picture. The 4th side is occupied by 6 masks each of which is accompanied by

1. A large mosaic that is now part of the Lateran collection; it is the classic example of the type known as 'asarotos oikos' or 'unswept floor'. *Bullettino*, 1833, 81.

the attributes appropriate to its character. The work is fine, but I cannot say of how many pieces to the square inch. One of the best things however attached to the mosaic is the name of the Author in ancient letters ΗΡΑΚΛΙΤΟ ΗΡΓΑΣΑΤΟ which last word the Learned Society will remark is usually replaced by ΕΠΟΙΗΣΕ & of which more shall be said hereafter. The fragments are evidently of the kind mentioned by Pliny XXXVI. 25, speaking of Sosus who was the great mosaic Artist of Pergamus, & who made the celebrated drinking Doves. He executed pictures called, House Sweepings, *asaroton oikon* or unswept house, that is composed of the fragments which were usually swept away in a house after a dinner. Now it may be wondered what the Society of Dilettanti has to do with the word *Exergasato*, but its Commissioner Dr. Chandler[1] my predecessor copied in the Cave of Vari, an inscription, importing, that "Archidemus the Pheraean the *Nympholept* for the Nymphs of the Cave, this grotto did prepare." Mr. Wordsworth has just been there & has imagined instead of my ΦΟΛΑΔΙΣΙ Cave loving ΦΡΑΔΑΙΣΙ; ΕΞΗΡΓΑΞΑΤΟ he finds false quantity at the end of an Iambic & so proposes to read it which seems quite a new or barbarous word. His idea of the inscription would I conclude run thus "Archidemus the Pheraean the Nympholept *by his art* prepared this cave for the Nymphs." For the honour of the Dilettanti this new Roman mosaic shews that ΗΡΓΑΣΑΤΟ was really used. Wordsworths account of Greece is frightful & he was stabbed on Mount Parnes himself & plundered of all he had. He says however that at the arrival of King Otho it seemed as if tranquillity might be restored. There is a German epigram current there, the joke of which consists in saying that the Allies have taken away our Otto-man to replace him by an Otto-kind, the child Otho for the Othmans—Kind as You know being Child in German. They are seldom so lively. I will next give You some account of the discovery which Count Beugnot[2] of the French Embassy has made in the ancient Etruria. He was present at the opening of a

---

1. Chandler, Richard, D.D. (1738–1810). Appointed by the Society of Dilettanti to lead the first expedition to Greece and Asia Minor. Author of many works on Classical subjects including the first two sumptuous volumes of *Ionian Antiquities* published by the Society and an account of his travels in Greece and Asia Minor based on his journals.
   An abridged account of Chandler's *Travels in Asia Minor 1764–1765*, edited by Edith Clay was published by the British Museum in 1971.
2. Beugnot, Count Auguste Arthur (1797–1865).

Tomb near the Etruscan City of Vulci or Vulcium, & in it found an Amphora about 18 inches high.[1] My account is from the Chevalier Bunsen Prussian Minister at Rome & he says, "On this 7 yellow figures were painted on a dark ground of good drawing & with Etruscan inscriptions. One is as he writes πευταθλα. One side has a female figure near which is the Daemon or underground divinity of the Etruscans with horns. There is another such Monster with a rudder & the inscription ΨΑΡV = Χαρυ written from left to right, the former inscript, being in the contrary direction. Another Etruscan inscription illegible & unintelligible is found on the same. What Bunsen means by writing this I know not for he knows better, therefore he only sends me the account as he had it. The truth is that the people at Rome did not know that very ancient Greek was written from Right to Left, & called all that was so Etruscan. Of course the word whether correctly copied or not is Greek & the other with the rudder is nothing more than the Greek Charon well or ill written. As yet of the 4000 vases found near Vulci there is nothing to contradict the fact that all the five Vases are Greek or derived from Greek. The only two with real Etruscan letters upon them were imitations. The ground or paste was of the common black ware of Etruria, that is, black throughout, but the figures and inscriptions were painted upon them with red paint so as at a distance to have the appearance of the Common Greek pottery.

We have no intelligence of the Steam Vessel with Grecian Travellers since her arrival in Greece. The Neapolitans who believe in the doctrine of the evil eye or as it is called of the ill effects produced by *jettatore* on board except to receive an account of a series of disasters because there is a Dutchman[2] in the Ship

1. Also in *Bullettino*, 1834, 9. This is the Campanari tomb of Vulci; for a description, G. Dennis, *Cities and Cemeteries*, i, 465 f.
2. Mollerus, Jonkeer Nicolaas Willem, later Baron (1787–1865). Charge d'Affaires at Naples from 1806, Consul General 1827 and later Dutch Ambassador at Constantinople. Of Mollerus and his wife it has been written (see *Ramage in South Italy*, edited by Edith Clay. London, Longmans, 1965, p. 214) that they were 'two Dutch beings, as heavily built and as dull in intellect as that nation generally is'. It may be noted here that in Ramage's original book he refers to the kindness shown to him by Gell at Rome when he was on his way back to England from Naples in 1828. He records one occasion when they set off on an excursion together driving in style in a carriage with 4 horses to visit sites in the neighbourhood. Ramage's return journey was omitted from the abridged edition of 1965. See *The Nooks and By-Ways of Italy* etc., Liverpool, 1868, pp. 294, 299–301.

whose presence is considered to bring misfortune on any enterprise. This man went to Castell a Mare in the summer. He praised a Donkey on which was riding one of the French attachés & down he fell. He then met an Englishman & admired also his animal when immediately the girth broke & he got a fall. Lower down he met the Duke of San Teodoro on a fine horse, scarcely had he admired the animal than his feet slipped on the pavement & the Duke was nearly killed. He went to lodge in the Palazzo Policastro & the Duchess died the next day. He changed his lodgings & the Archbishop recommended the other lodgers to quit. They had better have done so for one night the roof fell in & the whole was deluged & when that was repaired the house took fire. The ancients had the same superstitions & I believe Millingen wrote a dissertation upon it[1]—I have the honour to be etc.—etc.— May 20 1833.

PRIVATE

[no heading or date]

My dear Sir,
    I find no difficulty in writing my letter of May 20 though I sent another at the beginning of the Month, nevertheless it can scarcely happen that materials will always be equally at hand, at least so it seems to me. However, I shall always be on the alert to catch all I can of antiquarian News. I should like to know whether this letter for instance is well received or gives pleasure or seems interesting to any of the Society. If it does my task may be easily accomplished, & to prevent repetition I keep a little register of the subjects touched in my 3 last letters. If any thing such as You hint be done, it would be much better in a small annuity or pension than in any other way & more honourable, with a grant half in earnest & half in joke, for as long as the Society was pleased with the Services of its Plenipotentiary. This was the original style of the Dilettanti—The name of Dilettanti was taken only to preclude the forms & regulations of a Club—
    I am yet in a fright about the Book. I have no hopes from Cambridge & had not time to get a letter to Browne nor to Rose[2]

1. Some Observations on an Antique bas-relief etc., *Archaeologia*, XIX, 1818, 70–74.
2. Rose, Hugh James (1795–1838). Theologian and Vicar of Glynde who d. at Florence. Author of several works including *Inscriptiones Graecae Vetustissimae* etc., Cambridge, 1825.

before the thing must have been decided, & I am in additional fear that the spelling in the map will have played the devil with my reputation for accuracy. Mr. Temple has at length taken the Serra Capriola Palace & I took him the other day to see Miss Whyte & am to take him to dine at the Archbishops[1] on Sunday. The King has been on a Tour & having discovered the nakedness of the land is going they say to redress grievances in his Augean stable, & a pretty job it must be, but nevertheless the people are happier than under a Brummagan Solon. We now blockade Tunis with the Sardinians. Your Malt Tax[2] was very near shewing that Your government could no longer be carried on. I think Your friends have now arrived at the point when they might resign for no one else dare take their places. In the East, Your only chance as things now are, would be to support the Pasha, nothing else could save Turkey from becoming a province sooner or later. Your government mean to do the contrary & to threaten him. I am anxious to hear about the book lest Col. Vyse should quit the place before it is settled. The Dutchman is Mollerus, the Dutch *incaricato* here who is in a fright lest some one should tell Metternich.[3]

Ever Yours,

W.G.

For the illustrious Society of Dilettanti

Naples, June 8 & 12 1833.

My dear Sir,

I have just received Your letter informing me that my last had been received in time & had contained matter not unacceptable to

1. Capecelatro, Giuseppe, Archbishop of Taranto (1744-1836). The Archbishop was greatly loved and revered and kept open house in the *palazzo* Sessa at Naples. He had two immense tortoise-shell cats, which perched on stools beside him at table eagerly watching his hand for bits of bread and purring most affectionately.
2. On 26 April 1833 Sir W. Ingleby proposed the reduction of the Malt Tax, but the Government was defeated by a majority of ten votes. Lord Althorp, the Chancellor of the Exchequer, offered to resign but the Prime Minister, Lord Grey, advised the King not to accept it. The Government therefore remained in power; however the Malt Tax was finally abolished by Disraeli in 1852. See Miss H. Martineau: *History of the Thirty Years Peace, 1816-1846*, vol. iii, p. 87. We are indebted to Sir Charles Clay for this reference.
3. Metternich, Prince Clemens Wenzel Lothar (1773-1859) Austrian Chancellor and Foreign Minister.

the Society. There will be an opportunity through Mr. Temple I hope of transmitting this, though like the Comic Annual which must at last fail for want of more new jokes, I scarcely know whether antiquity or the arts will furnish sufficient matter for any thing worthy of being submitted to the Illustrious Body of Dilettanti. First however, it is necessary to state that the illusion of Pliny's fleet at Pompeii is for the moment totally dissapated, for I visited Castell a Mare the other day, when Colonels Robinson & Howard Vyse examined one of the masts and penetrated through the earth, the *lapillae* & the mud, till they came to the pebbles which they judged to have formed the bottom of the Sea long previous to the great eruption which destroyed Pompeii. The supposed masts were by no means confined to the spot indicated by me in my former letter, but have been observed on sinking wells for the purpose of irrigation in many places within half a mile of the Bridge & nearly between it & Pompeii. The experiment has been made at a place called Joje which is nearer to Pompeii than most of the others. The masts which had been seen at the bottom of wells from 13 to 15 inches in diameter, giving hopes that at a certain depth the galleys would be found of considerable size. It was observed also that all yet seen were of cypress wood perfectly sound & yet retaining the peculiar smell of that tree with the original elasticity. Moreover all these Masts inclined from Vesuvius & towards Castell a Mare [sic], as stranded ships in such a convulsion of nature & with a retiring sea might—naturally have fallen before the storm. I am now obliged to have recourse to a figure in order to render myself intelligible. [sketch] The modern vegetable earth ceases at the depth of 11 palms. There is one foot of water in the well & the mast has been cut down to that level. The water rises all over the plain to the height of the stratum of *lapillae*, because that material is not at all compact & affords like a sponge little receptacles for the moisture. The consequence is that the Wells never want water nor can be emptied, as the fresh supply falls in from every side. In the boring, at the distance of 8 palms from the wells mouth, the mast, or a bit of wood which might have been the mast, was found 30 feet from the surface. The instrument used, was that employed in what the french call Artesian wells. What appeared to be decayed roots were found in one instance at the depth of 20 palms, & these continued till about 27. If the mast yet retains its bark cannot now be distinguished. Supposing these data correct the boring seems to prove that the ancient vegetable earth lies immediately under the *lapillae*, & is that which is here termed Clay or mud with roots, & that there once had been sea in this spot at the depth of 46 palms. The clay or mud with roots was bearing its cypresses & other plants at the moment of the great eruption, when it was covered with lapillae from the mountain. Also it will be evident from the figure that had there existed a ship or a Deck at right angles with the mast, such planks would have been found either perfect or decayed before the Augur arrived at the depth of the most ancient Sea. On boring a fourth time, the Colonels found reason for thinking that the mast might have been less inclined than it is here represented, & consequently that the bit of wood found at a depth of 30 palms might not have belonged to it, but the roots still seemed most decidedly to prove that not a mast but a cypress tree was there buried. I fear therefore that our Roman fleet must be considered as having vanished for the present. In most of the wells in this part of the plain, such trees have been found, but the story of one upon which was found a hoop of iron seems not now to be credited. It may be worth while trying a second of these trees, & if the result be similar, we may conclude that the plain was thickly studded with cypresses in the flourishing times of Pompeii. A few days ago on the occasion of the marriage of the Grand Duke of Tuscany,[1] that Sovereign amused himself with an excavation at Pompeii during which a third fountain was discovered, far exceeding in beauty the two formerly known, & into which the water fell from a statue, of good workmanship, & which remains on the spot, but which I have not yet seen. I am told the difficulties as to drawing & measuring at Pompeii are much increased as the new Minister of the Casa Reale though a supposed liberal is going to write something himself on the antiquities. We have here Mr. Baillie & Doctor Hogg just returned from Egypt, Nubia & Syria. I had lent them Hamiltons *AEgyptica* with which they were delighted, & would find no fault except that in one place it was asserted that Camels were introduced in a picture. On examination they found no camels but horses loaded, & it has been decided that no Camel is found in any ancient sculpture of Egypt, a circumstance quite unaccountable. Mr. Hay[2] who has been for some years living in a tomb at Thebes

1. Leopold II, Grand Duke of Tuscany who m. 1833 Maria Antonia, sister of Ferdinand II of Naples. For his visit to Pompeii see *PAH*, ii, 272.
2. Hay, Robert (1799–1863). Egyptian traveller and archaeologist. Was 4th s. of Robert Hay of Drumelzier and Whittinghame. In Egypt between 1826 and 1838. Presented to the British Museum 49 large vols of architectural and other drawings relating to his expeditions, also collection of Egyptian antiquities.

has several artists constantly employed & they say has many thousands of drawings. They have brought two M.S.S. one Greek the other Coptic, both at this moment in my possession. They are books, not rolls, but written on papyrus. The Greek is ill written with accents & contractions & is Christian after the 8th or 9th century. The Coptic is better written & in it I see the names of Caius & Paulus therefore it may be Law. The Greek is Divinity, & neither I fear is of consequence. Among the curiosities from Egypt or rather Nubia these travellers who have spent some time at Abu Simbel at the great temple, have brought an addition of two lines to Bankes's famous inscription from the leg of a Statue which they have cleared of sand to the bottom.[1] It is incredible that Bankes should have seen what he did & yet have seen no more of it, if it existed in his time. He ought to be consulted. Dr. Hogg says that Mr. Bankes only excavated a sort of well in the sand & so might have not seen what was below. Mr. Hay has cleared the whole, down to the ancient pavement. Till Mr. Hay came nobody, not even Wilkinson[2] had seen the inscription. I send You the rest of it, as it is quite unknown in England. I must add that the copies of which I have several are all made by persons unskilled in Greek, but I shall send them as they are given, only observing that Bankes's [inscription] was sense and what they now write is nonsense, so that the remainder must be well studied before it can be trusted correct. [Here Gell discusses the lettering of the Greek inscription] Dr. Hogg says the execution of the letters is not what might be expected in a public commemoration. The two new lines will afford food for Critics, & will I think be interesting in London. The last news from the Steam Boat with 80 Grecian travellers, is from Nauplia. They have of course had constant disputes in so unruly a republic, but only two duels are as yet decided to be fought when the voyage terminates. The French on board unite into a Club to bully the Captain in a body. Those who went by land across the Morea were furious at finding few people & no house with its roof on,

1. Bankes, William John of Kingston Lacy (1786–1855). Travelled in Egypt and brought back to his estate an ancient obelisk from Philae. M.P., 1810–12, 1821–25, 1829–35. Elected to the Society of Dilettanti 1821.

The inscription was reported by Gell also to the Institute, *Bullettino*, 1833, 131. This is the famous temple of Ramses II, recently moved bodily to save it from being flooded in the Nile Dam project. The inscriptions are not the hieroglyphic texts found in the sanctuary itself, but the signatures left by Greek mercenaries in the early sixth century; see R. Meiggs and D. Lewis, *Greek Historical Inscriptions* no. 7.

2. Wilkinson, Sir John Gardiner (1797–1875).

though I told them how it was before they set out. The consequence is that all dine & sleep on board, while in Port & the Vessel cannot be cleaned. Even at Nauplia there were no accommodations for 80 passengers. Imagine them therefore at Vostizza [Aegion], Corinth, Eleusis or the Piraeus where they and all Europe expect operas, Pianofortes, & Billiards. With profound respect for the Illustrious Society believe me my dear Sir

Ever yours

William Gell.

Ended 12 June 1833.

PRIVATE

June 8/33.

To Mr. Hamilton.

I don't know that so little a slip of paper can cheat the Post but I will try. I received Your letter yesterday from Mr. Temple. I have sent You the result of the examination of the ground for Ships for the Society. They were so anxious about it at one moment that I conclude they will like to know the result, though highly unfavourable. It affords ground for curious speculations, but the roots in the stratum called clay & mud prove that that stratum was the soil of the country in Pompeian times beyond a doubt I think. I hope the Dons will not steal my work for the penny magazines. If they are so long in judging of it the appearance ought to be favourable but I fear they will never give money for it. They may offer to print it but I should never get a farthing by it that way. Ye Gods what a map of Greece it is. Very little better than any other, & it has waited 20 years for AEtolia & Acarnania which yet remains white paper. I shall be forced to publish all the interesting parts in detail in Bunsen's *Archaeologia*,[1] which I shall copy from my great map $\frac{1}{2}$ inch to a mile which I reduced with immense care & trouble & eyesight into the little one, & I rather think I shall be obliged to publish some thousands of angles for the map of Greece only to shew that I took them from every place & every point. It is I fear of no use to pretend to make money by writing any longer unless one writes a novel or a Life. Ones own life would be most entertaining if one dared write all one knows. Pray

1. The *Bullettino* or *Memorie* of the Instituto di Corrispondenza.

if it be but a line, let me know how my letter is received, The Society may make what use of it or them they think proper, but I like to know how they are relished, as I have not as yet at all altered my style on writing to a Body. Ridley Colbourne[1] was always a most aimable person. Believe me most truly & sincerely Yours with regards to Mrs. Hamilton.

W. Gell.

NAPLES. July 29/33.

Dear Hamilton,

You must be so tired of the Book & of so many more last words on the subject that I think You will be only too happy to put it into the printers hands to get rid of it forever. I send a passage about Veii from the last discovered fragments of Dionysius unknown in England. Please to see if I have not sent it before & if so cut it off & fasten it into the article Veii. The other article or note to be added to the Alban Lake seems to me of such consequence as the corroboration by an experienced thinker of my observations, that I am persuaded You will not grudge the trouble of inserting it with a wafer in the article of Lake of Albano, for nobody has as yet thought much about the facts or observed on the spot.

As to the M.S. the fewer persons have it the better. I have no hopes from Ch. Wordsworth though he is a very interesting person but the University of Boeotia as Dr. Clarke used to call it cannot be changed. Deighton the Bookseller[2] is of much more consequence according to Browne. I shall even fear Murray will now not accept our proposition, & the only chance I have of profit is evidently the magnanimous offer of Colonel Howard Vyse who offers 100£ for the printing of it which I may claim when the work is fairly undertaken & which I must accept in part of the 300£ which I owe Torlonia, & which I made sure of obtaining with ease. As to writing any more either for Public Private or Dilettanti I abjure it,

---

1. Probably Nicholas-William Ridley-Colborne (1779–1854) who was raised to the peerage as Baron Colborne of West Harding, co. Norfolk, 1839. Peerage now extinct.
2. The Cambridge Booksellers now Messrs. Deighton, Bell and Company. The 'Bell' association was entered into in the latter part of the nineteenth century and their premises have always been at 13 Trinity Street.

for it is evidently useless as a means of stopping the gaps in the pittance of a Younger Brother, so I intend to be idle upon principle for the rest of my life. Should this chance to cross on the road a letter of Yours containing news of better hopes, You will be amused with this suicidal resolution, but just now I am disgusted with Topography & all other sorts of graphy so there we will leave it—

As to the letters to the Dilettanti I make out from Your last letter that I need not trouble myself with any more at present, for the Society has already two in hand & in August they do not meet. It is all very well for I know of nothing at the moment new in the shape of arts or antiquities to communicate. I hope You will get the Brondstedt bronzes[1] which are beautiful though sufficiently costly. We have here no chance of meeting with subscribers as nobody I know has a sixpence in the world to spare. It will not be uninteresting to You to learn that Wilkins[on] who certainly except Champollion[2] knows more of hieroglyphics than anyone is now at Leghorn in his way to England. He was 12 years in Egypt & was the first person who knew what was known of the subject who went there. I had the pleasure to instruct him in all Young had discovered, & I send him all Champollions discoveries afterwards as they appeared. Salt[3] profited by these also & though he might say he never saw Champollions book he had seen from me all it contained & whenever he went alone was mistaken. Wilkinsons experience & knowledge is immense & I shall send him in a letter to You that You may at once pop him into the midst of the literary world instead of letting him languish unknown for many months as he would without such introduction. His know-

1. Brondsted, Chevalier Philip Oluf, Counsellor to the King of Denmark and devoted student of Greek architecture. Published *Travels and Researches in Greece*—d. 1842.

In 1833 funds were raised by the Society of Dilettanti to buy the so-called 'Bronzes of Siris', consummate examples of Greek metal-work, and for their publication. Brondsted was given £1,000 for the originals and £100 for engravings. *Die Bronzen von Siris* was published at Copenhagen in 1837. See Colvin and Cust, *op. cit.*, pp. 177–79.

2. Champollion, Jean François (1790–1832). Egyptologist. This must refer to his famous *Précis du système Hiéroglyphique* (Paris, 1824), in which he set out his decipherment of hieroglyphics.

3. Salt, Henry (1785–1827). Traveller and Orientalist. Was Secretary to Lord Valentia (later Lord Mountmorris) while in Ethiopia and India, and illustrated Lord Valentia's *Voyage and Travels in India, 1809*. Later Salt returned to Ethiopia as H.M.B. Envoy and published his travels. Both these books were illustrated with portfolios of coloured prints of great merit by Salt.

ledge will amply repay for any trouble You may bestow upon him & he returns to Egypt in a year. He is now in quarantine & if I cannot make him come here he will go direct to England, on escaping from the Lazzaretto. I conclude Mr. Hudson Gurney[1] is the depository of many of his papers which I sent to Dr. Young[2] who was much interested in them as well he might, & who has published some of them in the folio of the Hieroglyphic Society.

One thing I have just heard of Mr. Wilkinson, which will certainly give pleasure to Antiquaries. He applied ladders to the Statue of Memnon,[3] I mean the Vocal statue, which as You know has been broken & afterwards repaired. Probably Cambyses broke it, & the Ptolemies restored it. However he found that the Vocal stone, is really a piece of another & a resounding species, placed on purpose on the breast of the figure with a little niche in which the person who produced the sound was concealed, and who struck it with a piece of iron. Whether there were several pieces or only one stone I cannot tell You as my account is from a person neither very observant or very musical but it would have been as easy to have placed 3 or 4 stones & to have made a full chord as one note if such a sound was desired. The discovery strikes me as exceedingly interesting and as worthy of being communicated to the Dilettanti or Literary as any thing I have ever heard. So use this as You think fit till Wilkinson arrives himself who may give a detailed account of his discovery. By the bye, let the Learned say if the Statue was celebrated for its music previous to the time of Cambyses, if such notice can be found for if not it might have been rendered vocal only at its restoration. However anyone who now will get a ladder may perform the miracle for the benefit of those who stand below. Wilkinson has also copied a great many more of the inscriptions on the Statue than have yet been published. No more of the masts of Plinys fleet or the Cypress trees have yet been examined nor perhaps is an examination necessary for the first was decidedly a Tree growing in vegetable soil & covered with the tufa of an eruption. Col. Robinson I believe gives up the

1. Gurney, Hudson (1775-1864), eld. s. of Richard Gurney of Keswick Hall, Norfolk. Antiquary and verse-writer, M.P. for Newtown, Isle of Wight 1816 and sat in 6 successive Parliaments. F.R.S., F.S.A.
2. Young, Thomas (1773-1829). Distinguished physician, physicist and Egyptologist. In 1787 was classical tutor to Hudson Gurney who wrote a Memoir of him in 1831. His portrait was painted by Lawrence.
3. Also reported by Gell to the *Bullettino*, 1833, 130. This statue is that called the 'Vocal Memnon' of Thebes; it has been described by Strabo and many times since.

matter & Col. Vyse is going to England in a few days. The Baths of Vesuvian water at La Torre though warm or rather tepid, were too cool for me to venture to bathe when I got there. I have as yet seen no positive proofs of the wonderful sanitary effects produced by them. The water to drink is a palatable sort of such liquor as one finds in an oyster newly opened & has the same smack of shell fish & sea water a little warmed. But it is not unpleasant & I believe perfectly innocent either of good or evil. Lord Selsey[1] thinks himself the better for drinking and bathing but I see very little difference in him except what Summer & very moderate attempts at temperance in Wine might have produced. Most of the World is at Castellamare—Miss Whyte who is very well I have just seen at La Cava where I have left her with Matthis[2] younger than ever at the age of 80 & Miss Mackenzie.[3] Craven has bought a Convent at Penta[4] halfway between Salerno & Avellino in a pretty mountainous country very triste in my opinion & there he is spending much money in making improvements. The Greek Steamer is arrived at Malta to perform quarantine & they

1. Selsey, Henry John Peachey, 3rd Baron Selsey of Selsey (1787–1838).

2. Matthias, Thomas James (1754–1835). Satirist and Italian scholar. Sometime treasurer to Queen Charlotte and librarian at Buckingham House. Retired to live at Naples. Gell referred to him as 'obstinate as twenty pigs'.

3. Mackenzie, Hon. Frances Catherine, 2nd d. of the last Lord Seaforth. The Scottish earldom of Seaforth came to an end in 1716 when the estates were forfeited, but a barony was created in 1797 for Francis Humberston Mackenzie (b. 1754), M.P. He died without male issue but had six daughters. His eldest d. married Sir Samuel Hood, and her grandson was recreated Baron Seaforth in 1921, but died s.p. 1923.

There is a letter in the National Library of Scotland at Edinburgh (MS 6363, f. 119) from Sir William Gell to Miss Mackenzie written from Naples giving no date except, 'Monday', and addressed: 'Madamigella Mackenzie, Palazzo Calabritto', which says:

Dear Miss Mackenzie, I shall be at your door tomorrow morning at 11 and take you as far as Pompeii with my own horses, as we shall have then have passed the last Dogana. I then calculate that by taking a carriage (which it is to be hoped will be yellow and painted with flower pots) from La Torre we shall get on to La Cava. If not, we must stop at Nocera to wait, and you will go and see the circular temple which you have seen twenty times. My coachman insists on an open carriage if we go all the way with horses, which seems likely at present, but I daresay it will rain—today being so provokingly fine and then a closed carriage will be better—at all events at eleven, I shall be with you on Tuesday morning—being most truly yours, W. Gell.

We are indebted to the Trustees of the National Library of Scotland for permission to publish this letter.

4. Near Fisciano.

have had only one duel on board between a Philippist & a Carlist. Irby[1] writes that he saw King Othos entry into Athens which was fixed upon for the Capital & a new City was to be begun immediately. Mahommed Ali says that before 6 months are over it shall be as safe for franks to walk about Damascus in hats & coats as in London. Dr. Hogg who is just arrived says he had no difficulty at that once headquarters of Musulman bigotry. I have no more to add than to entreat that if not already done You would finish the affair of the Book *anyway* quickly & that You will believe me ever most truly & much obliged

Yours

W. Gell.

29 July 1833.

Naples. ? Oct. 1 or 2, and Oct. 22, 1833.

My dear Sir,

It does not indeed seem that our letters are ever likely to begin with any other expression than "I am sorry to say" as Yours usually do. I despair on the subject of the book & though very little is known as to it or rather nothing in these parts yet I should think it highly probable we shall see all the marrow of my production in print with some other name before my work & map appear. The Colonel, I mean Vyse, is most kindly anxious about it but he has already advanced 100£ on the publication which seems likely never to take place, or to be repaid till I come of age, which is a moment seemingly not fast approaching. You send no lamentations over the mislaid fleet at Pompeii which seems given up for ever by the two Colonels. I have sent a note for the Bunsens *archeologia*[2] at Rome about Wilkinsons vocal statue which has been received with great delight & another article as to what was a Kylix [Here Gell gives a sketch of a Kylix], so if You please if You have a tea cup with two handles let it henceforth be called a Kylix.[3] The people want to make

1. Irby, Hon. Charles Leonard (1789–1845), 6th s. of Frederick Irby, 2nd Lord Boston. Capt. R.N. but retired in 1815 due to ill-health—travelled in Egypt with Belzoni and Beechey and explored Abu-Simbel. In 1826 returned to the Navy with command of *Pelican*, later in *Ariadne* took part in the Battle of Navarino.
2. Not published.
3. Published as *Corpus Inscriptionum Graecarum*, i, no. 545; cp. Richter and Milne, *Shapes and Names of Greek Vases*, 25.

the great mosaic Gauls & Romans,[1] and why? [sic] because on the
flag say they is a Cock consequently the nation is Gaulish, as if the
Gauls punned in Latin. One follows another wiseacre, so as the
Persians had several standards, viz a Sun, a Buffalo, [sketch] & many
others, and as Hesychius & Suidas say the Cock [sketch] was a
Persian Bird, & all the good folks had represented the figure thus
[sketch] I thought I might as well go & examine minutely the fact &
see whether the thing might not be a Ram which was a Royal Persian
Standard. I send You here a positive facsimile, 18 stones of this
size, of which 4 are white & the rest light or dark yellow, by which
You may see how little claim the Gauls could have to the bad pun,
& I shall be glad if You or any of Your learned Correspondents
[Mr. Urban][2] could invent any figure of animal or vegetable of
which 18 stones could ever have formed a part. This is the whole of
what remains, upon a red ground. Even if Cocks combs were white
& yellow & not red this could never be converted into one which goes
thus [sketch] What can it have been. *NAPLES Oct. 13 1833.* I
began this when I rec^d Yours & I can't tell what day it was some
fortnight ago. The Galt & Spurzheim[3] faction have long vowed that
the head of Raffaello at St. Luke's at Rome[4] had none of the desired
characteristics & have at length succeeded in getting an order for
the exhumation of the body in the Pantheon which proves they
were right for the head was found in the coffin & not in bad
preservation. Raffaello it seems ordered that Lorenzo Lotti should
make a statue of the Virgin to be placed on his tomb in one of the
ancient Tabernacles of the Pantheon, the 3rd on right hand on
entering. The coffin to be placed in the pedestal. Fragments of
coloured *stucco* were found, certain rings of metal, an iron pin or
una stelletta di ferro but it may be *spelletta*, & some *fibulette* shew
that he was buried in a robe. The skeleton was well preserved. The
head quite perfect and though the muscles were gone yet the softer
parts sufficed to recognize the features of the great painter. The
cranium has been taken in plaster. It appears that the frequent

1. The Alexander mosaic; cp. above p. 66.
2. This seems to be an obscure joke.
3. Franz Joseph Gall (1758–1828) and Johana Friedrich Spurzheim (1776–1832).
Famous phrenologists and authors of *The Physiognomical System of Drs Gall and
Spurzheim.*
4. See *Nel Centenario di Raffaello Da Urbino a' di' XXVII DI MARZIO
DEL MDCCLXXXIII*, Roma tipi della stamperia del Senato MDCCLXXXIII
in which appear two plates of the skull of Raphael: also two others of his
skeleton lying in the tomb reproduced from the original drawings by Barone
Camuccini.

innundations of the Tyber have caused an argillaceous deposit even in the skull. The bones have been carefully packed into a leaden case, to be placed in a sarcophagus of marble given by the Pope from the Vatican museum. The reputed cranium of Raffaello shewn in the Academy of St. Luke is proved to have been that of Don Desiderio De Adintorio, a man of Talent who travelled in Palestine & on his return founded the Society of Artists called Virtuosi in the Pantheon, or that of St. Luke in the year 1542. I think all this curious & interesting & it ought to be so to the Dilettanti in particular, to which learned body I beg You to recount the particulars as I have them from Nibby himself who was an eye witness & the overseer of all the operations. I find You must have heard something of this but not equally authenticated. It appears that Raffaello was not only the great Painter, but Sculptor, Architect & Antiquarian, & that in the last line, he had undertaken the gigantic task of making a restoration of the Ancient City of Rome in a Model & had completed the first Region, when he died. This of course would be invaluable from his hands, and on the consideration that in his time the antiquities were standing in so much higher preservation, & many buildings the very sites of which are unknown. I am applied to to find out what is become of the papers, drawings, elevations plans & perhaps models belonging to this work which are said to be in England in the hands of Lord Leicester.[1] What Lord Leicester? [sic] Queen Elizabeths Lord Leicester, or the Late President of the Antiquaries or Who else for between the times of Raffaello & the present there may have been twenty of the name & not a few of different families, unconnected with each other. Pray see what can be done, made out, or conjectured on the subject, or if any trace of such very important documents can be discovered. The Romans insist upon it that somewhere in England they ought to be found & You will discover a great treasure if You can find them out, invaluable for archaeology & the happy possessor. I am sorry that You have by no means even yet escaped all the trouble of my after thoughts for I must get You to send to Mr. Lockhart the passage which may be of

1. Leicester, Thomas Coke, 1st Earl of (1698–1759) who acquired a manuscript or architectural drawings attributed to Raphael (Holkham MS.701). Dr. W. O. Hassall, the Librarian at Holkham, to whom we are indebted for this information, tells as that he has never heard of any model by Raphael as having been at Holkham nor is it mentioned in an early nineteenth-century guide book. Lord Leicester was elected to the Society of Dilettanti 1740/41. See W. O. Hassall: 'Portrait of a Bibliophile II, Thomas Coke...' in *The Book Collector* viii, 1959, pp. 252–55.

some consequence to the little account of Sir Walter Scott, which You will find on the top of the last fold of this page, & I must also beg You to cut it off as well as to cut off & wafer on to my preface a passage which I think of great consequence after having studied Niebuhrs second volume which I have just read.

A friend of mine Dr. Hogg is just returned from Egypt & I have got a Coptic book of perhaps 100 leaves, in the form of a book & on papyrus. I fear it is only law or divinity for I find the names [Here Gell transcribes] which must be Cyril or Alexandria, but it must be valuable as having only the translation of certain parts of the Bible in Coptic every new word is an acquisition. I fear nobody exists who would be so capable as Champollion was of turning the thing to a good account. The conquest of Syria by Mahomed Ali has quite altered the state of those Countries & he swears that before he has been in possession of Damascus one year it shall be as safe for Franks in hats & coats as it is now at Alexandria, & the fact is that it is now become so & all attempts at pillage & robbery have ceased. Instead of the Pasha there or at Tripoli there is now a commandant who kisses the firman of Mahomed Ali & becomes answerable for Your safety. It would be a most excellent moment for executing the plan I once had of making a real Map of Palestine, which was set aside by the "untoward accident" at Navarino.[1] I once had the opportunity of being useful to the great Soldan of Egypt who by Ismail Giblachter his Commodore sent me word he would be very kind to me if I came to Egypt, & I doubt not would remember his promise. I feel much interest in making out what could be discovered of the cities conquered by Joshua & in constructing a real map of the country, & as one may as well be ill in one place as another I should be tempted in my old age to undertake it if I could meet with the proper encouragement, taking my time about it & giving my employers the map & the documents, for their money. I would take from Jaffa to the South end of the dead sea for one extremity. Thence to Damascus for my eastern boundary. Thence to Sidon for the north & my fourth side should be the Sea. Only think that as yet no one knows whether there be or be not any remain of the Temple or altar or sacred place on the top

1. Gell alludes to the fateful Battle of Navarino (11 October, 1827) by which the Turkish and Egyptian fleets were destroyed by British action, largely accidentally. In the King's Speech of January 29, 1828 (echoing no doubt the conciliatory views of the Prime Minister, the Duke of Wellington), it was referred to as an 'untoward event', a phrase that became famous.

of Mount Gerizim of Samaria which was set up in opposition to Jerusalem, & 10000 such desiderata occur without a chance of being satisfied unless I go myself for I know no one who has the patience united with the practice necessary for the examination & communication of the Facts. Consider this & mind I cannot put a foot to the ground but must trust to slaves & asses for locomotion & then You will at least allow I am zealous. I hope You will have seen Wilkinson eer this & Col. Howard Vyse will appear in about a fortnight. Stoke, Colnbrook, Bucks is his direction, but he will I doubt not come to You. At Pompeii there is nothing new but a pretty fountain with a little Silenus throwing out water, & a beautiful Titian like picture of Perseus shewing the head of Andromeda, I mean of Medusa to Andromeda reflected in the water.[1] As to the book it is a subject for despair. Surely the Provost of Eton & the Master of Rugby would be able & willing to set it agoing—Wordsworth is very kind & he may know what is best but waiting is very bad both as to the money & the fear of the whole appearing in a penny magazine some fine day after that You say of the Dilettanti etc. etc. etc. I beg You will present my compliments to all my Constituents & tell them at the expense of Your eyes & Your recollection all the news I have sent in this long epistle. Ever yours,

W. Gell.

For Mr. Lockhart—

While at Rome, Sir Walter also became acquainted with Mr. Ganz a German who had long resided in London. This gentleman became so great a favourite, that Sir Walter promised to make him the present of a work which he mentioned as nearly compleated & called *Il Bizzarro*, a Calabrian story. On second thoughts however he said the book was not quite finished & that He would transmit it from some place at which He might stop on His way to England. It is possible that the Work was never committed to writing but that it consisted only of a short story which Sir Walter had conceived in his own mind. On the other hand papers or notes may hereafter be discovered which may relate to that object & which may be rendered intelligible by the knowledge of this anecdote.

1. Perseus and Andromeda are from the *Casa di Arianna*, below p. 156; the others are not easy to identify from Gell's account, but a figure of a silene was found at this time in the House of the Grand Duke and another of a satyr in the House of Meleager.

Not having met Mr. Ganz at Sir Walters house, the circumstances had escape my memory till I was reminded of it by accidentally meeting him some time afterwards at Naples.

W. Gell.

Place this in my preface after "This most ingenious author reasons from the monuments antiquity served to confute his system of incredulity.[1]

It can scarcely be considered safe to trust to the reasoning or conjectures of an Author who ventures to contradict the early history of Rome, while he places Fidenae on the right bank of the Tyber, which was notoriously on the left, & of infinite importance to the authentic continuity of history, as the position of that City on the Roman side of the stream afforded a safe & convenient passage into Latium, to its Veientine Allies, & a circumstance of which the Etruscans reaped the advantage while Fidenae remained the enemy of Rome".

followed by—"If History be valuable" etc.

Naples. Dec. 10, 1833.

My dear Sir,

A Courier has been waiting here for the last 6 weeks by whom I hope to be able to send this. I am waiting at this moment for Mr. Lytton Bulwer[2] the Author of *Pelham* etc. etc. who has been sent to me in a letter & who having a great experience in the wiles of the art of Booksellers offers to give his advice on the subject of our *Roman Topography*. I don't much admire writing or writers who merely pander to the passions of the Mob & who if the Soup is not good lay it to the influence of the Aristocracy but he seems in person quite different from England & the English so I shall tell You in this what new lights he may throw on the science of Publication. First of all he has already told me that nothing can be published which will not make two volumes so as to be sold for a guinea for the advertisements for one volume cost as much as those for two though the work cannot be sold for so much. You will

1. The words did not finally appear in Gell's book.
2. Bulwer-Lytton, Edward George, 1st Baron Lytton (1803–1873). Novelist and poet. Colonial Secretary 1858. *Pelham* was published in 1827.

learn from this how much he himself is interested in that excess of patriotism which urges him to make himself popular by crying out in Parliament for the abolition of taxes on Science & Literature, but as I am very apt to imagine that all outrageous patriotism proceeds from private motives we may as well learn as many tricks of the trade as possible while looking on. By the bye one of the best things in His book is the unmasking of who are the British public who pronounce what is the opinion of the English nation. He says these are tenth rate scribblers who write from garrets & who can get no other employment than writing such nonsense. I shall proceed with my letter as he does not arrive. In Sicily has been found a vase about 10 inches high [sketch] & nearly this shape. The ground is of a beautiful deep rose colour. The ornaments round the lip are finely gilt & half figures in miniature so well done that they seem portraits are painted in natural colour. I suspect that the colours are not burnt in & might be washed off but this I do not assert as I have only seen a drawing of it.[1] Next in Apulia, I don't remember the name of the Village has been discovered a treasure of ancient armour. The accounts would lead one to suspect something like the perfection of Brondstedts armour just purchased by the British Museum.[2] I am told five suits have been recovered in good preservation highly & finely wrought & one being of a colossal size— it is probable they were used in some procession & that the largest was a Trophy. I shall send You a better account when I am able to obtain further information. Can You believe it the Roman fleet at Pompeii is revived. I sent to Colonel Howard Vyse to inform You as soon as I heard the story. It seems Colonel Robinson had satisfied himself that the discovered remains were those of ships & not of cypress trees, but he wisely concluded that every sort of obstacle would be thrown in his way if his opinion were avowed, so he reported that only trees had been discovered. He has lately purchased the land himself and after the papers were signed he no longer hesitates to announce his opinion. I have just heard also that the King has given an order to excavate "the Ships" & I know not how the two accounts correspond. I give You therefore the account as I receive it. You can have the kindness to communicate the history

---

1. One of a series of painted vases found at Centuripe; the example was described in *Bullettino* 1833, 5 but now is lost. See B. Pace, *Arte e Civiltà nella Sicilia Antica*, ii, 171–2.

2. The armour was published in *Bullettino*, 1834, 36 ff and is now in the Museum in Naples. Brondstedt's armour is in the British Museum: Walters, *BM Catalogue, Bronzes* 39 ff. Both are from Ruvo in Apulia.

of the Ships & the armour to the learned Members of the Dilettanti & to such as You may think will feel most interested in the discovery & prosecution of the excavation. I told You that before the level of the galleys is reached by digging, it seems that the level of the sea water causes the substratum of all the plain to be inundated. This stratum is composed of small stones or *lapillae* which permit the water to return as fast as it is cleared out so that it is doubtful whether the excavation can proceed without damming or caissons.

I have just seen the second Volume of Niebuhr who places Fidenae on the wrong side of the Tyber, & must request of You to add to the history of the Alban Lake & ? Emissary the passage which I now send & hope You can cut out or wafer in. Cut also off I pray You the passage on the Allia & put them at the end of the Article Allia. Mr. Bulwer says the best people for my book are Bentley, New Burlington St. whom we have I think tried. Also Saunders & Otley in Conduit Street, Volpy in Red Lion Square & Whittaker in Ave Maria Lane. He says Mr. Knight[1] of the Society for the diffusion of knowledge has been already ruined & Bankrupt & therefore has no money to give otherwise he would be likely to treat. Mr. Bulwer is to write himself to his Bookselling Constituents & I hope may make out something—of which I will let You know when I know any thing myself—I cannot help thinking nobody would go to Rome without our work if it were once published & great numbers of people are come this year so that I find the engraved map is called for by many. I should not wonder if I find myself disposed to make a plate of the Battle of the Allia which is one of the most interesting of Roman subjects. I am in such haste for the Courier that I can only hope You will be able to read this—Ever yours most truly sincerely

William Gell.

Mr. Auldjo of Mt Blanc hopes You have got his book on Vesuvius— he is just come in & says it is printed in England also.

Naples. Jan. 31 & Feb.6, 1834.

My dear Sir,

I write so little a scribble that I shall be able to say all I have got to say in half a sheet of paper, for as the information is to be

1. Knight, Henry Gally (1786–1846). Traveller and writer on architecture. M.P.

had I think it not useless to add to my work wherever You think it would be well to place it, the whole of the opposite page [Notes on the Roman State from the latest Accounts].[1] You can cut it off & it will give You but little trouble to just put it in my M.S. Wilkinson wrote that Murray has undertaken it at last. I am glad of it on any terms as it would have in some way or other have evaporated into some of the penny magazines. I wrote to Colonel Vyse that Mother Starkes[2] being in two volumes is a reason for mine not being so & here is Dr. Watson[3] full of oriental Parisian learning just come from Paris who is in a fury that there is any idea of not making the work at least a decent volume or two & I think he is right. I am glad You protect Wilkinson who must have seen more of Egypt & besides went better prepared for it than anyone since the discovery of hieroglyphics. I see you have been reading his Memnon & my rose coloured vase. You know that writing entertaining letters in succession is as bad as being Editor of a Review or a magazine which must at last break down for want of matter. I have sent Colonel Vyse an account of the last discoveries at Torre della Annunziata[4] which I think prove that the Ancients knew of the source & had done something to shew their reverence for it. You know They have scooped out of the Tufa rock 70 feet high, a place large enough to erect Baths

for Aldborough 1824–28, for Malton 1830 and for North Nottinghamshire 1835, and 1837 until his death. F.R.S. Elected to the Society of Dilettanti 1817.
1. We omit the account that Gell here summarises from the published annual figures. But we quote the reflections he gives on the conditions of the Papal States at this time:
'The advantages and ameliorations which are produced in other states can never be hoped for in a country absolutely destitute of all claim to public or private credit. The national Debt was expunged by Papal decree, and His Holiness enjoys the power which he exercises without scruple of postponing the payment of debts however contracted for three or five years which is frequently renewed for life or sine die, & which naturally puts an end to all confidence between man and man.'
2. Mariana Starke, *Travels on the Continent*, was the *vademecum* of all European wanderers at this period. Her book went through eight editions between 1820 and 1833.
3. Watson was medical attendant on Sir William Drummond when he was British Minister at Naples in 1801–3 and 1806–9. The doctor was an eminent linguist who had lived for 5 years in Paris before taking up residence at Naples.
4. For a summary, see *Introduction*, p. 32. The only other contemporary witness is R. Liberatore, 'Delle nuove e antiche Terme di Torre Annunziata', in *Annali civili del Regno di Napoli*, vol. VI, 1834, 95–109; whence N. Corcia, *Storia delle Due Siclie*, II, 290. These have been analysed by A. Maiuri, *Rendiconti dell' Accademia di Archaeologia...di Napoli*, vol. 34, 1959, 75 ff.

etc. In enlarging this they have made another excavation & found a circular sort of well lined with bricks A

After pursuing this to a certain depth as far as B the workmen fell into a cavity & reported that the well had no support— However, the day after Colonel Robinson was let down into the place to examine it when the water rushed in so that he was glad to escape, & to be drawn out—Five or 6 Doric columns of marble were found & certain Boucranii

which I have myself no doubt were a frieze, but I have not yet seen it myself. The Columns are marble. They imagined that they had found a Tower

in the walls of the Town of Oplontis, but I rather think my theory more probable. I imagine therefore that after an eruption the proprietor of the spring dug for it over the known site of the *AEdicola* & was obliged to support his excavation by bricks in a circle like a well, placing the same on the entablature as a foundation—By this means they for a time recovered the use of the spring. The pillars & bulls head frieze could never have been in a wall and the well could not have existed upon the Temple till the earth or Tufa had buried the original building—I have therefore little doubt that my theory will prove true. The water seems to be like the medicinal spring recently discovered by Gen. Nunziante[1]

1. This was General Vito Nunziante; see the memoir by his relative, Ferdinando Nunziante, 'Il Generale Vito Nunziante' 1775–1836 in *Archivo Storico per le Provincie Napoletane*, n.s. II (1962), 135–165; III (1963), 192–275. He was throughout keenly concerned with exploiting commercially the mineral wealth of the kingdom of Naples, in advance of others. He established an extraction

below. I conclude that the ancient baths will be found as they proceed. I have asked the General to do all that is possible to save the *AEdicola* which he told me he was in hopes of doing entire. In a few days it will be more exposed & I shall go & see it myself. At Pompeii beyond the house of the great Mosaic picture a *Vicolo* to the left has been opened & in it two skeletons were found seemingly caught together in the general ruins or precipitated as their heads were downwards. In the same *Vicolo* in little Shrines of their own are 3 or 4 *Phalli* which I have not yet seen but which are said to be curious.

Mr. Bulwer is departed this day by the steamer for Marseilles. Mr. Lockhart has never acknowledged the receipt of my *Scottiana* nor thanked me in any way for it, & I don't know whether he has published it, whereas Lady Blessington says it would be much sought for & give pleasure to many. I have sent her a copy desiring that if Mr. Lockhart has it not or does not use it She would sell it to the highest bidder & let it be published. I hear the life is published but that it is very scanty in one little Volume. People seem to think Lockhart is *una Bestia feroce* & that it is no wonder he has taken no notice of my compliance with Miss Scotts desire to write. I have supplied a few more anecdotes & probably could find as many more if I were to set about it. We are full of company & the stories of the Duke of Devonshires[1] illness in the papers is for the present untrue for he called on me today & only used a stick now & then. He shewed me a root of Ruby perhaps Zaphir more of the colour of pale Amethyst uncut, a hexagon Crystal two inches long. Mr. Ramsay says there were no fewer than six Lords at Church on Sunday but several of them are but small ones—Ranelagh,[2] Elliot,[3] Combermere[4] & Co. They don't do much for the public, but Lady Strachan has opened her new house with a tremendous Ball with the whole Court, fireworks, 2 Balloons etc.

---

of sulphur and alum on the island of Vulcano, and of other deposits of sulphur in Calabria; he was also responsible for draining the plain of Rosarno and the area of Modern Pescara; see *art. cit.* 265 ff.

1. Devonshire, William George Spencer Cavendish, 6th Duke of (1790–1858): died unmarried.

2. Ranelagh, Thomas Heron Jones, Baron Jones of Navan, 7th Earl and Viscount (1820–1877).

3. Eliot, Edward Granville, 4th Baron, later 3rd Earl of Saint Germans (1798–1877).

4. Combermere, Field-Marshall Sir Stapleton Cotton, 1st Viscount (1773–1865). G.C.B., C.H., G.T.S., K.S.F., K.S.I. Governor of Barbados, C-in-C India and Constable of the Tower of London.

etc. They say Rothschild[1] is resolved to eclipse her so we are likely to see sport. M^{rs}. Dodwell is become Countess Spaur & Bavarian Minister at Rome.[2] Chiavari writes that She is with child. I find the expected Courier has been here 3 months & no one knows when he will go so you must excuse this by post as Wilkinson alarms me by saying that my Book is printing. Where are the proofs of the map. I am already late for the post but believe me ever yours W. Gell finished Feb 6 1834

Rome 30 March, 9, 10 April 1834

My dear Sir,

I have delayed so long in sending You any thing relating to the Arts or Antiquities of Italy, the cause has been that during the winter at Naples nothing very interesting has been brought to light, but before I quitted Naples on the 25th of March I thought it would be right to inspect the operations at Pompeii & to look at Colonel Robinson & General Nunziantes excavations at the newly found mineral waters of La Torre. The Bank has been cut down facing the sea to the depth of 70 or 80 palms, & the substance was generally a thin coating of lava about 6 feet deep under which lay the *Tufa* which equally proceeded from Vesuvius. The remains of a great square building seemingly of Roman work has been discovered perhaps 30 feet above the sea. Only the exterior walls have yet been seen, but from some fragments of glass, ground on one side, I think there can be little doubt that the edifice has been a Bath erected for the sake of the Thermal waters now re-discovered—The glass is plate glass & was rendered not transparent by grinding, that persons upon the roof might not look down upon those who were bathing in the *Calidarium*—A *Calidarium* could not have existed without glass windows, on account of retaining the heat, & I found at Pompeii in the *Thermae* exactly similar bits of glass[3]—In an excavation which seems to have laid open a vaulted crypt the arches of which were supported by square piers was found the skeleton of a small child in a vase of rough pottery. The Mouth not having been large enough for the insertion of the body

1. A branch of this famous banking house had been established at Naples by Baron Carl Meyer Rothschild. See *The Rise of the House of Rothschild*, London, 1928.
2. See Dodwell, p. 41, n. 4.
3. Presumably in the Forum baths: cp. Nissen, *Pompeianische Studien*, 135.

the bottom of the Vase was knocked off & the Child placed as
You see in the

& the whole placed upon a piece of marble instead of the original
base. The whole edifice has been made up of fragments of still
more ancient buildings & there is nothing which seems of a good
Time or of good workmanship. In front of this building & containing mineral warm water on a level with the sea is a well,
down to which a passage & narrow flight of stairs has been cleared.
The well is built with Roman bricks & is circular above & pentagonal below. Out of this had been made those exaggerated reports
of five columns not one of which exists. There is however in the
wall of the passage the marble fragment of a Doric frieze not
horizontally placed but taken from some anciently ruined portico
& employed perpendicularly in the wall like any other stone. This
frieze had triglyphs & bulls heads & Rosone thus

but had nothing remarkable & out of this had been invented the
whole story of Doric columns. There was a supposed inscription
also in very soft stone reemployed, but on examining it I found
that it was not Roman nor Greek & if it were not merely scratched
with a pickaxe it had more resemblance to arabic than any other
writing, so that I began at the moment to imagine we might be
standing on the ruins of a Saracen Bath erected while the orientals
were in possession of Nocera. Nevertheless the fragments of letters
were not cufic which they would most probably have been in that
case but they were carved like those of modern Arabic.[1] The water
in the well is by analysis found to be precisely like that lately

1. Gell's careful observations here correct his earlier reports. Liberatore's article
also speaks of the five columns, inaccurately. The re-used fragment of Doric
frieze, and Gell's insistence on the re-used material elsewhere in the building,
are strong arguments for a late-imperial date for the whole complex: perhaps
third or fourth century A.D. (so also Maiuri, *op. cit.* 78). The presumed 'Arabic'
inscription remains a mystery.

discovered by boring & for the sake of which the Baths are now building—Having seen Colonel Robinson I can say that the whole story of his buying the land supposed to contain the Fleet is untrue, but he has negociated the permission to excavate. The Hopes of finding the Galleys are again revived for the Colonel has at length discovered the man who was said to have taken from one of the interred masts a hoop of iron. This man is a carpenter belonging to the Dockyard of Castellamare & deposes, that he himself sawed off the top of a mast which was discovered at the bottom of a well. He did this for the sake of an iron cap which was fitted onto the top of the mast in the way here shewn

& had rings affixed to it by which the Shrouds were fastened as I have here represented them—Not only this he found, but near it, the skeleton of two persons who had chains affixed to their legs & whom he considered as real Galley slaves of the time when the ship was buried—The masts if such they be are perfectly sound & not at all decayed, so that Colonel Robinson intends to fasten upon one of them a strong tackle with which he hopes to draw it out. He says if they are masts this will easily be done, but of course if they are trees with roots the thing will be impossible— This seems to be the real state of the case at present & I conclude as the subject had excited a great deal of interest in England not only the Dilettanti but many others through that Society will have pleasure in learning that any hopes which may have existed may be considered as more within the probability of realization than when I last wrote. At Pompeii several *Phalli* which had been covered with plaster & so hidden from view have been discovered by the plaster falling off this winter. Why they were hidden after they had been sculptured remains a mystery, perhaps the existence of these objects had an effect on the security of the house whether seen or not. In a newly found house with a doric court has been found a *Tablinum*[1] painted in black & high enough to have had a row of windows above the roof of the peristyle as I am persuaded they always had—in this upon a white ground are three pictures, one a sacrifice to Mars, another to ————(sic), & a third to Juno. The last is quite beautiful, consisting of winged cupids

1. Also in *Bullettino*, 1834, 141.

146

playing with a Peacock at the foot of a sort of Trophy dedicated to the Goddess. The excavation is now proceeding slowly towards the Gate of Nola in a line from the Temple of Fortune. The soil is very deep & the street seems to promise some good houses. The intrigues among the Supervisors & in general all those who are concerned in the excavations, to prevent strangers or even each other from drawing or measuring the Pompeian antiquities are incredible & the only object in making the discoveries would seem to be that of preventing them from being known or made use of by Antiquaries of any Nation whatever.—For a long time I endeavoured to take an account of every thing as it appeared, but now that works of expense can no longer be undertaken in England the necessary funds for evading these absurd dog in the manger practises, fail, & I cannot watch the excavations longer, for here all must be done by bribery. I will not close this without telling You what has been done in the Forum & procuring if I can a sight of the Head of Raffaello or the cast from it.—*April 9*—I have not been able to see Raphael's head,[1] but I find that it was not by the will that the body was discovered, on the contrary they dug in several places & even under the high altar & in all found bones confused—Under the statue however they found an arch walled up in the manner I have shewn in the other page

The back part of the skull was a little broken with its own weight. I hope to send You its phrenological qualities. I must now give You the account of the Forum & Clivus in the remaining bit of paper if possible as it is much talked of by Antiquaries. The road did not turn sharp round the western angle of the *Tabularium* but admitted another building, the *Athenaeum* of Adrian[2] at that place. This discovery has deranged all the Theories & the columns

1. Discovered when the Tomb was opened, see pp. 134–135.
2. Gell's sketch accompanying the name makes it clear that this is the *Portico* of the *Dei Consentes*, identified shortly after this time when its architrave inscription was recovered: *Bullettino*, 1835, 33 f. Gell's remarks on the poor work in the columns are fully justified; the surviving masonry is of late date.

now called *Tabularium* are found to have been a covered portico paved like a street with the *Tabularium* on a story above them. I wish that could be put in my book which I hear from Mr. Terrick is sold—Most truly yours

W. Gell.

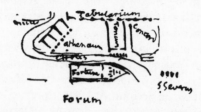

"I hope You will be able to understand this—3 rooms of the *Athenaeum* are dug out. The columns are of marble & corinthian— I suspect not good."

10 April. Please to judge whether it be worth while for the Society of Dilettanti to pay the postage for the information contained in this & do not read it if it be not likely to entertain them. Of course you know that the Royal Family of Naples is here & that 3 days after the holy week are [to] be dedicated to a sort of Jubilee for them.

Now that my paper is full I have got some account of the Etrurian Tour of Mr Jocelyn Percy[1] & Don Flavio Chigi.[2] At Toscanella[3] 3 sepulchres have produced 30 sarcophagi. At Cervetere[4] several *Tumuli* have been found to cover fine sepulchral chambers cut in the *Tufo*, not painted but of curious architecture; in one is a sort of foot stool. There are many of these *Tumuli* & they produce fine Vases.

Rome 19 April 1834

My dear Sir,

I write in the greatest hurry as I expect every moment a Courier of Col. Vyse who is to set out for Civita Vecchia this evening. I

1. Possibly Hon. Joscelin Percy, C.B. (1784–1850), 4th s. of Algernon Percy, 2nd Baron Lovaine of Alnwick and later 1st Earl of Beverley. M.P. for Beeralston, Devon 1806–20. Rear-Admiral 1841.
2. Chigi, principe Flavio, later Cardinal and Papal Nuncio at Paris.
3. Modern Tuscania. For these sarcophagi, *Bullettino*, 1834, 50.
4. At Caere the principe Ruspoli began his epoch-making excavations in this year: *Bullettino*, 1834, 49 f. and 97 f.

had already sent the Col a letter by him in which I had said much of what I have to say to You & am now in too great a hurry to say much more. I had rec^d a letter from Mr. Bulwer to say he had succeeded with Messrs. Saunders & Co & I heard a week ago from Don Terrick[1] that You had finally settled with those Authorities. I am very grateful for the long trouble You have had about it. I fear it arrives too late to save my Roman Villa which after my trees are grown up into groves & my garden is beautiful I cannot afford to keep if books wont sell. As to the Scott memoir, say nothing about it to Mr. Lockhart for I understand he is very sulky & says he has rec^d all the information previously from other hands— rather a difficult thing considering that our conversations generally took place in a carriage & only between us two. But Lady Blessington & Mr. Bulwer have got the M.S. between them & the Lady has made out that Lockhart does not mean to publish it, so I have left it to them to do what they like as it is a folly to lose what might be got for the said M.S. & to be besides unworthily treated. You English may be very moral for ought I know but I will say that whenever I have united with Literary persons for any literary purpose I have always been cheated & I have no doubt been abused after I had taken 9 10th of the whole trouble. Let him therefore alone—As to the *AEdicola* it is all come to an end by a personal examination but I have sent You an account of it by Post for I could find no other conveyance. The Courier is come. As you say the letters are well rec^d at the Dilettanti. I will write more in a short time for there are some circumstances which are interesting. Mr. Hare is just come in & sends Compliments. Believe me gratefully yours

W. Gell.

NAPLES June 3rd 1834

Caro mio—I received Your letter from Mr. Temple on my return to Naples. It contained as You say no good news with regard to the payment of the 300£ & a philippic instead against the accuracy of my M.S.S. which it appears You have at length discovered to be pretty nearly nonsense, & almost all contradictory. The last accusation I suppose may have been justified by the Authors

---

1. Hamilton, Terrick (1781–1876), y.s. of the Archdeacon of Colchester and bro. of W. R. Hamilton. Diplomat. Elected to the Society of Dilettanti 1830.

change of opinion, or understanding his subject better as he proceeded in the work—So that it be right at last it will do Messrs.
S & O [Saunders & Otler] good to employ a poor Scholar who
does not understand greek & Latin to overlook the M.S. & pretty
work he will make of it if You do not assist him & overlook him—
The Dilly Dandy [Society of Dilettanti] had originally engaged
to superintend that part of the business in London. The Lockhart
Scotts who want to make out that Sir Walter was a divine personage
& free from the faults or infirmities of human nature find my
anecdotes too true, though I have purposely, as they were written
for Miss Scott omitted everything which bordered on the ludicrous
—I believe that there was plenty of that in Sir Walters character
at all times for I now find that Hogg the Ettrick Shepherd[1] who
knew him well has written a great many anecdotes which shocked
the family, & which he has published in America. First I very
much doubt whether Sir Walter was a very extraordinary man, &
secondly if he were so I think the history of his decay must be
quite as interesting as the account of his glory, & would give an
air of truth to the account which it must want without it. The
account of Mr. Lockharts intentions as he has described them to
Lady Blessington I have from Her—The end therefore of the Life
of Lockhart will be vitiated by wanting truth in fact & in representation.

I went to Tivoli before I quitted Rome to see the new operations
upon the river. As it had not then rained for three months the heat
about the 20th of May was that usually experienced in August. The
hay had entirely failed, that is there was not the slightest attempt
at long grass & the cattle were turned out onto the lands usually
set apart for mowing—I remember Prince Poniatowsky[2] who
possessed a good deal of that sort of property about Rome saying
that the rent was always equal for if there was not a good crop
the price of hay rose in proportion, but this year there is
absolutely nothing. There has however been rain in the mountains
& I believe everywhere except in Campagna for I find this Kingdom
greener & more flourishing than I ever saw it before. At Tivoli the
government has undertaken at an enormous expense to cut two
channels in the form of gothic arches [sketch] in the hard limestone
rock of Mt Catillus. These begin about 100 yards above the old fall

1. Hogg, James (1770–1835). Scottish poet known as "The Ettrick Shepherd".
2. Possibly the son of Prince Joseph Poniatowski (Polish War Minister and
later Marshal of France) who was attached to the court of the Grand Duke of
Tuscany and who was created principe di Monte Rotondo.

of Bernini & are to conduct the Anio to a spot in the mountain about 100 yards below the temple & about level with it on the opposite Bank, whence it will fall in a tremendous flood into the old bed of the river, so as not in future to risk the undermining of the rock of Tivoli. This may however or may not be the consequence for the force will be prodigious. The old fall is to be filled up with rocks and earth which may be all accomplished till one of the usual floods takes place, when it remains to be seen how much of the river can be disposed of by means of two tunnels about 50 feet wide. On the whole it appears to me a terrible job but somebody will get rich by it. In the meantime the whole Town of Tivoli seems to be in a state of poverty & decadence almost unequalled even in the Roman State, & that is saying much. At Rome there is really an appearance of prosperity greater than usual as if money was to be had though they say there is not money to go on with for a month & they have at length pawned the customs which are their only dependence for daily bread. The houses however are white-washing without & rents are doubled within, & some of those ruinous little villas beyond the gates seem to be refitting & putting in order while the Piazza di Spagna which ought to be called Piazza d' Inghilterra is quite furbished up anew & 3 or 4 houses in the Town are rebuilding whereas I never recollect more than one at a time in other years—The fear of reproach for Nepotism has prevented the Popes from setting up their own families & adding a prince or a Palace to the holy city for several of the last reigns, & the newest of the Nepoti, Braschi, is quickly returning to the penny & oblivion whence the family sprang. It appears that some of Pope Braschis[1] purchases were not well made & that there are reclaimations of consequence. The later Popes have enriched paviours, valets & such sort of people, who soon vanish without any permanent good to the City or the state. What is curious is that almost all the *Mercanti di Campagna* who ruled the public in matter of provisions are notwithstanding their own monopoly Bankrupts. The Villa Borghese[2] is so changed that You would not know it again—First we have close to the Porta del Popolo a magnificent entrance with a lake or a broad avenue. The gate is [sketch] a pretty exact copy of our *propyleum* of Minerva Polias at Priene twice over & the effect would be good had not the

1. Pius VI (1775–1799). The palazzo Braschi fills the whole of one side of the *piazza S. Pantaleo* and was built in 1780 for the nephew of Pius VI—it now houses the *Museo di Roma*.
2. Being rebuilt at this time to the plans of Luigi Canina.

architect forgotten the wall between the fronts & made a transparency of the whole like the late & much abused colonnade at Carlton House. Thus [sketch] instead of [sketch] The consequence is that the whole appears an unreal mockery & on approaching the gate from the interior of the Villa the windows of the opposite English chapel & Fenili [sic] seem to adjust themselves between the pillars of the Borghese colonnade. The Prince has taken a great taste for the Villa & passes there in improvements the greater part of the day. Moreover the drives for the public are to be prolonged into other parts of the Park & Raffaells house & a great deal more land is already added to the original plan. In our Kingdom Capua has capitulated to escape the sacking & ravishing that would have evoked from a more obstinate resistance & the two armies during an armistice had a *fête champêtre* under the trees at Carditello which was as I hear very pretty & not productive of anything more than Wineshed.[1] Our King whose habits of frugality are so praiseworthy in these degenerate times had occasion to go on a day of *fête* to Naples, & kindly told Filangieri[2] that his Tent & conveniences were at his disposal if he had a mind to ask his friends to dinner. The General invited some 40 to this Royal feast, but when the morning arrived he discovered that only the Royal pots, pans & dishes & plates, were at his disposal & that what was to be eaten on them must be procured & paid for by himself. However the Guests were invited & there was no remedy, so he paid dearly for his honours, & returned shortly after to the Capital crowned with laurels.

There came at last rain to refresh Rome & restore the climate to its usual state in May & on the road I found the dust laid & the heat never oppressive. The corn in the Campagna was stunted & the ears only half size but here everything is flourishing. I tried to stop at Fondi to examine the palace of Giulia Gonzaga & the affair of the Barbarossa.[3] I really found a Coffeehouse called & inscribed *Caffè di Barbarossa* which is historic, & I went & drew

1. An insurrection nad been planned for August 1834, to break out in revolts in Capua, Salerno and Aquila; it was forestalled by the arrest of the ringleaders. Gell refers to events that are apparently connected with it.
2. Filangieri, conte Carlo, principe di Satriano and duca di Taormina (1784–1867).
3. The Corsair, Ariadeno Barbarossa, after landing at and devastating Sperlonga, besieged Fondi on the night of 5–6 August 1534. He wished to carry off the famous beauty, Giulia Gonzaga, wife of Vespasiano Colonna, and take her as a gift to the Sultan. However she succeeded in escaping and fled to her other estates either at Campodimele or Vallecorsa.

& examined the window whence the Countess escaped in her shift and about which I mean to write a Romance when I come of age. Such a set of people I never met with even in Greece & I drew what I wanted with the utmost difficulty though I was protected by Doctor Sotis chief Physician of the Town to whom I was recommended by the Archbishop of Taranto. I wrote to You about Raffaeles skull & with some difficulty & negociation, as a mystery & a favour was made of it, Dr. Verity[1] got a sight of the cast which was taken from the original—As to the other head, it is known to be that of Don Desiderio the founder of St Lukes academy.[2] Dr. Verity will publish his remarks on the skull, so in the meantime I send You a few of his observations for the benefit of Your Constituents who may be interested in such researches, premising that No 10 is the medium of all the qualities & that what exceeds 10 is considered a full quantity & all below 10 is small—Amativeness 18—Philoprogenitiveness 16—Concentration 16. Adhesiveness 16—Combativeness $16\frac{1}{2}$—Destructiveness $14\frac{1}{2}$. Secretiveness 19—Construction 16—Selfesteem $15\frac{1}{2}$—Love of Approbation 18—Caution $17\frac{1}{2}$—Benevolence 10—Veneration $15\frac{1}{2}$ —Firmness Conscientioness & Wonder each 15—The skull by no means large & Hope only $14\frac{1}{2}$. We had a very curious examination of Thorwaldsen[3] at my house. He has one of the largest heads ever seen & has very little imagination veneration or hope all which would have made him a better Sculptor in all probability. Let us hope neither You nor Your friends care about phrenology & what a bore You will think it. I was much amused with the remark upon Terrick by the Doctor who had no idea of his pecularities. He was found to have very little conscientiousness or hope "which in You Sir are likely to produce a disposition to dispute and argument in conversation." Terrick himself burst into a fit of laughter at hearing so true a description of himself & of course denied the science which Combe says all who want these two qualities are sure to do—I

1. Verity, Dr. Robert. Author of *Changes produced in the Nervous System by Civilization, considered according to evidence of physicology and the philosophy of History*. London, James Leach, 1851. Dr. Verity was summoned by Lady Cowper to go to Madrid to attend her son, Viscount Fordwick who had been taken ill when staying with his uncle, Hon. Frederick Lamb. (*Letters of Lady Palmerston*, ed. Tresham Lever-London, 1957, p. 153).

The *Accademia di S. Luca* was founded in 1577 by Frederigo Zuccari. Gell's reference to 'Don Desiderio' is not understood.

3. Thorwaldsen, Albert Bertel (1770–1844). Sculptor who lived at Rome 1797–1819.

remember however that You patronized Dr Baillie[1] at Rome of whom someone said "If you want to know Mr. Hamiltons opinion of You You may learn it from Dr. Baillie." Lady Coventry[2] calls Terrick Sir Cerberus, & he is just gone to Florence after a trip to Palestrina which he declares to be a mere humbug & as to the walls they were built very ill by Dodwell by way of supporting a theory which he had conceived. I forgot to say that at Tivoli in digging for the Tunnel[3] they had found a number of sepulchres with inscriptions & a very great quantity of *opus reticulatum* supporting the Via Valeria, & a bridge two arches of which remain above Bernini's fall, but the whole was curiously buried under the soil, though now restored to daylight. I never saw so much of the *opus*— You are aware that the Anio threatened to undermine the Temple on which account & for fear of more damage to the Town they say the new works are undertaken. I hope also that You understand that the river anciently formed a lake or *Barathrum* under the Temple when the *Grotta* of Neptune was all under water, but a great flood burst the dam which held up the pool between the Sibyl & Vopiscus & left the pool & *Grotta* nearly dry by which means the fall was divided into 2, one above & one below the Temple. My paper is ended & how glad You must be for You are tired of reading & my letter is too discursive & too little redolent of Art to entertain the D.S. at least in my own language. Therefore it rests with You to retail the facts to those whom they may concern & thus saying these words the blessed Saint expires.

Ever yours

W.G.

March 10th 1835
[Heading with engraving of Maison de Tasso a Sorrento] (Pl. XIIIa)

I have been waiting for some centuries to inform You of the arrival of the ship with the Books from Messrs. Saunders & Co & also till the 15th of February was well passed when we shall have a right to touch 150£ of the Money—Of the books You should have taken Your copy & the Colonel Vyse his before they were

---

1. Baillie, Dr. Matthew. Physician who attended George III from 1810 to 1820. Lady Charlotte Bury (*op. cit.*, vol. ii, p. 16) records Dr. Baillie's comments on the skull of Samuel Whitbread (1765–1815) after his suicide.
2. Coventry, Countess of, see *Appendix* C, n. 3.
3. For the finds made while driving a tunnel under the tall spur on which the Temple of Hercules stands, cp. *Bullettino*, 1834, 161 f.

packed up for Naples which I thought was a matter of course. They are, as I hear safely arrived in the post & undergoing quarantine. Shall I send You copy & Col. Vyses home again, or would that cost more than they are worth or how can I make You my donation in the best way, the mistake being committed? Answer this—I have seen Auldjo's copy & think altogether the Book is as well got up & looks as creditable as one could expect in these hard times, when if things hold together at all one has reason to be thankful. I was highly flattered in my old age by Bulwers dedication of his Pompeii[1] to me & think the Book itself is as well fitted to the place as circumstances permitted. I own I consider the Tragic Poets house since I read the novel, as that of Glaucus & have peopled the other places with Bulwers inhabitants in my own mind which I believe is a proof that his Tale is judiciously applied to the locality. I wish the blind Girl however had not seen sometimes so much better than the rest of the world. With regard to Your Villa of Pollio in the sea at Posilippo Mr. Laing Meeson made plans & elevations & sections of the whole with an Architect who drew everything out in a regular manner. His Son might give You the papers as he has I imagine no taste for such matters. I once went & drew it for Sir Walter Scott & as I have heard some of the building has fallen down since. The Talbots called it the *Casa degli Spiriti* but I know not where they found the story of the Ghost. If I ever get well enough however I will attack the place again & send You the result. I sent You at the time of the great eruption an account of what took place near Ottajano. Of course we expected an account by Monticelli or some of the Big Wigs, but none that I have yet heard of has ever appeared & Auldjo who is wet nurse to the mountain was in England. My account therefore of what I saw is the best I have yet seen. I hope You received it, for You have not mentioned the having done so. They are working at Capri, but though all Their geese are like Dr. Clarkes Swans, I have not yet heard of any thing of importance being found. At Pompeii they have done something at the Street called that of Fortune & have almost cleared a new house between that of the Faun & the great Mosaic of Alexander & the Wall. There is in it a fine peristyle the columns of which were I believe all overthrown but they have been re erected & make a great shew. In the Street of Fortune some 5 or 6 great houses have been excavated with pictures & pavements. Some of the pictures are of

1. *The Last Days of Pompeii* (1834).

great merit, one of Perseus shewing the head of Medusa & Andromeda[1] reflected in the water is touched in the style of Titian & some which seem portraits are finely executed or rather were for they are now very much reduced in value by the admission of the air. Some of these I have managed to copy & may possibly save from entire oblivion if times should improve in England, but the chief object of those who now rule in Pompeii seems to be the preventing of the fruits of the Excavation from being useful or ornamental to themselves or others. There is the largest painting yet seen in one of the houses,[2] but by no means the best. The subject is a hunt of beasts with the horizon taken very high. A man fights a Boar, a Lion, a Bull etc.—Near this is a little crooked *Vicus* which has in it five or 6 *phalli* visible on the Walls. I intend sometime or other to shew that such was the Sign of high Pelasgic nobility. I fear the Baths at La Torre have now lost their reputation though General Nunziante has spent a great deal of money in erecting baths & accommodation, but I have heard of no cures this year. Do I beg You get the money from the Bookseller pay 100£ of it to Colonel Vyse with many thanks from me—Somebody in one or two of the Reviews has spoken very kindly of the work & I am much obliged to them—Nunziante by the bye who is always digging & boring has found a rock of fine white marble near Policastro[3] with a descent to the sea & in the Abruzzi he has discovered quantities of coal, petroleum & sulphur, the latter strangely mixed. The coal is very fine but as yet only in knots & masses like waggon loads & called in England loads. You can have no idea of the improvements in the City. Chiaja is now all as wide as it used to be in the widest part & I should think if it were ever finished it would be the finest thing in Europe. It is now in a wonderful Chaotic state with hundreds of workmen & millions of stones & clouds of dust. I was in a tolerable state of health or rather of suffering till about a month ago when my Gout seemed to take a turn into Asthma & Dropsy which was no change for the better & which I am inclined to think ill of. The only doubt is whether it was discovered in time or only too late, the Doctors as I hear & Dr. Heath who is with the Ponsonbys think they can do me good. By the bye I see from Wm Ponsonby[4] that the

1. From the *Casa di Arianna*, cf. above, p. 137.
2. From the *Casa della Caccia*. Helbig, *Wandgemälde* 1520.
3. Actually near Lagonegro, see F. Nunziante, *Archivo Storico per le Provincie Napoletane*, 1963, 270 for details.
4. Ponsonby, Hon. William (1787–1855), 3rd s. of 3rd Earl of Bessborough. Created Baron de Mauley 1838. Elected to the Society of Dilettanti 1821.

Whigs are terribly alarmed at their own works & M[r] Ellies[1] was no less so. We have had Tories & among them L[d] Stanhope.[2] What a crisis things seem to be in. Kind regards to Mrs Hamilton & all the family & pray believe me most truly & faithfully

Yours

W.G.

Naples March 25 1835

It was most provoking that under pretence of Cholera the letters were just withheld till I had sent mine off to You when Your last with the account of the payment & Your permission to draw on You arrived. I have now under the advice of Cotterell who is supposed to understand such matters sent to Colonel Howard Vyse a letter with a draft on You for one hundred pounds to pay him what I owed him upon the Work, & I have given a draft to Cotterell & Iggulden[3] the Bankers here upon You for the remaining 50£ for my own use. I trust this will not be inconvenient but is as nearly as may be the way in which You directed me to proceed. As I wrote to You so lately as the day before yesterday I am not likely to give You much news, but the Mountain has broken out on the side opposite La Torre & the last time I saw it a long line of smoke shewed that the lava was already at the foot of the cone. The eruption is yet going on & this is its third day, & John Auldjo as high priest of Vesuvius is visiting & examining both night & day with a troop of *dilettanti*. The box of books from Messrs Saunders & Otley really did come by the Ship *Swallow* & arrived safe at Naples. I am quite sorry You did not at least take Your copy & give the Colonel his before mine set out for I see no manner by which they could ever return now.

The other day there was a most fortunate *Scavo* at Pompeii, I don't exactly know where.[4] Two good sized drinking cups of Silver were found with figures in high relief. Twelve smaller ones

---

1. Probably Rt. Hon. Edward 'Bear' Ellice (1781–1863), m. 1809 Lady Hannah Althea Bellesworth, sister of 2nd Earl Grey. Politician.
2. Stanhope, Philip Henry, 4th Earl (1781–1855).
3. Cotterell and Company were wine merchants and bankers at Naples whose London agents were Bingham, Richards and Company, 8 Kings Arms Yard, Coleman Street, E.C.2.
4. These were a hoard of silver vessels, found in the house called the *Casa dell' Argenteria* (VI, viii, 21–22). *Bullettino*, 1835, 38 f.; *PAH*, ii, 304 f.

of Silver & some 29 Coins among which they pretend were two or 3 others in gold which were once so rare that one of Copper sold for 20£. These articles are described as a great prize but I have not yet seen them myself. Winter as usual is doing all it can to encroach upon the months of spring & though the poplar buds are bursting there is no hope at present of any great change likely to be useful to invalids, & I am told, to myself, who labour under an asthmatic dropsical gout without any organic defect. We have had here Captain Lyon[1] who means to swim down the Euphrates & has taken Malta in the way. I have a letter from Theodora Makri[2] nee Vitali at Athens who says Athens is indeed the Capital & the residence of the King who gives Balls & makes the world very agreeable to the inhabitants who are building & flourishing— Tupper, a Guernsey man, & friend of Cockerells[3] is married & here on his way to Athens to see how things go on in the new regime. Gen. Church[4] was at Athens but his employment is not mentioned nor how he goes on without money since the Russians would not receive him. When the Bavarian loan is gone we shall see how things turn out, in the meantime Gropius[5] owes me 600£, in hard cash which has now I believe positively the fact. I have done all I can to direct Travellers to the Zerynthian Cave in the Island of Samothrace, which was the headquarters of the Pelasgi & where I expect to find something very historic & very antiquated written in a sort of Osco-Etruscan Alphabet. I see one of the reviews is highly pleased with my researches, the next however will [paper torn & missing] be angry so one may as well be quiet. What

---

1. Lyon, Capt. George Francis (1795–1832). R.N. and traveller. Was in command of *Berwick* at Siege of Gaeta 1815. Later went on expedition to Tripoli and North Africa and wrote *A Narrative of Travels in North Africa in the years 1818, 1819, 1820.* Oxford 1825. He m. 1825 Lucy Louisa d. of Lord Edward Fitzgerald, s. of 1st Duke of Leinster.

2. Macri, Theodora. A widow with 3 daus., Teresa, Mariana and Katinka with whom Byron and Cam Hobhouse lodged at Athens. It was to Teresa that Byron wrote *The Maid of Athens*. She was only 13 when Byron met her.

3. Cockerell, Charles Robert (1788–1863). Architect, archaeologist and author. Travelled in Italy, Greece and the Levant, and m. 1828 Anna Maria d. of John Rennie.

4. Church, General Sir Richard (1784–1873). British Military Resident in Italian army against Murat and became Governor of the two Provinces of Bari and Otranto—commanded the Greek forces in the War of Independence and later defended the Ionian Islands.

5. Gropius, Georg. Prussian painter and vice-consul at Athens. See Adolf Michaelis: *Ein Jahrhundert kunstarchäologischer Entdeckungen*, 2. edition Leipzig 1908, p. 34 f.

say the Dilettanti? Poor Sothebys death though one expected it is unpleasant. I believe he was tolerably old. The Archbishop of Taranto is 93 & 6 months & is quite well as is Matthias at 85 who has just been in & sends his love to You.

Believe me ever

Most truly Yours

W. Gell.

Appendix A

John Auldjo's Account of the Cruise of the Neopolitan steam-packet Francesco Primo *from Constantinople to Naples in 1833.*[1]

John Auldjo left Naples on 6 April 1833 in H.M.S. *Actaeon* which was carrying Lord Ponsonby[2] to Constantinople to take up his post as H.B.M. Ambassador there. After visiting various places in Greece, the ship reached Constantinople on 1 May. Auldjo remained there for more than a month and gives a very interesting and often amusing account of life at the Supreme Porte.

On Sunday 9 June Auldjo went down to Pera and found the steam-paddle-boat *Fransesco Primo* lying proudly in the centre of the Horn. 'At the Consul's I found Taylor, and near the house, Lord Wiltshire,[3] Ruddel, and Hatfield: every lodging-house, every thing which went by the name of an *albergo* was occupied; and such an immigration of visitors (sic) with purses full of money, and pockets crammed with note books, had probably never happened in Stamboul before. The Prince of Bavaria[4] and his suite occupied the Palace of Austria.' Auldjo acted as *cicerone* to the travellers who, as well as visiting the sights of the city, went for a short cruise into the Black Sea. The Austrian Ambassador[5] gave a grand fête, dinner and ball in honour of the Prince of Bavaria, but 'all attempts have failed to procure him an audience of the Sultan, who will not receive him, because he says, naturally enough, "What has he to do

---

1. *Journal of a Visit to Constantinople and some of the Greek Islands in the Spring and Summer of 1833*, by John Auldjo, Esq; F.G.S. London, Longman, Rees, Orme, Brown, Green & Longman, 1835.
2. See p. 55, n. 4.
3. Wiltshire, John Paulet, Earl of (1801–1887), suc. as 14th Marquess of Winchester 1843 m. Mary d. of Henry Montague, 6th Baron Rokeby of Armagh.
4. Maximillian (1811–1864), son of Louis 1, Kg. of Bavaria and Theresa of Saxe-Hildburghausen who succeeded as Maximilian 11 on the abdication of his father in 1848. As Crown Prince he gathered around him at Hohenschwangau near Füssen an intimate society of artists and men of learning, and devoted himself to scientific and historical studies. He married Maria Hedwig d. of Prince William of Prussia and had 2 sons.
5. Freiherr Bartholomaeus von Stürmer. Austrian Ambassador at Constantinople 1832–50—raised to rank of Count 1842.

with me, or I with him? He is a brother of the King of Greece[1] granted: but why come to intrude himself here? I will not see him; it can do no good." '

On Sunday 16 June the Prince reviewed the Russian troops who were encamped on the 'Giant's Mountain' on the opposite side of the Bospheros. He was received by a guard of honour; Count Orloff,[2] the general, and a staff of officers superbly dressed in Polish, Russian and Turkish uniforms.

Since *Actaeon* was remaining some time longer in port, Auldjo decided to return to Naples in *Francesco Primo* and they left Stamboul on Sunday 23rd. 'What a motley crew! A royal prince; Spanish nobles; Italian counts; French marquises; Dutch chevaliers, and, I may proudly add, English gentlemen. We had also a quack doctor from Paris; a gaming-house-keeper from Milan; a clergyman, poor as an Apostle, from Iceland, a grim-looking student from the University of Göttingen; a Danish baron, music-mad; a singing count from Sienna (sic); a crazy architect from Paris; and two Russian noblemen. There were only two ladies;—a Russian countess, who read nothing but Homer, and made classical mistakes; and a Bavarian lady; whose great merit was her inclination to render herself agreeable. Then there were the chief Captain, the second captain, and the sub-captain; the manager, second manager, and sub-manager. However, two things most necessary to the establishment were still wanting; namely, a good cook, and an honest steward.'

'The vessel carried a Neopolitan pennant, and was armed with six brass cannon, a very sufficient stand of small-arms, and a Forest of boarding-pikes, in case we should be attacked by any of the pirates infesting the Greek Archipelago. An awning was spread over its spacious deck, under which we lived like a swarm of flies, fifty in number, feeding on detestable provender, and sleeping in beds remarkable for uncleanness and their innumerable parasitical tenants!'

On the 25th they arrived in Smyrna and 'as soon as we came in sight of the *Madagascar*, which was lying in the harbour or roadstead of Smyrna, a boat put off from it towards the steam-vessel, and in a few moments the King of Greece was in the arms of his brother.' The Prince thereupon transferred with all his suite to the *Madagascar* and the royal pair left together on a short cruise. The travellers remained at Smyrna until the 30th, then sailed for Chios and Syra where they put in the next day and were immediately ordered into quarantine for 7 days. The King and

1. See p. 101.
2. Orloff or Orlov, Prince Alexis Fedorovich (1787–1862). Russian statesman; took part in the Napoleonic Wars from 1805 to Siege of Paris and was in Turkish War of 1828–29 when he rose to rank of Lieut. general. Was Russian plenipotentiary at Peace of Adrianople and appointed Russian Ambassador at Constantinople in 1833, at the same time holding appointment as commander-in-chief of the Black Sea Fleet.

Prince had already arrived. In the evening of 3 July a grand festival and ball took place, the *Madagascar* sailing immediately afterwards. 'It seems rather extraordinary that the Prince of Bavaria had not the inclination, as he certainly had the power, to put off these fêtes until the passengers of the *Francesco*, with whom he had sailed for two months, and to whom he was now under some obligation, could have participated in them.'

The travellers left on 6 July for Tinos, Mykonos, Naxos and Antiparos. Auldjo here devotes many pages to a vivid description of the expedition that was made to the remarkable grotto at Antiparos. 'Close under the western shore, where the island of Paros terminates in bold perpendicular cliffs, lay the little island of Spotico; while all around, the sea bristled with rocks as far as the eye could reach. On one side of a steep path, which we were now slowly ascending, the guides pointed out a huge fissure or break in the rock, which they said was the platform in front of the grotto. At the further end of this cavern, behind a vast stalactite, reaching from the roof to the ground, and suggesting to the imagination the idea of some gigantic sentinel before the pit of Acheron, yawned a low narrow opening, the interior of which presented to the view a more than Egyptian darkness. Around this spot were assembled a band of Kirtled Greeks, provided with ropes, ladders, and flambeaux. Our appearance was the signal for a general uproar: each commenced talking, screaming, and fighting for possession of the ladies, and every now and then edging in a word of French or English, by way of additional recommendation.' The exploration of this most interesting and often rather frightening cavern took many hours since the party left the ship at 4 a.m. and did not embark again until 11 p.m. Auldjo ends his fascinating account by remarking, 'I am not a little surprised that the two ladies who accompanied the party had courage to descend to such a place. In my opinion, excursions like these are by no means adapted to either the mental or corporeal delicacy of the fair sex; and, however disagreeable the position might have momentarily proved to them, it was impossible to witness the tall slender figure of one of them, grasped in the arms of a bearded swarthy Greek, now squeezed against the wall now almost astride upon his shoulders, without indulging in the laughter such a spectacle was well calculated to inspire.'

Proceeding on their journey, the travellers came to Melos on the 9th where they were joined by the Royal party in *Madagascar*. Auldjo was invited on board in the evening and appears to have 'enjoyed a pleasant *confab* with the officers.' However, he remarks, 'There is a striking difference in the temper and dispositions of the two royal brothers; the one being greatly beloved, while the other is disliked by every person in the ship. The King is very kind and affable, giving no unnecessary trouble, and mixing freely with the midshipmen and sailors: many a luncheon has he partaken of in the *den* of the former. His brother, on the contrary, is all fuss and superciliousness: and the very first morning after he embarked, the captain was compelled to read him a practical lecture on the necessity of complying with the established regulations.' It seems the Prince had appeared for breakfast $1\frac{1}{2}$ hours late whereupon the Captain merely remarked that he 'was sorry he had lost his breakfast, particularly as it was a long time to dinner, and the regulations of the ship precluded his having any meal served before that was ready. The Prince frowned and looked marvellously discomfited; but, pocketing his lecture, he made an apology, and went sulkily on deck.'

The next day the King and Prince parted, the latter re-embarking in *Francesco Primo* and the King returning to Nauplia. The steam-packet then sailed on her way via Cerigo, Cape Matapan and the Gulf of Coron to Zante where they refuelled and landed ten passengers; four of them British officers belonging to the garrison of Corfu, and the other six, being disgusted with the boat, thought they would better themselves by transferring to another steamer bound for Ancona. Early in the morning of the 14th, the ship was in sight of the Calabrian mountains and in the afternoon entered the harbour at Syracuse. After a few hours delay the ship left in a gale for Malta where she arrived and passed into quarantine at 10 o'clock in the morning of 15 July. The whole of the great *Lazzaretto* was prepared for the travellers who 'landed in a hurry; the object of every one being to secure a good room for himself, as, with a piece of chalk in hand, he wandered through the vast corridors of this immense building.' The Prince of Bavaria was accommodated in Fort Emanuel—'His Royal Highness never deigned to visit us; indeed, it could hardly be expected he should do so, when he did not even condescend to pay his respects to the ladies in the fort, or the party there established, though living within the same walls himself.' On 30 July Auldjo says he 'rose early, for the steam-packet from Corfu had arrived in the night, and, lo! all the passengers who quitted us at Zanta were on board her.' The expected steam-boat for Ancona had met with an accident at sea and, although passing within sight of Zanta, did not put in.

July 31 saw great festivity at Valletta. 'His Excellency the Governor[1] entertained His R.H. the Prince of Bavaria, the Prince of Butera,[2] other noblemen and gentlemen, and passengers in the steamer, at a grand dinner at the palace.'

The whole of the garrison was afterwards reviewed on the Florian parade; 'and, certainly, in no quarter of the world could a finer body of troops be seen, than those composing the garrison of Malta; consisting of a detachment of the Royal Artillery, the Royal Fusileers (sic), the Royal Highlanders, the 73rd and 94th regiments, and the Royal Malta Fencibles.'

---

1. Major-General the Hon. Sir Frederick Cavendish Ponsonby (1783–1837). He m. Lady Emily Charlotte, y.d. of Henry, 3rd Earl Bathurst in 1825. Was Governor of Malta 1826–35. Lady Emily Ponsonby d. in 1877.
2. See p. 97.

'In the evening, Lady Briggs[1] gave a magnificent ball, at which His R.H. the hereditary Prince of Bavaria, Prince Butera of Sicily, and the other *distinguished* personages who came by the steamer, were present.'

Auldjo relates that 'the whole garrison was greatly offended at the conduct of the Prince (who seems to have been a detestable character), who never acknowledged the salute of the officers, nor the lowering of the colours to the ground in passing his royal person. Every one besides stood uncovered, and the populace cheered loudly, while he displayed a sort of contemptuous indifference, and remained motionless as a statue.'

On 1 August the *Francesco Primo* sailed for Alicata where the Prince of Butera, who had estates in the neighbourhood, was landed, the steam-boat proceeding on to Girgenti where, half-an-hour after midnight, the travellers set off to visit the temples by 'that light, "which mingles dark shadows into gentleness".' In spite of a fine, clear night with the moon shining with an intensity of light, and after rambling across the country and getting lost in olive groves, the party were at last obliged to take a guide. While they were still visiting the temples the Eastern sky began 'brightening with the beams of the morning sun, and its reflection tints each mouldering column with a purple light. The moon slowly resigns her influence over the scene, and a splendid prospect of earth and sea bursts upon the eye, as the sun springs upwards from behind the ruins, like the presiding deity of the spot.' And so the travellers were privileged to see these magnificent temples both by the light of the moon and of the rising sun. It must have been an unforgettable experience.

The prince of Butera rejoined the party on the evening of 2 August having come overland from Alicata and the ship sailed for Palermo which was reached the next evening. They were too late in arriving to obtain *pratique* and 'had to endure the mortification of hearing the hum of enjoyment arising from every part of this gay city, without the possibility of being partakers in the amusements going forward. The marina was well illuminated, and the distant sound of music, which ever and anon came softened over the waves, communicated an air of enchangement to the scene.' However, they landed early the next morning and Auldjo established himself in an hotel where, two years before, he had spent a pleasant fortnight. He writes that 'after visiting every object of curiosity in Palermo, I surrendered myself to that pleasing indolence in which every one appears more or less to indulge. Nevertheless I could not resist the temptation of making an excursion to Prince Butera's villa, in order to catch a glimpse of her who had soared so high and sunk so low (duchesse de Berri).[2] She came to the window while we were in the

---

1. Wife of Admiral Sir Thomas Briggs (1780–1852). The Ball was given to celebrate the award of the G.C.M.G. to the Admiral.
2. Berri, Maria Carolina Ferdinanda Luisa, duchesse de (1798–1870), elder d. of Francis I, Kg. of the Two Sicilies. She m. 1816 Charles Ferdinand de Bourbon, duc de Berri, 2nd s. of Comte d'Artois later Charles X. The duc de Berri was

garden; and a Carlist, who formed one of our party, seemed to gaze at her as though she had been a deity. A dispute having arisen about some trivial circumstance, she stormed with rage, and her gesticulations were perfectly furious. She is a perfect Neopolitan.'

The Duchess later expressed a wish to go to Naples and the *Francesco Primo* delayed departure for a day or two to suit her convenience. Eventually, on Friday 9 August 'we bade adieu to Sicily. The Duchess came on board with her husband and suite, Count Menars,[1] and the Prince and Princess. Her face is by no means a handsome one; and she is very short, thin, and vulgar-looking. Nothing in her personal appearance marks her out for a heroine, or is calculated to inspire her followers with the awe and respect with which they seem to worship her. She soon sat down to whist with her husband, Butera, and the old Princess St. Theodora,[2] but the game received many unpleasant interruptions from the pitching and rolling of the boat. Each time the fit came on, she sprang upon the bench on which she had been sitting, and, after bending her head *sans ceremonie* over the vessel's side, quietly sat down again to resume her cards. This rather unroyal and unlady-like exhibition occurred repeatedly, and we were impressed with the idea that her manners altogether were very unfitting her rank and station.' Later Auldjo reports the calming of the seas and says, 'The heroine of La Vendée is sleeping in her arm-chair; the faithful Menars reposes at her feet; and her husband, whom she hardly seems to notice, is sitting on a bench beside her.'

---

assassinated in 1820 and the duchesse gave birth to a posthumous son later that year (she had borne a daughter earlier). The baby was christened duc de Bordeaux but later was usually known as the comte de Chambord, and as Henri V was Kg. of France for 1 day on the abdication of his grand-father in 1830. The duchesse de Berri and her children followed Charles X into exile in England, but she was determined to recover the throne for her son. She grew bored with exile at Holyrood House and returned to Italy leaving her children behind; however in April 1832 she returned to France and disguised as a servant entered the regions of La Vendée and Brittany to rouse the loyal inhabitants to rebellion. Her followers were defeated and, after remaining concealed in a house at Nantes for 5 months, she was betrayed and imprisoned in the Fortress of Blaye. It soon became evident that she was pregnant and she then acknowledged a secret marriage with conte Ettore Lucchesi Palli, principe di Campofranco (1806–1864), a member of the royal household of the Kg. of the Two Sicilies. After the birth of a daughter, she was released and returned to Sicily. The Berri children were brought up by their childless aunt, the duchesse d'Angoulême and made their home with her at Frohsdorf near Vienna.

1. Mesnard, Louis–Charles–Bonaventure–Pierre, comte de (1769–1842). 1814 aide-de-camp to duc de Berri and was with him when he was assassinated. Accompanied the duchesse de Berri into exile in England, and re-entered her service as chamberlain after she had been released from the castle of Blaye, remaining with her in Italy. He returned to France in 1840.

2. See p. 101.

The next day, 10 August, they sighted Capri and after four months of travels, Auldjo sailed back again into the Bay of Naples—one presumes that the Prince of Bavaria remained at Malta since neither Auldjo nor Gell report his returning to Naples.

Appendix B

*A Sketch of the Character of Sir William Gell, by James Ramsay, Esq.**

'The merits of Sir William Gell as an author, chiefly on subjects of antiquity and topography, are already sufficiently known and appreciated by the public. The fruits of much patient research, of ingenious conjecture, of great personal activity and industry, with admirable graphic illustrations, his works are valuable helps to the student, and an accurate guide for the traveler. In attempting the more difficult task of delineating his general and private character, as deduced from an inter-course of many years, if I am conscious of any bias, it must be in favor of one with whom I have spent so many delightful hours, unalloyed by the recollection of even a passing cloud; for to me he was uniformly kind and attentive. Yet I will endeavor to be impartial, though at the hazard of incurring the reproach of being rather severe.

'Sir William started in life with the advantages of a handsome person— of a fine, open, placid countenance—of a prepossessing manner—of a remote ancestry, and of an extensive connection with the best society. He traveled at a period when travelers were rare, and thus early acquired a distinction which he continued to maintain. Possessing general, though superficial information, both literary and scientific, including some acquaintance with the Oriental languages and hieroglyphics, he sketched beautifully, had a taste for and some knowledge of music, and excelled as an easy, off-hand, unaffected correspondent; indifferent, indeed in-sensible, to the graces of composition, yet universally courted for a style of *naïveté* "beyond the reach of art". Although, however, led by the course of his studies into classical inquiry and reference, the character of a profound scholar will not be assigned to him, notwithstanding his general reading; he had little taste for literature, and never seemed to feel the beauties of poetry. I should say, indeed, that, in other respects, his taste—meaning by this term a delicate and just perception of the beautiful —was far from being refined, and that that defect was apparent in all, even his personal decorations, by a preference for gay, gaudy colors, striking contrasts, and meretricious ornament.

'To the depth of thought Sir William would have no just pretensions. He rarely made a general reflection or observation; all his conclusions were particular. On many of the important questions by which the world is now agitated, he had no steady, fixed opinions; he had neither the boldness to form, nor the courage to avow his sentiments, which were very liable to be temporarily influenced by the last speaker, the last writer.

'In his political principles he was decidedly aristocratical, with a strong predilection for "rank, fortune, and fashion," our besetting sin!

'But it is in a companionable, sociable point of view that the memory of Sir William Gell will be most fondly cherished, his loss most deeply lamented by his surviving friends and acquaintances; for there he shone without a rival, with a charm peculiarly his own. To a considerable share of wit and humor—to a natural tact and penetration, improved by a long intercourse with the great world, to the habits and bearing of a "high-bred gentleman," Sir William added an unceasing flow of lively, playful language, sparkling dialogue, and brilliant repartee upon every topic which formed the subject of conversation, and this, his great forte both in company and *tête-à-tête*, was endless. Placing people of all classes on a footing of easy familiarity, and thus unlocking their confidence, he drew from them a perpetual supply of materials for his own combination— "toujours variées toujours renaissantes"—his house became the resort of all ranks, ages, and sexes, and his mornings one continued levée. The equanimity of his temper under the pressure of bodily infirmity, often of acute suffering, enhanced the value of a cheerful, humane, benevolent, charitable disposition, and even the shafts of sarcasm and of ridicule, in which he occasionally indulged, left no sting, because it was felt that they were the offspring of no malignant spirit. With all his resources, however, Sir William languished in solitude; he breathed only in the atmosphere of society; even his literary and other occupations were sometimes carried on in company, while conversing with those around him.

'He was fond of being looked up to as a patron and protector, and somewhat jealous of the ascendency which he thus sought to preserve.

'It has been said that, as in thinking, so in feeling, he was a stranger to any great depth; and certainly he seldom betrayed much emotion, or even expressed much interest in the fate of others. It is a remark of his friend, Lady Blessington, in one of her books, that "persons the most remarkable for general kindness are those who have the least feeling."

'Emulous of fame, he aspired after notoriety and display; and the latter was sometimes evinced by introducing subjects with which his auditors were very imperfectly conversant, in order, as it seemed, that he might excite their surprise and command their applause.

'In an argument he was easily vanquished; in a forward remark as easily checked; by superior powers painfully eclipsed. Sir William liked to be the presiding genius. In his acquaintances, visitors, guests, with a few exceptions, he preferred variety, novelty; and when these had lost the power of pleasing, he willingly resigned them, "like the last month's magazine," for others more attractive.

'Hence he was deemed by some people rather selfish, not quite sincere, and not sufficiently mindful of past favors; but in endeavoring to exhibit the various traits of a distinguished character, we ought always to bear in mind that they include many from which no human being is entirely exempt.

'Amid a boundless acauaintance, it may be questioned whether Sir William Gell had many really and truly attached friends, his affections were infinitely subdivided, frittered away; but he was a kind and indulgent master.

'He seemed to be a great favorite with the fair sex. They gathered—flocked around him; they confided in—they confessed to—they consulted him as a superior being! Yet all the youth, beauty, grace, accomplishments, whose homage he was constantly receiving, did rarely, in my hearing, call forth an admiring, never one enthusiastic, one impassioned sentiment. They might be "well-looking," "well-mannered," "a pleasing person," that was all. I often asked him *who* was the most beautiful woman he remembered to have met with. He replied that "he thought he should say Lady Blessington." Still, his behavior, attentions to, correspondence with ladies, were excellent, polite, and kind. In estimating character, we judge partly from what people do and say, and, *which frequently escapes them,* from what they do *not* do and say!

'In these peculiarities and other foibles we have, alas! only to recognise the imperfections from which none are free; but the verdict of an immense majority will decide in favor of the amiability, the charms of the character of Sir William Gell, and will confess he has left a blank which it will be difficult, if possible, to supply.'

'There are several busts of Sir William Gell, but none of them a good likeness. With the exception of a less aquiline nose, he bore a strong resemblance to the statue, said to be of Aristides, in the museum of Naples.'

*(Madden., *op. cit.*, vol i, pp. 330–333.)

Appendix C

Account of a Picnic at Veii.[1] (Pl. IX)

May 7 [1830]. 'A picnic to Veii. Gell, Mills, Dorlac, Hamilton,[2] Catel, Lady Mary,[3] Miss Coventry,[4] E. Cheney and myself. The day was very hot. Gell made us ride many miles, which Lady Mary walked. Some of the views of the ravines are very picturesque. Gell took us up on what he and other antiquarians pronounced to be the citadel. Mills was very cross at bumping so long on a donkey. His humour broke out while I was spelling an inscription at the citadel to Gell. "Ah, Torquitia Priscia, a good old Roman name," said Gell, "we shall find out more about her. Go on, what letters follow that name V.M—." Mills whispered to me, H-U-M-B-U-G: We then rode to see a very curious natural bridge called Ponte Soda. The way was bad, the sun was hot, we often lost the path, and Gell, who was our only guide, did not seem to recollect at all which way we ought to go. Mills lost patience and temper. After we had seen it, on coming back towards the Isola Farnese (for that is the modern name of Veii), Gell pointed to another bridge, and said to Mills, "When you were last here, that is the place you took for Ponte Soda."

"Oh, yes," replied Mills, "I certainly believed it to be so, because you told me so; it was in the days of our mutual ignorance." We came home in tolerable time and passed the evening at Lady Mary's.'

1. *Journal of Henry Edward Fox, afterwards last and fourth Lord Holland, 1818–1830*, edited by The Earl of Ilchester, London, Thornton and Butterworth, 1923, pp. 373–74.
2. Probably Terrick Hamilton mentioned in Gell's letters.
3. Lady Mary Deerhurst, Fox's future mother-in-law. She was a d. of Aubrey, 6th Duke of St. Albans, and m. as his 2nd wife in 1811, George William, Viscount Deerhurst (1784–1843), who succeeded his father as 8th Earl of Coventry in 1831. Lady Coventry died in 1845.
4. The Hon. Mary Augusta Coventry, later known as Lady Augusta Coventry whom Henry Fox married in 1833.

Bibliography

The Topography of Troy and its vicinity illustrated and explained by drawings and descriptions etc. London. Longmans, 1804.
The Geography and Antiquities of Ithaca. London, 1807.
The Itinerary of Greece, with a commentary on Pausanias and Strabo, and an account of the Monuments of Antiquity at present existing in that country, compiled in the years 1801, 2, 5, 6 etc. London. T. Payne, 1810: 2nd ed. containing a hundred routes in Attica, Boeotia, Phocis, 1827.
The Itinerary of the Morea, being a description of the Routes of that Peninsula. London, 1817.
Views in Barbary—taken in 1813. London, 1815.
Pompeiana. The Topography of Edifices and Ornaments of Pompeii (with J. P. Gandy). London 1817 and 1818, 2 vols. New ed. London. Rodwell and Martin, 1824, 2 vols. Further edition by Gell alone giving the results of excavations since 1819. London 1832: 2nd ed. 1852.
Vues des Ruines de Pompeii, d'après l'ouvrage publié a Londres en 1819, sous le titre de Pompeiana. Paris, 1827.
Narrative of a Journey in the Morea. London, 1823.
Le Mura di Roma disegnate da Sir W. Gell, illustrate con testo note da A. Nibby. 1820.
Probestücke von Städtemauern des alten Griechenlands...Aus dem Englischen übersetzt. Mit 47 Abbildungen. München, Stuttgart, Tübingen. 1831.
The Topography of Rome and its Vicinity with Map. London. Saunders and Otley, 1834, 2 vols: revised and enlarged ed. by Edward Henry Bunbury. London, 1846.
Analisi storico–topografico–antiquaria della carta de' dintorni di Roma secondo le osservazione di Sir W. Gell and del professore A. Nibby. 1837 and 1848.
Antiquities of Ionia, Vol. I^2 (1821), Vol. III (1840) and Vol. V (1915) contain contributions to the letter-press and illustrations by Sir W. Gell. Published by The Society of Dilettanti.

Although many of Gell's note books and sketch books relating to Italy seem to have disappeared, the following, and other *Gelliana*, are extant:

Abbotsford. MS of *Notes to save Sir Walter Scott the trouble of looking out information about Rhodes.* (See p. 74, n. 1.)

Athens. British School of Archaeology. Notebooks and sketch books relating to Greece and Asia Minor. See *BSA.* XXVII, pp. 67–80 and XXVIII, pp. 107–127.

——. The Gennadeion Library. 3 MSS.

Barrow-in-Furness. Public Library. MS. of *A Tour in the Lakes Made in 1797*, ed. by William Rollinson. Newcastle-upon-Tyne. Frank Graham, 1968.

Bristol. University of. 1 note-book: MS diary of a tour in Greece beginning 29 April 1801: 1 note-sketch book giving itinerary Hull–Cuxhaven–Weimar–Trieste–Padua–Venice.

Cambridge. Downing College Library. A copy of Wilkin's *Antiquities of Magna Graecia* (1807) has pasted into it two designs by Gell.

Derby. County Record Office. Colonel John Chandos-Pole of Newnham Hall, Daventry recently handed over a collection of papers and other items relating to Gell, but he still retains certain letters and other relevant material.

Edinburgh. National Library of Scotland. Certain letters and papers.

London. British Museum. Many sketch books and note-books relating to Greece, Asia Minor, Spain and other parts of Europe except Italy. These are in the Dept. of Greek and Roman Antiquities. See L. Binyon: *B.M. Catalogue of Prints and Drawings*, vol. ii, 1900.

——. Mr. Brinsley Ford. Original MS *Farces Written by William Gell, Esq., M.A., F.R.S., F.S.A. and Member of the Society of Dilettanti and Fools for the Theatre Porkington 1808. The Beauty and The Beast and The Cave of Trophonius.*

Naples Biblioteca Nazionale. 'Gli avanzi di Veij illustrati del Cav. Sir William Gell al Cav. Augusto Kestner.... Con la pianta di Veij e aggiunte d'osservazione dell' editore (Od. Gerhard), e la sequente nota e I carta contenente aggiunte autografe dell' autore in inglese.' (Ref. 186. L. 16⁷).

Oxford. Bodleian Library. 1 sketch book and 5 note books acquired among 29 items sold by Messrs. Winifred Myers in 1927.

——. Griffith Institute. 3 note books containing heiroglyphs, King lists, etc., copied from monuments in Rome or Britain, including some items in his own collection.

Rome. Biblioteca dell' Instituto di Archeologia e Storia dell' Arte. Autograph letters, notes, drawings and letters to A. Nibby.

——. British School. 3 sketch books relating to *Topography of Rome*: 1 working note book relating to *Pompeiana*: 1 sketch book of the English Lakes, Scotland and Ireland.

Windsor Castle. 2 vol. MS verse translation of the *Odes of Horace*, bks I and II, written by Sir William Drummond and illustrated by Gell—Presentation copy to King George IV.

Wirksworth, Hopton Hall. Album of sketches of the British Isles, Italy and Greece: album of drawings of Haddon Hall, also various other items relating to Gell.

The following publications are relevant to Gell's work:

John Auldjo: *Journal of a Visit to Constantinople and some of the Greek Islands in the spring and summer of 1833*. London. 1835 (2 drawings by Gell and the Dedication to him).

E. D. Clarke: *A Letter to Mr. Archdeacon Wrangham on the character and writings of Sir G. Wheler, Knight, as a traveller*, printed in Otten's *Life of Clarke*, vol. ii, appendix (drawing of Eleusis by Gell).

J. C. Corson: Gell's *Reminiscences of Sir Walter Scott's Residence in Italy, 1832*. London and Edinburgh. Nelson, 1957.

INDEX OF PERSONS AND PLACES

(For economic reasons, the Index has been confined to the text: relatives of persons in the text, who only occur in the notes, are not indexed, and there are no cross references.)